Cha Ghill!

Herb Hamilton

HERB HAMILTON

Queen's
Queen's

Alumni Association of Queen's University   Kingston, Ont.   Canada

For Norine

ISBN 0 9690332 0 6
Legal deposit 3rd quarter 1977
National Library of Canada
Design Peter Dorn
Printed in Canada

When upon his retirement in 1975 an honorary degree was conferred upon Herb Hamilton, the citation read: 'He has been and is the one and only "Herb", the unique incarnation of the Queen's spirit.' Now in *Queen's! Queen's! Queen's!* Herb has distilled that spirit in a personal history of the University, drawing upon his experience and memories from more than four decades as student, counsellor to the Alma Mater Society, alumni director, and editor of the alumni publication *The Queen's Review.*

A humorist by description, Herb has included accounts of many amusing incidents and most of his favourite stories, as well as sketches of memorable Queen's characters such as Dr. McNeill, Alfie Pierce, Dollar Bill, and Leonard Brockington, not to mention the seven Principals with whom he was associated and a host of others.

To all who have been at Queen's sometime or other during the last 45 years, this book will bring back many vivid memories and will add to these many fascinating insights into life at Queen's over that period.

Ronald L. Watts
Principal and Vice-Chancellor

Wallace R. Berry photo

Acknowledgements

The idea for a book of my personal reminiscences obtained its impetus from the Board of Directors of the Alumni Association, including George Perrin, George Toller, Evelina Thompson, Russ Kennedy and Eric Jorgensen, among others. From the wings I got encouragement from Harvey Marshall, Ernie Hurlbut, Jim Courtright and Harry Hutton, one-time Director of Extension.

The hired hands in the Douglas Library Archives were most helpful – Rosemary Gibson, Anne MacDermaid, Ian Wilson and George Henderson – as was Kay Roushorn in the office of the University Secretary. And a special vote of thanks is due those members of the Alumni Office staff, Faye Patten, Vivienne Duffey and Anne Rutherford, who did the typing despite a heavy workload of their own.

I am most grateful to those who took the trouble to read the MSS in whole or in part and who saved me from some misstatements: Dr. Norman Miller, Bernard Trotter, Mary Medland, Murray Gill, Russ Kennedy, Peter Dorn, Frank Tindall, and Johnny Edwards, among others. And, of course, I was most fortunate in having as editor Cathy Perkins Morton, who painstakingly worked over the script, as well as making innumerable suggestions for improvements of all kinds.

To these and to all those who helped in any way, I say Thank you very much.

Herb Hamilton

Contents

Foreword

In this account of my years at Queen's I have tried to record some of the facts one would not expect to find – and which indeed would be out of place – in an official history, already well provided by D. D. Calvin and E. Pearson Gundy. The history which was started by Hilda Neatby and which is being completed by F. W. Gibson will add new lustre to the story of Queen's. My account is of a more personal nature, and my philosophy might well be summed up in the Chinese proverb quoted by Sean O'Casey in the final volume of his fascinating autobiography: 'You cannot prevent the birds of sadness from flying over your head, but you can prevent them from building nests in your hair.'

One fact that stood out was the quality of men who served as Principals of Queen's. Whenever there was a Principal to be appointed and whatever the problems of the day, the Trustees were always able to come up with the right man. Judge John Matheson once summed it up neatly: 'I think it's fair to say that there's no institution in North America where the principalship is more highly conceived and imagined. To some degree all our administrative structure depends on absolute excellence at that level.'

The Principals I have known, seven of them, were not interchangeable. Each was right for his own time. Nor can there be any practical comparison, any more than one can compare the heavyweight boxing champions of yesteryear with those of today.

Each Principal was different, but there were some common denominators. Each had a wife who patiently and competently gave support, who acted graciously as the official hostess, who served on committees on campus and in the community, and who kept a candle burning in the window for her itinerant spouse. Each Principal had the ability to make tough decisions; no wavering or uncertainty here. Each had an influence that extended far beyond the campus, and, indeed, contributed to the stature of Canada as a nation. Each had a lively sense of humour that served as a safety valve. And what was of utmost importance to an Alumni Secretary was the fact that each took a very real interest in maintaining close contact with the graduate body.

When I was a student I had one ambition, and that was to put as much distance between me and my native Kingston as was possible. I graduated when the Depression was in full flower, and I never did make it out of town. When the opportunities later presented themselves, I was no longer interested. Queen's had become a way of life.

I did have one frustration that I will eliminate here and now, and that was the lack of opportunity to answer a question that was never asked and for which I had a seemingly off-the-cuff reply.

The question: 'Have you lived in Kingston all your life?'

The answer: 'No, not yet.'

I
The Queen's Spirit –
How to colour,
sing or
yell it

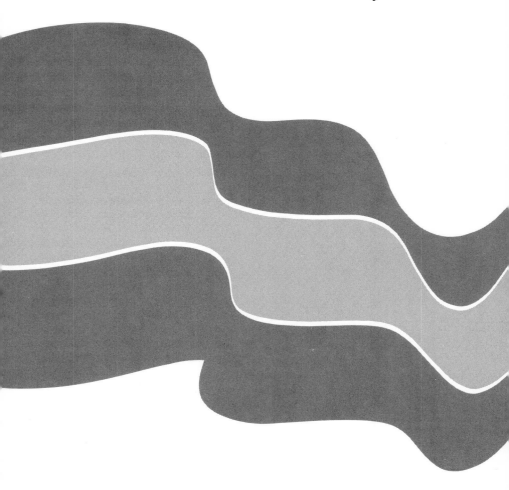

Alfred E. Lavell, Arts 1891

1-2-3! Sis! Boo! Yah!

Breathes there the Queen's man, or woman, with soul so dead, whose adrenalin does not start flowing freely at the sound of the Gaelic war cries in the Queen's yell?

True, those who raise their voices in tribute to their alma mater probably do not know the meaning of the words, and even fewer could spell them, but these are merely details. The yell is a common bond, a rallying cry, a defiant challenge hurled into the very teeth of any and all opposition.

To me the Queen's yell conjures up memories of warm, sunny, autumn afternoons in the old George Richardson Stadium as the Golden Gaels engaged in mortal combat with the warriors of a rival institution. The fierce Gaelic cries were right at home in that gladiators' arena, and served to heighten the excitement and the drama of the encounter.

The yell has a long and honorable history. It dates back to those days when the football team was a comparatively new campus endeavour and the need emerged for something more sophisticated than the Sis! Boo! Yah! yell then in use.

The Alma Mater Society recognized the need and on October 3, 1891, appointed a committee to produce something suitable. Only the names of two members are known: Alfred E. Lavell and S. Alfred Mitchell, selected to represent the faction pressing for a yell that would reflect the University's Scottish origins.

An approach was made to two students who could talk the 'language of Eden' – Donald Cameron and F. A. McRae. After some persuasion they gave a Gaelic translation for the college colours and 'Queen's forever'. For a war cry to complete the yell, the services of a student named McLean were pressed into service. McLean knew his Ossian, but he was lukewarm about the use of the sacred language for such base purposes. His resistance overcome, he read through a list of possibilities. When he came to *Cha Gheill!* he hit a responsive chord.

'What does that mean?' asked Lavell.
'Nil desperandum!' was the reply.
That was it. The search was over. And so the yell was composed:

> *Dearg! Gor'mus! Buidthe!*
> *Oil Thigh na Banrighinn gu Brath!*
> *Cha Gheill! Cha Gheill! Cha Gheill!*

which translates as:

> *Red! Blue! Yellow!*
> *Queen's Forever!*
> *No Surrender!*

and phonetically:

> *Jarg! Gormoos! Boo-ee-ee-ee!*
> *Oil Thigh na Banree gu braw!*
> *Kay Yi-al!*

This yell was adopted by the committee on October 9 and by the AMS on October 10, 1891, after some opposition from those who wanted Queen's to stay with the yell then in use: '1-2-3, Sis! Boo! Yah!' At another meeting on October 24, at which Lavell was not present, the AMS substituted 'Queen's! Queen's! Queen's!' for 'Jarg! Gor'mus! Buidthe!'

Dr. Lavell always regretted this change. He said so at the time and he confirmed it many times afterwards. He felt that the eliminated words were the best part of the yell; if properly rendered they constituted a fearsome cry. He always hoped that some day the original yell would again come into favour. Others shared this point of view, among them Dr. B. K. Sandwell, one-time Rector.

And so the Queen's yell came into existence. The Gaels who had made their substantial contribution were not interested in the results of their collaboration. They felt it was a defamation of the Gaelic, particularly in the manner in which it was mispronounced. The *Journal* on November 7, 1891, sourly predicted: 'The new yell as it will probably appear about the year 1901:

> *Oilyvanblaricom*
> *Kawhig! Kawhig! Kawhig!'*

When he was resident in Toronto, Dr. Lavell faithfully attended the alumni Branch meetings and at one of these he was called upon to relate the history of the yell and to demonstrate the proper method of delivering it. His listeners learned they had never known the proper pronunciation, cadence, or tempo or had a true conception of the full possibilities of *Cha Gheill!* as a Scottish battle cry.

In 1931 Dr. Lavell was invited to the campus to tell the students of the background of the yell and to instruct them on the proper rendition. At a well-attended meeting in Grant Hall, at which I was present, Dr. Lavell gave a dramatic demonstration. He explained that the *Cha Gheill!* should be pronounced 'kay yial', and there should be marked and prolonged stress on 'yial', pronounced as two syllables.

I can still see the good Doctor carried away by emotion as he demanded: 'Can you imagine the warriors of Clan Macgregor going after the Macdonalds with their dirks and yelping "cayell, cayell, cayell" like a bunch of mongrel pups? If the *Cha Gheill!* is given in two long beats it makes all the difference in the world.' And, of course, it does, and sounds like the shout of defiance it was meant to be.

An interesting appraisal of the yell was made by Dr. W. H. Fyfe, Principal of Queen's 1930-36 and then Principal of Aberdeen, in an address 'Scots in Canada' over the BBC network in 1937:

Another feature of the football game which novels and films have made familiar in Great Britain is the yell. Each university has one or more of these slogans, and during the course of the game the cheerleaders spring out in front of the stands and with passionate gesticulation of arms and legs conduct a stentorian choir of undergraduate students – aged alumni, too, and even professors are not too dignified to help in swelling the roar. In cold print these yells sound singularly fatuous. But Queen's is fortunate. She has a Gaelic yell. It is little understood and universally mispronounced, but it forms a rousing slogan and retains even in the hoarse throats of these excited 'football fans' some relic of the dignity and beauty which seems to be inseparable from Gaelic speech.

Dr. L. W. Brockington had his own translation of the Gaelic:

Scots who hae wi' Dr. Wallace bled
And to the devil wi' Toronto.

At one time it was possible to determine the vintage of graduates by the tempo with which they delivered the *Cha Gheill!* Those of a certain era would give it a rapid rendition, while those who had been exposed to Dr. Lavell endeavoured to give the slower and more forceful treatment. Over the years, however, each generation has tended to beat out its own time, and even add an additional 'Queen's!' or two as the spirit moves them, and such distinctions are no longer possible. Currently, the student body is using a rapid tempo running the words all together, but such is the strength of the Gaelic phrases that they survive the ravages of the Philistines.

Such minutiae might be of interest only to collectors of trivia were it not for the fact that the yell is a manifestation of what is known as the Queen's spirit, and even those who take such matters lightly are wont to admit that something called the Queen's spirit really does exist. To belong to Queen's is to belong to a not-so-secret brotherhood, in the view of the majority, and contributing to this tradition is the Gaelic inheritance.

For many years there was a Gaelic Scholarship of $60 a year, founded by M. C. Cameron, M.P., of Goderich, Ont., and awarded to the best Gaelic scholar or speaker at Queen's. This was still offered in my time, but eventually was withdrawn because there were no qualified examiners on the staff, to say nothing of a dearth of students proficient in Gaelic.

What of the principals of this history? Dr. Lavell, who made a lasting contribution in many ways (not the least of which was his almost singlehanded efforts to found the Arts Society – for which he was rewarded with defeat when he ran in the first election for the presidency) graduated from Queen's with a B.A. in 1892. He was ordained in the Methodist ministry at Victoria College. He held charges at Walsh, Ayr, Norwich, Waterloo, Niagara Falls and Brantford. In 1916 he went overseas as Padre of the 125th Regiment. After attaining the rank of Major he was invalided home, following service in Europe and Macedonia. After a term as senior chaplain of Saskatchewan, Dr. Lavell was named executive secretary of the Ontario Board of Parole in 1918 and moved to Toronto. In 1931 he accepted the post of Provincial Historian, and, in the next four years, wrote books on the educational, medical, and penal institutions of Ontario. He retired in 1935 and died in 1951.

Dr. S. Alfred Mitchell graduated with his M.A. and the gold medal in Mathematics in 1894 and obtained his Ph.D. at Johns Hopkins. As Director of the Leander McCormick Observatory of the University of Virginia, he became famous for his knowledge of astronomy and as an observer of eclipses. In 1945 he retired as director emeritus. He was regarded as one of Queen's most distinguished graduates, and in 1958 he was awarded the Montreal Alumni Medal. Queen's and the University of Western Ontario gave him honorary LL.D. degrees. A loyal Queen's man all his life, he took a lively interest in his alma mater, and in the 1920's he established the S.A Mitchell Foundation for Research in Physics. He died in 1960 at the age of 85.

Donald Cameron, a Theological student from Prince Edward Island, came by his knowledge of Gaelic naturally; he could speak it before he could speak English. He was a football player and champion athlete of the University. A highly promising career was cut short by his death from typhoid fever in the spring of 1892.

Queen's College Colours –
The indestructible song

The famous Lichty cartoon neatly sums up about all there is to say about college songs. Very rarely do the music and the lyrics combine to reach the inspirational heights for which they are intended. The melody is apt to be better than the lyrics because it has been borrowed from popular and lively airs in the public domain, while the lyrics have been composed by dilettantes who have laboured long and hard to include every cliché about loyalty, Alma Mater, ivied halls, invincibility and courage – a form of shameless chauvinism. When graduates try to recapture in song the rapture of their college days they are prone to failure because the words invariably are less than memorable.

There are some memorable songs, of course: the University of Maine's *Stein Song*, Cornell's *Far Above Cayuga's Waters*, the u.s. Naval Academy's *Anchors Aweigh!*, Notre Dame's *Victory March,* Yale's *Whiffenpoof Song,* plus *On Wisconsin* and *Rambling Wreck from Georgia Tech.* For the most part, however, the typical college song has become what *Time* magazine once labelled the Great Mumble. Nobody knows the words.

The college song is a North American phenomenon. Only in the United States and Canada does the tradition flourish. Canada's contribution is somewhat less than top flight. 'Old Toronto, mother ever dear, All thy sons thy very name revere' is a sample from the University of Toronto; 'Great our affection, though feeble our lays,' is the apologetic tribute from old McGill; 'Western, Western, Western U, College fair and square; Arts and Meds are strong for you, deny it if you dare,' is the challenge issued by the University of Western Ontario; while at the University of British Columbia they boast, 'All other men acknowledge us masters.'

It would be a source of great pride if this scrivener could claim that Queen's had a truly great song that would put all others to shame. Alas, this is not possible, although we do have a richer heritage than most. Early in the history of the university it was a custom

"Old Alma Mater-r-r, Hmmmm de-duu-u-u classic halls, Frmmmm aa-aaa-a-a ivied walls, Grmmmm ba-laa hopes and fears, Brmmmm dee-dmm after years, Alma Mater thee-e-e..."

Grin and Bear it by George Lichty, Courtesy of Field Newspaper Syndicate

for the students to sing in the halls between classes, and out of this tradition emerged a repertoire of songs peculiarly Queen's. Some were stolen or borrowed, some were totally Queen's, a few even had merit.

Here are titles: *Alma Mater, On the Old Ontario Strand, Queen's Football Song, Queen's College Colours, A Song of Queen's, Alma Mater, Queen's, Our Chrysanthemum, The College Motto, Here's to Good Old Queen's!, Litoria, The Maidens' Song, Queen's Victory March, Freshmen's Song.*

In 1903 these songs and some of the standards of the time were collected in book form and published by Whaley Royce & Co., Toronto. In 1955 the same firm brought out for the Alumni Association a more modest song book, but with much the same content. It was after this that Dr. Graham George, resident musician, made a selection of the better Queen's songs and had the Glee Club record them. The Club also sang some of these songs at Convocations.

At time of writing the songs of the past have again lapsed into oblivion, with the notable exception of *Queen's College Colours*. This song, composed before the turn of the century, has received general acceptance as the Queen's song. The tune is that of *The Battle Hymn of the Republic*, which has been borrowed by at least three other universities. The refrain is the Gaelic *Oil Thigh na Banrighinn a' Banrighinn gu Brath*, a show-stopper if there ever was one, and one that gives the yell its distinction. The verses are something else again – amateurish, boastful, sophomoric.

In all fairness, the song was not written for the ages. It was born of an effort to inspire the football team to avenge an unexpected defeat at the hands of Varsity in 1897, and to stir up and encourage the demoralized team and supporters. Queen's had gone to Toronto, full of confidence, and had been rudely repulsed 18-5.

Drastic action was indicated. At the weekly Saturday night meeting of the Alma Mater Society the student body sat in solemn conclave. Out of the deliberations arose the suggestion for a powerful slogan that would inspire the team to rise to superhuman heights in the forthcoming return engagement in Kingston. Alas, the magic formula did not emerge.

By the following day, however, a fight song had been composed, or, more accurately, a song already in use was resurrected and rewritten. With the ubiquitous Alfred Lavell, who always seemed to be in on these affairs, a committee rewrote the song *Queen's College*

Colours, and it was eagerly received by the student body. Here is the song as the 1903 song book has it:

Queen's College colours we are wearing once again,
Soiled as they are by the battle and the rain,
Yet another victory to wipe away the stain!
So, boys, go in and win!

Chorus:

Oil thigh na Banrighinn a' Banrighinn gu brath!
Oil thigh na Banrighinn a' Banrighinn gu brath!
Oil thigh na Banrighinn a' Banrighinn gu brath!
Cha-gheill! Cha-gheill! Cha-gheill!

Varsity's not invincible, they tremble at the news
Of Queen's College colours and are shaking in their shoes.
Yet another victory, the chance we dare not lose.
So, boys, go in and win!

McGill has met defeat before, they've heard the same old tale
Of Queen's College colours, boys, the ones that seldom fail,
Remember Captain Curtis and the conquerors of Yale,
So, boys, go in and win!

There may be other colours to the breezes oft unfurled,
And many another college yell by student voices hurled;
Queen's College colours are the dearest in the world,
So, boys, go in and win!

Dr. Lavell told me that the words in line three of the second verse originally were, 'We're out for the pennant, boys, the chance we dare not lose' and that the word 'colours' in the same verse should read 'prowess'.

Whatever, the song caught on and, while it may be just a coincidence, Queen's won the return game.

The surprising fact is that although the song was produced for a specific moment, it has survived the vicissitudes of time down to the present day. It is still taught to the freshmen, it is still played at football games and other gatherings, and it is still, but not so surprisingly perhaps, sung at reunions, where all can come resoundingly on the chorus, even if they have to hum the verses. So what's new? The *Journal* for November 2, 1908, said: 'An attempt was made to sing *Queen's College Colours* but, *horrible dictu*, hardly anybody could get beyond the first verse.'

11

In later years Dr. Lavell expressed surprise that his song had survived. In 1938 he wrote: *Some of the others who were associated with its production may still be living. If so I think they will agree with me that it should be placed in the ash-can. When it was proposed to include it in the Song Book I objected to Norman Carmichael, chairman of the committee in charge. He agreed with me that it was mere doggerel, and that much of it expressed that inferiority complex and resultant foolish boastfulness which characterized Queen's for a long period. However, others on the committee thought it should go in, and it did, with its fine, familiar, stolen tune.*

Over the years efforts have been made to provide Queen's with a more sophisticated anthem. Dr. L. W. Brockington, when he was Rector, was determined to sponsor a more distinctive song, but his efforts came to naught.

About 1928, George Ketiladze composed the music and Harold Sprott wrote the words for *Sing to the Praise of Queen's University*, which showed a lot of early foot. Ketiladze was a man of many talents, a White Russian from Tiflis, who had found his way from war-torn Russia to Queen's in an adventure story that deserves preservation. He was a fine pianist, a magician of considerable skill, and the perennial Intercollegiate heavyweight wrestling champion. He wrote a lot of the music for the annual Frolic, and such was his popularity on campus that when he came up with *Sing to the Praise* the search for a suitable anthem seemed to be over. It did enjoy some popularity for a year or two, and then it faded from view, while *Queen's College Colours* persevered with scarcely the loss of a beat.

In 1940 J. R. Miller produced a melody, to which words were provided by G. F. Allison, described as a stirring Queen's song. Said the *Journal*: 'One spring evening last term this clever pair were on the piano-seat thumping out this catchy melody. Throughout the common room, feet began tapping, bridge-players stared at the piano and several kibitzers strolled over to watch the performance. ... Thus a hit made its debut, nonchalantly presented and ardently received.' A sample:

Queen's marching forward, Queen's to the fore.
So it's fight, fight, fight, fight, fight
And you will lead the way to victory once more.
Cheer, cheer them onward, help them fight through
And we'll win and then we'll cheer again
For the red, and gold and blue.

Whatever its merits, the song did not catch on.

Another challenger arose in 1949, called the *Golden Years*, composed to the tune of *The Whippenpoof Song*, with lyrics by Ron McLaughlin and Debbie Pierce.

It was a favourite of Principal R. C. Wallace. The words were:

When the leaves are gold and crimson
And the lake is summer blue
Of the years which pass so swiftly, held so dear
Do we pass our lives together
And for red and gold and blue
Alma Mater do we raise our Gaelic cheer.

Soon the Gaelic cheers are fading
And the echo slowly dies
And the time when we must part is near at hand.
Then we know the hours are fleeting
In the short span of our lives
In the limestone halls upon Ontario Strand.

We shall come to the end of the Golden Years
Oil Cha Gheill
And we'll say good-bye, as our smiles hide tears
Oil Cha Gheill
Then will friends and familiar scenes
Live in our minds as they once have been
Gone too soon is our life at Queen's
Oil Cha Gheill. ...

It was a haunting refrain and had a rousing reception. It enjoyed a modest vogue for several years and then it, too, faded away.

The winner and still champion: *Queen's College Colours!* It has survived all attempts to drive it into the discard, not the least of which was a recording made in 1975 by a firm that had not done its homework; the song emerged with all the pizzazz of a funeral dirge. The Gaelic war cry came out more like a limp-wrist salute.

But this too will pass. By now I have every faith in the indestructibility of *Queen's College Colours*.

13

The Tricolour

Queen's College colours we are wearing once again,
Soiled as they are by the battle and the rain;
Yet another victory to wipe away the stain,
So, boys, go in and win!

Two years after I joined the staff of the Alumni Association, I wrote an article for the *Review* on 'The Origin of the Tricolour'. I said that the word 'Tricolour' had been identified with Queen's for so many years that it was somewhat difficult to conceive of a period in the University's history when there were no official colours.

Now, as I write this 37 years later, it is evident that Tricolour as a synonym for Queen's, particularly in athletics, has been superseded by 'Golden Gaels'. Somewhere over the years, the gold has become the predominant colour, although the blue and the red are still very much in evidence.

Perhaps Tricolour as a cognomen lost favour when a radio announcer of the Queen's-*Whig-Standard* radio station CFRC in the Thirties invariably referred to the football team as the 'great Trickler machine'. This is merely conjecture, of course. After all, the same announcer pronounced Honolulu as Honalulla without permanent damage.

Be that as it may, for the first 40 years of existence Queen's struggled along without any colours to call her own. Nor was it much of a handicap. The enrolment was small. There were few athletic teams. As late as the 1880s the Association football team played in whatever sweaters and knickers the players could contribute from their own stores, and the total effect was that of a rummage sale.

In 1879-80 a fine new Arts (now known as the Old Arts) Building was constructed. Enrolment had doubled over what it had been a few years before, and there was a growing pride in Queen's and all that it represented. With this new awareness came a need for identification, a demand for college colours which the athletic teams could wear proudly.

The *Journal* of February 21, 1880, contained this editorial:

There is a question that has often been asked the students: Why has Queen's no college colours?: which was almost invariably answered, Because it hasn't. Now while the subject is not one of the greatest importance, we still think that the adoption of some colours would be agreeably entertained by all the students. When our number was small it was perhaps judicious not to wear any distinguishing mark, as it would have shown that paucity too plainly. Now, however, that the undergraduates have so increased that the old buildings are no longer able to hold them, why should we not have some mark by which we should know each other, and the citizens, generally, know us? There are particular occasions, moreover, when colours are extremely convenient. How our football team has existed so long without some badge we hardly know. Had it been an aquatic club there is no doubt that distinctive colours would soon have been chosen; and it is surely as much a convenience to a football club, rather more – for, in a football match, players become so inextricably mingled that without distinctive colours it is impossible at times for the onlookers to distinguish friends from foes, while in a rowing match those acquainted with either of the opposing parties could always distinguish them.

Then, also, were our Athletic Association at all a live institution, distinctive colours would be desired, and in case the newly formed Snow Shoe Club decided to have any kind of uniform, the requisite colours would be the first things chosen. We might suggest to the officers of the Snow Shoe and the Football Clubs, in case they determine to select colours, to meet and decide on the same that the colours may not represent the clubs so much as the College; the form of wearing will be sufficient to distinguish the clubs.

By 'football' the *Journal* meant what is now known as soccer. Rugby football was not introduced at Queen's until 1882. The *Journal* of 1883 commented:

Some time ago our Association footballers met in solemn conclave and decided in what colours they would next session appear before an admiring world. The suit is as follows: dark-red stockings, white knickerbockers and dark-blue jerseys. ... The Rugby men have not yet decided their costume. Judging from last year's beginning they can take care of themselves and are going to make a lively scrimmage to come out near the top. The colours of both teams when chosen should at once be registered.

As far as the soccer players were concerned, they did not feel bound by their original decision, and shortly after agreement had been reached as recorded above, they appeared in a game at Brockville wearing black rather than dark-red stockings. And within a month of that engagement they showed up for a match at Cobourg wearing blue jerseys, dark trousers, and red polo caps.

The outfits worn by the first rugby football team, in 1882, appear to have been adopted or borrowed from the soccer players. Without helmets or pads of any description, they look quite vulnerable by today's standards.

The question of colours continued to be a live issue. In the *Journal* of December 2, 1884, the editor writes:

We are frequently asked the question, What are the college colours? For our part we must confess ignorance on this point, though every student is ready with an answer which, while it may satisfy himself, does not coincide with what his neighbour supposes to be the true answer.

Old graduates tell us that once upon a time the Alma Mater Society undertook to select college colours and did so, but there seems to be a good deal of uncertainty now as to what the choice really was. This is a point on which there should be no doubt, and the only way to settle the question for good and all is to make a new selection. The Alma Mater Society is the source from which the choice should emanate.

Action finally was taken on January 12, 1884, when a committee consisting of the president of the Alma Mater Society and the presidents and captains of the football clubs was formed to decide upon the college colours. A few weeks later the question was settled by the passing of a motion that Queen's adopt the colours appearing in the University crest – namely, gold, blue, and red. The *Journal* wryly commented: 'How the footballers will incorporate this in their costume is awaited with interest.'

Pictures show that the designers used the three colours in narrow bands. A Pittsburgh, Pa., newspaper in 1899 commented: 'The visitors presented a rather odd appearance, because their skating costume contains such a combination of colours as to make the players look like animated sticks of candy or skating barber poles.'

Later the styles changed to three broad bands, of which, in 1903, the *Journal* said, 'At any rate, no one will be in doubt as to what Queen's colours are.' Over the years there have been all sorts of experiments, with the tricolour usually being incorporated in some form or other. In recent years the football uniforms have been predominantly gold, hence Golden Gaels.

It will be noted that nothing definite was said about the order of the colours. The *Journal* contains a report of a rugby match in Ottawa on October 15, 1884, in which reference is made that 'the red, blue and yellow of our kickers [sic] contrasted well with the black and amber of the Metropolitans.' Two years later the *Journal* mentions the official colours as red, yellow and navy blue, and, again, in the same issue, as red, blue and yellow. A letter to the editor in 1888, signed 'Heraldry', states that the colours were, properly, golden yellow, red, and sky blue.

The Gaelic yell adopted by the AMS on October 12, 1891, translated as:

Red, blue, and yellow!
Queen's for ever!
Won't yield! Won't yield! Won't yield!

At the very next meeting the line listing the colours was dropped.

It was not until 1923 that the proper order of the colours was established with any authority. In a letter to the *Journal*, the late Col. C. F. Hamilton of Arts '90, an expert on heraldry, wrote that the yellow must come between the blue and the red if the rules were to be observed.

Now, our arms are an adaptation of those of Edinburgh University, with a change in tincture and an important 'difference' added to show our juniority. The field is golden, with a blue St. Andrew's Cross, and with the golden book at the intersection of the arms; the thistle remains in one of the compartments, but the rock and castle disappear, and in their stead are a rose, a shamrock, and, to give a Canadian touch, a pine tree. Around the whole shield is a border, or 'bordure', of red, garnished with crowns; the border in especial being a mark of cadency. The line of descent is clear; the blue field and silver saltire of the Scottish nation; the silver field and blue saltire of the University of Edinburgh; the golden field and blue saltire, with the red bordure added, of Queen's.

The University 'Colours' thus are the gold, the blue and the red of the arms. So far as these can be regarded as having priority, presumably the first place would be taken by the gold, as furnishing the field, with the blue coming next as the colour of the principal charge. In arranging a flag or ribbon, it is essential that the gold (or yellow) should come between the other two; heraldic usage and aesthetic considerations united in demanding this.

The Alma Mater would do well to insist that the ribbon, the football flags, and the other devices be regularized. ... if changes are to be made, a brighter shade of red might well be obtained than the rather heavy crimson of the ribbons of the writer's day; heraldic red is scarlet, and scarlet and gold make a good combination.

The matter of the proper shade of colours has been largely a matter of caprice. When the AMS adopted an official blazer in 1937, the

SAPIENTIA ET DOCTRINA STABILITAS

crest was mounted on a tricoloured bar on the breastpocket. To make sure that the colour used for the blazer, Queen's blue, would not be allowed to vary with the passing of time, it was fixed at wavelength 4660 Augstrom units, a scientific and exact method of determining the colour forever.

Alas, and alack, for the hopes for eternity. The blue so designated proved to be too light a shade for popular taste, and gradually the official blazer came to be a navy blue, with either a felt or a metallic-wire crest. For many years this blazer, with grey flannel trousers, was accepted as the equivalent of a dinner jacket at the so-called formal dances.

While all this was taking place, the girls came up with a most attractive blazer of their own: white flannel, with the crest in all its tricoloured glory emblazoned on the breast pocket.

During the time of Principal W. A. Mackintosh, the crest was registered with the Heralds' College at a cost of approximately $600. For some reason known only to those in charge of such arcane mysteries, there was a difference in cost of $50 as to whether the crowns on the bordure were open or closed – and that, my friends, is how the open style was said to be adopted, in the interests of economy.

The legend at the bottom of the crest reads: *Sapientia et Doctrina Stabilitas*. The most commonly used translation is 'Wisdom and knowledge shall be the stability of thy times.' 'Stability through wisdom and learning' also has its supporters.

A poem entitled *Aberdeen*, by Thomas Hardy, dated April, 1905, reads:

'And wisdom and knowledge shall be the stability of thy times.'
Isaiah xxxiii.6

I looked and thought, 'All is too gray and cold
To wake my place-enthusiasms of old!'
Till a voice passed: 'Behind that granite mien
Lurks the imposing beauty of a Queen.'
I looked anew; and saw the radiant form
Of Her who soothes in stress, who steers in storm,
On the grave influence of whose eyes sublime
Men count for the stability of the time.

In recent years the Alumni office used a special pin bearing the Queen's crest for the identification cards issued to the 50- and 60-year graduates at the time of their anniversary reunions. The Latin inscription reads: *Sigil Senatus Univers. Regina Ap. Reg.* , an abbreviation for the Latin which appears on the seal on the graduation diplomas: *Sigillum Commune Universitatis Reginalis Apud Regiodunensis Victoria MDCCCXLI Regnanate*. For those Philistines who never had the cultural advantages of sitting at the feet of Dr. R. O. Jolliffe, and I'm one of them, it means (courtesy of S. E. Smethurst): 'The official seal of Queen's University at Kingston in the reign of Her Majesty Queen Victoria 1841.'

Now you know.

II
In my time...

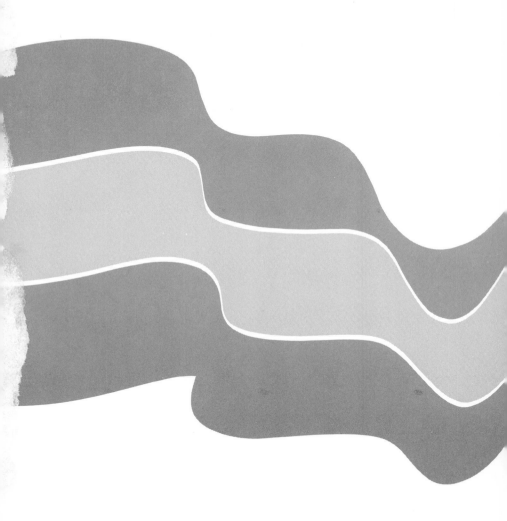

R. Flynn Marr photo

The depression years meant hard times, not only for the administration, which had to make do with less and less, but for the students, some of whom tried to get along on below-subsistence levels. Some didn't get enough to eat. Some lacked adequate clothing and went through the winter months without overcoats and wearing gym shoes. Few were hard-up enough, however, to have to wear blue jeans; that was left for the more affluent days of the Sixties and Seventies. Some found it necessary to interrupt their courses and stay out for a year while they built up a stake.

Employment was scarce, both for students and graduates. Construction jobs paid 35c an hour for an eight-hour day. One summer I got a job as a waiter in the officers' mess at Petawawa Military Camp, $2 a day all found – a real plum, as I was easily able to save the $70 needed for my fees. When a student graduated he was on his own. There were few, if any, prospective employers visiting the campus. You paid your own way to Toronto, Montreal or wherever, and sat for hours outside a company personnel office door waiting for an interview, which was not always granted, even then. As Principal Fyfe once commented: 'Graduating in a time of depression is rather like emerging from a comfortable homestead into a thick and chilly fog.'

Kingston girls were in great demand as dates, whether they were co-eds or not, because they provided a conduit to an ice-box which might yield a substantial snack. An invitation to Sunday dinner was an event to be cherished.

Yes, those were hard times, yet the students, with the resilience of youth, managed to enjoy themselves. They were ingenious in finding low-cost entertainment or in making their own. Bridge was a popular pastime; there were always a few tables in action at the Students' Memorial Union day or night. There was no parking problem, because the number of cars could be counted on the fingers of one hand. Not to worry. If the students were underprivileged, they did not seem to know it. Queen's was a happy place.

It was possible to find board and room for $5 a week, but the going rate was a dollar or two more. A student experienced in the ways of the world preferred to find a room in a location other than where he ate, on the far-sighted theory that if one didn't work out, he still had some of the amenities.

The women students had an advantage in that a large number could be accommodated in Ban Righ Hall. All first-year students under 25 and not resident in Kingston were required to live in Ban Righ or one of its annexes, which gave assurance of a reasonable degree of comfort. All others were required to live in supervised rooming or boarding houses. They were not allowed to stay in any house where men were lodging.

The regulations in residences were strict: all first-year students had to be in by 10.15 p.m. every evening except for one 12:30 late leave a week, and one 2.30 a.m. a term. Other easements for special events such as concerts, lectures and theatres were available if approved by the Dean of Women.

There was considerable traffic through windows after hours, and there were other schemes to circumvent the rules, but no out-and-out rebellion or resistance. After a night warden had reported seeing a freshette kiss her athlete good night, the Ban Righ House Council ruled that such osculation was permissible if the girl had no objections. In 1937 the AMS Court cancelled social privileges and imposed a fine of 25c on each of the men students who had made a raid on Ban Righ, inspired no doubt by a desire to lift the veil of mystery on what went on in that No-Man's-Land.

COST OF LIVING

The *Journal* advertisements reflected the times. Taxis, mostly a one-man operation, offered 25c fares anywhere in town. The ubiquitous Chinese cafes offered meal tickets at special rates (e.g., Peter Lee's Grand Cafe, 14 meals for $3.80). You could get a special Sunday dinner at the Roy York for 55c. W. J. Arniel's Cafe, one of the few WASP establishments, provided board for $5 a week, $4 without breakfast. Many of the proprietors carried indigent students on the cuff when necessary, and at the end of the year some of the accounts were sizeable. The students regarded these as debts of honour and paid up when circumstances permitted, even if it took months or possibly years.

At Bibby's you could get a suit for $22.50. Across the street at the Fifteen Dollar Clothes Shop, suits were $17.50. A shirt cost $1.55 at Livingston's, while Abramsky's had a special: a free tie with every shirt at $1.69. Tricoloured sweater coats, *de rigueur* with the 'in' crowd, were $5 at Van Horne's. Dress shoes sold for $5.50 at Lockett's, and Zaks were $7 at Alan M. Reid's. Spats cost $1 up. Tuxedos rented for $2 and up, or could be purchased outright for $35.

Indoor golf was available for 25c a round. A permanent wave cost $1.95. Bell Telephone advertised long-distance rates at 100 miles for 30c. An ordinary fountain pen sold for $1.50, but a Sheaffer's life-time pen cost $10. Dresses, suits and hats could be dry-cleaned for 39c each. Atkins Hosiery and Lingerie Shop advertised women's stockings as 'pure silk, fullfashioned, ringless, non-run tops,' but withheld the price, if not the purple prose. Theses could be typed for 5c a page, double-spaced, with carbons 3c each.

Buckingham cigarettes sold for 10c or 20 for 20, but a carton of Camels, Chesterfields or Lucky Strikes cost only $1.15 over the border. During the winter months there was considerable student traffic across the ice in the St. Lawrence, down the old canal on Wolfe Island, over the St. Lawrence again to Cape Vincent, N.Y. – a distance, perhaps, of a dozen miles – for a spot of healthy exercise with a little smuggling as a dividend. The story is told that one year some of the natives on the American side were down by the river, poking a broom handle through the newly formed ice to test the thickness, when seemingly from outer space loomed a figure, carrying a suitcase, skating with giant strides, the ice bending beneath his weight. Only his momentum kept him from breaking through. As he reached shore he grabbed for the dock and clambered up, leaving broken ice in his wake. The visitor was Charlie Stanbury, a Science student, opening the season for contraband. He didn't smoke himself, but he could make a profit on his wares. Yes, he made it home again safely.

For those who could afford to go out of town, the King Edward Hotel in Toronto offered single rooms at $3 to $4 and doubles at $5 to $6. The Royal York advertised rooms at $4 and up. The Queen's Hotel in Montreal had rates starting at $1.50, with breakfast 25c – 75c, luncheon, 40c – 75c, and dinner 50c – 90c.

SIGNS OF THE TIMES

In 1930 the streetcar barns on Queen St. caught fire, and the students poured out of the audience at the *Frolic* production at the

Grand Opera House with the commendable, if misguided, aim of assisting the firemen. One year some adventurous souls painted the winter rolling stock with the Queen's colours, for which they were assessed damages by the unamused owners. In 1931 the streetcar tracks were removed from Union St., thereby marking the end of that colourful era.

On campus the risk of fire was ever-present. Many of the buildings, with their wooden interiors and large open stairways, were veritable fire traps. Smoking was strictly forbidden. In the Thirties, Kingston Hall (where the fire started from a cigarette butt dropped in the women students' lavatory), Fleming Hall, and the Students' Memorial Union were victims. At Kingston Hall, students were on the scene before the firemen, and managed to throw most of the faculty records out the upper windows, presumably in the interests of conservation, before their energies could be diverted into other channels. Insurance – and in the case of Kingston Hall, a grant of $150,000 from the City – made possible improved replacements. 'Queen's has always been fortunate in her fires,' commented Dr. McNeill succinctly. Prof. Alexander Macphail, head of the Department of Civil Engineering, once asked the Principal if he could have the next fire.

Paint and students proved to be another dangerous mixture. A car belonging to a friend of Principal Fyfe was liberally bedaubed as it stood outside Summerhill, an act that the *Journal* denounced as 'rowdyism'. When McGill students painted the goal posts in Richardson Stadium on the eve of a football game, the Queen's students invaded the McGill section of the grandstand the next day, bowling over friend and foe alike, and necessitating a public apology from the Principal, the president of the Alma Mater Society, and the captain of the football team. On visits to Toronto and Montreal the overzealous Queen's supporters painted such landmarks as Hart House, war memorials and other vulnerable targets, for which acts of vandalism they paid damages amid threats of an end to Intercollegiate football.

Guarding the goal posts was a tradition. The routine was for volunteers to foregather at Richardson Stadium on the eve of a game to repel invaders who might be expected to come over the wall in the dead of night. Most of the defenders huddled under the grandstand where they drank beer and played or watched the inevitable crap game, while scouts kept a lookout for invaders. By three or four in

Queen's – Varsity game, October 1954

the morning, when nothing had developed, most of the troops had drifted away, and the stadium was left alone in all its glory.

Somewhere along the line another tradition developed, and that was to tear down the Toronto goal posts. Queen's must be the only institution to adopt this policy, win, lose, or draw. There is some precedent after a winning effort, but the incongruity of razing the posts after sustaining a loss defies logic. All efforts to put an end to the practice have failed, and the custom prevails to this day.

On one occasion Toronto installed steel posts, but they were cut down and carried off almost as quickly as the wooden variety. The wonder is that in all the years this has been going on, very few injuries have been sustained, although the potential hazard of a jagged end ripping through a jugular vein is ever present. Warren Stevens, athletic director of Varsity, as a safety measure once offered, at least half seriously, to have a crew take down the posts right after the game and present each Queen's student with a sliver as a memento.

Athletics helped town-gown relationships. In the Twenties Kingston had an outstanding junior hockey team that went through to the Canadian finals with the aid of such Queen's players as Carl Voss, Gib McKelvey and Bud Macpherson. Howie Reid, a Kingston boy, later came to Queen's. Queen's Senior A hockey team was bolstered by players from Kingston: Joe Smith, Chummy Lawler and Frank Bellringer. Tricolour boxers, including Herb Dickey, Merve Peever and Leo McDonald, appeared on Oley Olsen's fight cards. Two local middleweights, Earl Gallivan and Ken Robinson, were highly popular with the campus fans as they traded punches in fights in the Gymnasium that are remembered to this day. Gallivan is now in the Canadian Boxing Hall of Fame. Bubs Britton, Harry Batstone, Bernie Tetro, Jake Quinn, Bob Elliott, and Chuck Fournier played on championship Kingston senior baseball teams, the Ponies, and Howie Reid, Bud Macpherson, Weenie Day, and Bill McKee, among others, also played with city teams.

Queen's always had a few strong competitors in field and track, but never enough to challenge Toronto and McGill. Then Bill Fritz and Jim Courtright showed up on the scene and suddenly Queen's became a force with which to reckon. Fritz in the quarter- and half-mile and Courtright in the javelin throw were world-class performers and represented Canada in the Olympics, the British Empire Games, and other international events. For two winters Fritz competed in indoor tracks in the United States, although badly handicapped by the lack of time and facilities to train. Some of his pals dug a path through snow in Richardson Stadium and Bill worked out there when he could. He won a couple of races against the best in the U.S., and he invariably was well up in front of the pack.

Excellent entertainment was offered by the Drama Guild, and the leading players became campus celebrities. Under the direction of Mrs. G. B. Reed and later Dr. William Angus, a wide variety of plays was offered. Among the leading actors and actresses over the decade were Lee Williams, Roland Browne, Walter MacLaren, Lebo Ware, Robertson Davies, Art Pettapiece, Arthur Sutherland, Lorne Greene, Gerry Chernoff, Hazel Okilman, Martha Johnson and Anne Macdonnell. Some, notably Lorne Greene, went on to a career on the stage.

The Faculty Players also provided popular fare. One memorable production was *Twelfth Night* , with such members of staff as Dr. John Orr, Dr. Hilda Laird, Dr. L. J. Austin, Prof. W. M. Conacher, Dr. Frederick Etherington, Dr. Rob Roy MacGregor, Prof. R. G. H. Smails and Clara Farrell and Margaret Fyfe, a student, in the principal roles, and others as walk-ons and spear-carriers.

As a change from the legitimate theatre, the students sporadically raided the local movie houses, particularly the Capital where Ernie Smithies was in charge. This followed a precedent set in the Twenties when the practice was to raid the Grand Opera House operated under the management of Dinny Branigan. Sometimes they tipped Ernie off, more often they didn't, and their visits were not always appreciated by the paying customers. Ernie was in the habit of issuing passes to members of the senior football team, and he was understandably annoyed, but unbelievably patient, with this imposition on his generosity. In time the local theatres extended matinee prices, 27c until 7:30 p.m., and this helped to solve the problem.

A typical bill might present Maurice Chevalier in *Love Me Tonight*, or Greta Garbo, John Barrymore, Joan Crawford, Lionel Barrymore and Wallace Beery in *Grand Hotel* , or Norma Shearer, Frederic March and Leslie Howard in *Smiling Through* .

Debating was a good drawing-card and sometimes attracted quite large audiences. When the touring Oxford-Cambridge team won from a Queen's team of Bob Young and Jack Weir, Principal Fyfe was sufficiently exercised by what he felt to be an injustice to write a strong letter of protest to the *Journal* .

Perhaps the most universal of diversions available was dancing,

Queen's Faculty Players, Convocation Hall

the prevalence of which Principal Fyfe deplored. There was a 'year dance' once a week on campus at $1.25 a couple. The Proms were $2 and the Formals $5-$6. The new Gymnasium, opened in 1930, with its vast expanses, posed a problem as far as decorations were concerned, but the students proved equal to the challenge. For one of the Science Formals, Frank James, Sc. '31, engineered a revolving 'crystal' ball that scattered patches of light over the dance floor and was received so enthusiastically that it became an annual feature. You could go dancing downtown at the Bellevue Winter Gardens for $2 a couple, including refreshments. The Roy York Cafe offered afternoon tea dancing for 25c a person. At the Riviera the tax was 75c a couple. A deluxe spot was the LaSalle Hotel, which featured the music of Sid Fox and his orchestra. Herb Simmons of Arts '39 had his own 10-piece orchestra: 'Simmons swings, smooth as a summer breeze and hot as a noonday sun.'

With all the opportunities to dance, it is little wonder that some of the students developed a distinctive style, known as the 'Kingston Crouch'. The *Journal* described this phenomenon: 'The lady partner rests her head on her partner's shoulder or on his cheek, meantime keeping her body away from his.' There was also a sophisticated manoeuvre known as the 'Ban Righ Dip'.

In the late Thirties a new dimension was added with the innovation of what was known as 'Sadie Hawkins' week. Founded on the popular *Li'l Abner* comic strip, the custom was introduced of the ladies taking the initiative in inviting the men of their choice for coffee, walks, and other inexpensive diversions. The climax of the week's festivities was a dance, The Dogpatch Drag, in Grant Hall, to which the students came dressed as Li'l Abner, Daisie Mae, Paw and Maw Yokum, Marryin' Sam, and other characters from the strip. On one occasion realism got out of hand when one of the jug-toting students was accidentally shot through the leg.

By-products of the football teams were the pipe and brass bands. The pipe band consisted of half-a-dozen or more pipers and drummers, occasionally with a student player or two when such were available, but with a backbone of Kingston musicians, including a high school teacher, a publican, and even a high school student (Reg Hanna, who subsequently became the Queen's bagpipe instructor). These appeared in kilty uniforms they provided themselves and so presented a reasonably respectable appearance.

The members of the brass band looked like poor relations in com-

QUEEN'S BAND

32

parison, and, because there were more of them, their motley appearance was emphasized. For a while they appeared in white duck trousers, if they had them, tricoloured pullovers, and tams. These uniforms, to use a euphemism, were succeeded by Queen's blazers and wedge caps. And then in the mid-Thirties, through the generosity of T. A. McGinnis, the bandsmen were outfitted with red tunics with blue cuffs, gold braid, blue shoulder straps, yellow belts, blue trousers, and blue caps with gold lining. The band was on its way to sartorial splendor.

A handsome and welcome addition to the campus was the building erected in 1937-38 to house the Biochemistry and Pharmacology departments. It was a gift from the estate of $380,000 left to Queen's by Dr. Agnes Craine of Smiths Falls, Ont., a member of that courageous and remarkable group of women who pioneered in Medicine in the 1880s. The sum of $125,000 was earmarked for the building, and the income from the remainder was left for the upkeep of the Department of Biochemistry.

One of the most explosive developments on campus was the announcement in the mid-Thirties that Dr. Hendry Connell, a Queen's graduate and assistant professor in the Faculty of Medicine, had discovered a cure for cancer by means of a biological product he called 'ensol'. The doctor himself was cautious in his claims, but he was forced into premature disclosures. Following extensive laboratory and clinical testing, the product showed indications of producing highly desirable results in arresting the disease. However, ensol failed to produce lasting results, and the manufacture and use of the product were eventually discontinued.

The eyes of the world were focused on the Queen's campus on August 18, 1938, when Franklin Delano Roosevelt, President of the United States of America, received an honorary Doctor of Laws degree in what the *Review* described as 'the most colourful and dramatic Convocation ever held in Kingston.' The ceremony took place in Richardson Stadium, and 5,000 people filled every seat on the grandstand side and overflowed into the bleachers. The President chose this occasion to make an historic announcement: 'I give to you assurance that the people of the United States will not stand idly by if domination of Canadian soil is threatened by any other Empire.' The words went winging around the world.

The Queen's University contingent Canadian Officers Training Corps was presented with colours by the John Hayunga Post No.

The Roosevelt Convocation in Richardson Stadium, August 18, 1938

1069 of the American Legion, in 1938, by Dr. George Hayunga, Med. '90, New York City, in a brief but impressive ceremony. Later Dr. Hayunga established a scholarship for highest marks in military subjects combined with high standing in academic courses. The first winner was W. G. 'Jerry' Hamilton, Arts '38, Sc. '40, who was later decorated in World War Two.

By the time the Thirties ended, the depression was over and Canada was at war. Government policy called for students to continue their university education and to qualify themselves further in order to be able to give more efficient service when the need arose. Principal Wallace announced that a complete inventory of the technical and scientific research facilities, equipment, and personnel of the University was being made so that, as problems emerged, men in the laboratories, at Queen's as elsewhere, might be ready to work out the solution.

To the students he said: 'At such time a feeling of gloom would be unreal to young men and women, and is to be deprecated. But, on the other hand, a note of simplicity and quietness in all our undertakings, the elimination of everything that may offend, and a wholehearted devotion to the tasks that are before us, these are things that are expected of us.'

MAKERS OF QUEEN'S

Four men who are listed among the 'immortals' of the teaching staff passed away in the Thirties, long after their retirement, and full of years: Dr. A. P. Knight, Dr. James Cappon, Dr. W. G. Jordan ('none more loveable'), and Dr. John Watson ('Queen's has had no more distinguished scholar on her teaching staff'). Dr. James A. Richardson, who had served the University as Chancellor with great distinction for ten years, died in 1939. During the decade other great losses were recorded in the death of Dr. John Macgillivray, Dr. A. B. Klugh, Dr. R. O. Jolliffe, Dr. J. C. Connell, Prof. G. J. MacKay and Prof. W. C. Baker. Through retirement Queen's lost the services of Dr. G. W. Mylks, Dr. Alexander Macphail, Prof. T. Callander, Prof. Duncan McArthur, who was appointed Deputy Minister of Education for the Province of Ontario, and Dr. W. T. MacClement, Professor of Biology and founder of the Summer School.

The Forties brought in a new set of problems. Canada was at war and the universities were floundering about trying to find out how they could best fit in for the greatest good.

At Queen's the administration and the student body were wracked by uncertainty. The staff was depleted. Enrolment went down. When at long last the war came to a close, another challenge arose, as the administration came to grips with an influx of veterans and a housing shortage. Almost lost in the shuffle was the celebration of Queen's 100th anniversary; almost, but not quite. The event was marked in most appropriate fashion, or what, long after the event, the student *Who's Where* in 1975 was to describe as 'one of the most elaborate and brilliant occasions ever held in Canada to that time.'

THE WAR YEARS

During the early Forties the campus was a busy place, with most members of staff and students involved in the war effort to some degree. The staff was decimated, as a result of enlistment, or being seconded for special projects in Ottawa and elsewhere, or engaged in important and secret research on campus, or in a wide variety of laboratory services, educational services for the men in the armed forces or courses for internees, and the like. Intercollegiate sport was dropped, but there was an intensified intramural program to take its place. Military training was compulsory for all physically fit male students; the Canadian Officers Training Corps was enlarged, and units of the University Air Training Corps and the University Naval Training Division were established. A continuous stream of young men passed through the halls under a Royal Canadian Air Force program; they were quartered in the Gymnasium. The Army sent a number of men to take a year's training in the scientific subjects, in uniform, and under Army pay. These were quartered in the basement of Kingston Hall.

One of the brave: King George VI awarding the Distinguished Flying Cross to Sqdn. Ldr. R.E.D. Ratcliffe, Med.'45. *Photo courtesy Whig-Standard*

38

Training was provided to fit women to enter any one of the women's services. Courses were given in nutrition and health and home nursing. Every woman undergraduate registered for work in one or other of a variety of special activities for at least two hours a week. Medical students in their clinical years were exempted from regular military training, but took special courses in war medicine and war surgery. Medical training was accelerated and became practically continuous. Picked men were admitted to first-year Applied Science from junior matriculation. Final-year men were given their degree on the basis of their academic record in order that they might be available to essential industry in mid-term of their final year.

Dr. Wallace reported:

The greatest pressure has been on Applied Science and Medical students. But the war has made heavy demands as well on women who are well educated and have some business training, and who are expert psychologists or sound economists. There is an emphasis as well on mathematics, chemistry and physics for the needs of the war, and on a good training in languages. The student in Arts, therefore, while not so definitely in the centre of the stage, is by no means supernumerary in the action. We cannot contemplate, with any degree of assurance, a world controlled by men who have a strictly scientific training, and nothing else.

Military records maintained by the Alumni Office showed that approximately 3,000 alumni were in the various services, and 164 were killed in action, died on active service, or were officially presumed dead. Honours or distinctions were won by 268, including the Victoria Cross to Major John Weir Foote, Arts '35, of the Canadian Chaplain Service. (Major Foote was the second Queen's man to win a Victoria Cross. Major General H. E. M. Douglas, a graduate in Medicine in 1897, received the V. C. for gallantry during the South African War.) In addition, hundreds of alumni served in a civilian capacity in Canada and elsewhere.

It is interesting to note that in World War One 1,600 alumni, students, and members of staff served in the Canadian and British Expeditionary Forces and 194 were killed or died while on active service.

CENTENARY CELEBRATION

With pomp, dignity, and panache, Queen's took time out from the war effort to mark the 100th anniversary during 1941.

A richly varied program of special events was presented, including a series of six lectures on 'Some Great Men of Queen's' and culminating in a three-day celebration on October 16, 17 and 18. Delegates came from all over Canada, the United States, and abroad to pay their respects – 'a tremendous galaxy of intellectual stars.' There were banquets, receptions, a service of thanksgiving and remembrance, a reception, dance, play, even a football game (non-Intercollegiate). There were speeches and addresses and presentations of formal papers by eminent men. There was a Centenary Convocation at which honorary degrees were given to 24 distinguished personages, and a special Convocation at which the Governor-General, His Excellency the Earl of Athlone, and Her Royal Highness Princess Alice, Countess of Athlone, received honorary degrees and the Governor-General gave a Rectorial Address. A highlight was a speech by Dr. W. E. McNeill, *The Story of Queen's,* which made a lasting impression on all who heard it and which should be required reading for all good Queen's folk everywhere.

A detailed history, *Queen's University at Kingston, 1841-1941* , was written by D. D. Calvin, a member of Arts '02, the last class to take degrees under Principal Grant. 'This is a stirring narrative which adds immeasurably to the pride of every Queen's alumnus,' wrote J. Wilfrid Eggleston, Arts '26. This is also required reading for anyone interested in the University.

In addition, the anniversary was marked by a Centenary Fund, a film, *Paths of Learning,* a *Commemoration Ode, Queen's University, 1941,* by Dr. George Herbert Clarke, head of the English Department and a poet of repute, and an *Ode of Remembrance,* music for a mixed chorus, organ, and pianoforte, composed by Frank Harrison, Resident Musician. There was also a biography of Daniel M. Gordon, Principal of Queen's 1902-1916, written by his daughter, Prof. Wilhelmina Gordon, Arts '05, LL.D. '50.

A. E. Prince, Professor of History, described the celebration as 'planned and executed with an infinite capacity for taking pains mounting to genius in organization. ... a memorable milestone in the history of Queen's.'

HARVESTING

Early in the fall of 1942 the shortage of manpower prompted an appeal from the Hon. Humphrey Mitchell, Dominion Minister of

Labour, to the universities of Ontario and Quebec to provide help for the harvesting in Western Canada, thereby preventing a serious loss to the wheat crop. Arrangements were made that the students would receive a minimum of $4 and board for each day they worked, free transportation to the West, and return transportation at a cost of $10. The students had to provide their own meals *en route*. They were to receive credit for classes missed and for COTC.

From Queen's, 182 answered the call. They set out in a spirit of high adventure, joining with the students from other universities on the way. They decorated the railway coaches with their respective school colours. When they arrived at their various destinations they did not always find their receptions well organized. The farmers, for their part, were expecting experienced personnel, and some complained bitterly about what actually materialized. For the most part, both sides made the best of the situation, and the results were good, on the whole. When their time was up the students returned, having been away an average of nearly a month. They felt that the experience had been educational and worthwhile, and most of them said they would go again if called upon under the same circumstances. Dr. Wallace was more guarded: 'It is hoped that other ways of securing help may be found, if similar conditions arise again.'

CO-OPS

The first co-operative rooming- and boarding-house appeared on the campus in 1941. E. A. Collins, Sc. '05, president of the Alumni Association, presented a property on Earl St., where Harkness Hall now stands, to be leased to a group known as Science '44 Co-operative Incorporated. There was accommodation for 16 students. They hired a cook, but looked after all other household duties.

Two years later a second house was acquired on University Ave. at the head of Clergy St. W., on a long-term lease from Dr. N. E. Berry, Med. '26. Known as Berry House, it provided accommodation for 19, mostly but not exclusively Medical students, just as Collins was mostly but not exclusively for Science students. All ate their meals at Collins House.

A third property was added in 1945 when a group of upper-year women, with the generous help of Dr. and Mrs. D. W. Boucher, opened the first women's co-op in a house at 144 Lower Albert St. Sixteen women students were accommodated here, and they, too, took their meals at Collins House.

The University entered on a new phase of experience with the enrolment of veterans. In the long summer session, April to September, 1945, there was a registration of 105 ex-service personnel. During the 1945-46 winter session almost half the student population consisted of veterans – 1,030 out of a total registration of 2,300. In the spring of 1946, 866 men and 27 women registered for the summer months.

In the fall of 1946 registration went over the 3,000 mark for the first time. One of the greatest problems was accommodation. Some students had to sleep in the Gymnasium temporarily. Nearly 100 went to the Stone Frigate at the Royal Military College, and ultimately this number was doubled. For married students the problem was compounded. A few couples lived in trailers parked behind the Gymnasium. Some crowded into accommodation for singles. Some set up housekeeping in nearby communities. Salvation for many was the LaSalle CWAC barracks (beside St. Mary's-on-the-Lake Hospital) which had been converted into 55 units for married students with children, as well as rooms for 100 girls. Still others found accommodation at the Kingston Plant of the Aluminum Company, where hutments were provided for single men and for married veterans without children. By the end of the decade the number of veterans had decreased and the problem of student housing had eased off.

One anticipated problem that did not develop was in the academic area. Many members of the teaching staff were frankly worried about the inability or disinclination of the veterans to cope with studies. Instead, the veterans proved to be excellent students, quite capable of holding their own and even leading in academic studies. 'At no time in the past experience of many of us who have had long contact with student life has there been such steadiness of thinking and ripeness of judgment as there is today,' reported Dr. Wallace.

The veterans had problems peculiar to themselves: pensions, gratuities, non-arrival of cheques for educational grants, change of university courses, dental and medical treatment, employment and the like. To help them cope, a new appointment was made in the fall of 1945 – that of Adviser to Ex-Service Personnel. The man was John S. Leng, a graduate of Queen's in Arts and Theology. When Rev. A. Marshall Laverty was appointed University Chaplain in 1947, he assumed the duties of this office along with many others. There was

Levana campaigning in the AMS election

a precedent for the Chaplaincy; the Rev. M. N. Omond, Arts '09, M.A.'10, Theol.'13, D.D.'47, was appointed to this position in 1919, but he was gone after one year. Padre Laverty, on the other hand, was to become an institution, an integral part of the campus scene.

Not the least impact the veterans made was through their families. Where before a married student had been a rarity, there were now so many student wives that they formed their own club and planned their own programs. In 1948, of 10 males on the AMS executive, the student-governing body, six were married and some were parents; there were three children. For a number of years Padre Laverty organized a Christmas party in Grant Hall for the children of married students, and a happy occasion it proved to be. In 1948 the DVA statistics showed there were 1,756 veterans attending Queen's; of these 556 were married, and there were 362 children. Many husbands were able to carry on as students only because their wives worked and helped to ease the financial strain, an arrangement that was known as going to school by 'the sweat of one's frau'.

Women's liberation was only a gleam in some mothers' eyes in the Forties, but there were significant break-throughs in some areas. In 1941 Dorothy Wardle became the first woman president of the Alma Mater Society; in 1947 Mrs. D. W. (Thelma) Boucher became the first woman president of the Alumni Association; in 1946 Dorothy Heartz became the first woman graduate of the Faculty of Applied Science, and Alice Bertram and Margaret Elliott the first members of their sex in 43 years to graduate in Medicine.

On other fronts there was little if any progress. The Journal for March 12, 1943, contained the following item entitled 'Co-eds and Slacks';

The Dean of Women requests the members of Levana to refrain from wearing slacks when attending classes, laboratories, the Library, or the examinations in Grant Hall. The University authorities will appreciate the co-operation of every woman student on the subject.

43

The brass and pipe bands came in for a lot of attention before and after the war. As both groups increased in size there just weren't enough uniforms of any description to outfit them, and the result was a make-shift hodge-podge of windbreakers and odd vestments. The Class of Science '41 turned over their rights to the lucrative Sadie Hawkins dance so that the proceeds could go to the bands. The student body agreed to pay a *per capita* levy, and this money was collected through the war years even though the bands were not operative. Shortly after the war, these funds, augmented by grants and loans from various bodies, including the Athletic Board of Control, and contributions from a few interested alumni, were used to purchase authentic Highland dress for both bands.

The tartan was the Royal Stuart, as was correct under the circumstances, with green Melton doublets for the pipe band and scarlet doublets for the brass band. The pipers, led by three Highland dancers, and the brass band, led by the luscious Marge MacGregor, the first in a long line of pulchritudinous drum majorettes, made an impressive appearance, late in the Forties, as they marched across Richardson Stadium in white-spatted unison, kilts swirling, sporrans swinging. From poor relations the bands became overnight the pride of the University.

SEPTEMBER 4, 1947, proved to be a 'bad day at Black Rock' for the Queen's community, when fire hit the Students' Memorial Union. The west half of the building was practically destroyed and the rest sustained heavy smoke and water damage. With the opening of the session only two weeks away, the emergency was met by Dr. John Orr and his Union committee and by Warden Jim Wright. In one of the speediest operations in the University's history, a kitchen was set up in McLaughlin Hall, dining-room facilities provided, and a common room made available on the day that registration took place.

Plans for a new and enlarged Union were already in hand, and construction began immediately, although no one knew where the funds were coming from. The formal opening was held in 1949, with the Governor-General, Viscount Alexander, unveiling the memorial tablet. The Memorial Room was dedicated by Principal H. A. Kent of Queen's Theological College, who had served as Chaplain in World Wars One and Two. For the first time women students were admitted to the building, and there were quarters for a Faculty

Fire at the Students' Memorial Union, September 4, 1949

Club. The Union was launched upon a new era of service for the entire University community.

The seven paintings in the Memorial Room, done by Miss Marion Long, RCA, were a gift from the Alumni Association as a record of World War Two. They depicted representative members of the armed forces. The oils were set in oak panels designed and arranged by Canadian sculptor Ted Watson. The literary quotations chiselled in the altar and stone panels of the room were selected by Dr. McNeill.

Almost everything cost more. By 1947 fees in Arts were $150, Science $225, Medicine $200. Student interest fees were $23, and covered health insurance, Students' Union, faculty society fees, the AMS, *Journal,* and athletic fees. Table board, where available, ranged from a rare $6 to a more prevalent $8.50. In an article in the *Review,* Gwen Herbst, Arts '43, wrote: 'Eating around at restaurants, as many do, is very expensive, with meals starting at 50c plus beverage.' Co-eds living in residence were still better off than most: $250-$300 for a double room and board and $275-$300 single.

In clothing, the windbreaker had replaced 'the old Queen's sweater', at about double the price, $12. A ready-made suit with one pair of trousers sold for $50. Grey flannels ranged from $12 to $25. Women's clothing was up in price, if down in style: a *Journal* poll solemnly reported that the average length of a co-ed's skirt was 14 inches from the floor as compared with 17 inches in 1946; an afternoon dress cost $20, cloth coats ranged from $40 to $100, nylon (formerly silk) stockings were fairly steady at $1-$2. Gym costumes, perhaps because of increasing brevity, were a bargain: a blue romper, short sleeves and open neck, cost only $2.50.

The little luxuries cost more. Twenty cigarettes sold for 33c; as a result many students rolled their own. A nickel wasn't much good any more, with soft drinks and chocolate bars selling for 7c. Toast and coffee were up from 10c to 20c and even 25c . As a concession to the times, the University permitted smoking in the main halls of all university buildings except the Douglas Library, Nicol Hall, and Ontario Hall; classrooms were still forbidden territory, however.

There was no shortage of employment, either of a permanent nature

46

or during the summer months. The demands of the services and wartime manpower controls took care of that. The only firms permitted to visit the campus and interview students were those few with high priorities, and then only after the selection board of the services had had first choice. As soon as the war was over and the restrictions lifted, prospective employers were quick to resume visiting the University. More and more companies adopted the practice. Students, particularly in Engineering, in the top third of their class could pick and choose, but the demand exceeded the supply for those with average qualifications, as well. The employers came to Kingston earlier and earlier in the school year to ensure that they would see the better students. In the fall of 1948 Queen's graduated a special class of 146 engineers, and these were quickly absorbed in industry. The demand carried over into the spring term, and most engineering students had positions long before they wrote examinations.

CULTURE

An anonymous donor established the $100,000 Dunning Trust Fund in honour of Chancellor Charles Avery Dunning 'to promote understanding and appreciation of the supreme importance of the dignity, freedom, and responsibility of the individual person in human society.' Dr. T. E. Jessop of University College, Hull, England, visited the campus early in 1948 as the first Dunning Trust Lecturer. He spent a month meeting students and staff in informal groups and gave three public lectures on 'The Freedom of the Individual in Society.'

Fifty years on campus were celebrated by the Queen's Drama Guild early in 1949, with a banquet, special Convocation, pageant of theatrical fashion, and a play. Raymond Massey, world-famous Canadian actor, was a guest of honour and received an honorary LL.D. degree.

The Guild continued to provide excellent fare. Staged were such attractions as *Arsenic and Old Lace* and *Candida*, and such Shakespearean productions as *Hamlet, As You Like It*, and *The Tempest*. Actors of note included Sandy Webster, who went on to a professional career, and Doug Dale, whose Hamlet was publicly acclaimed by Principal Wallace.

The Glee Club also broadened its horizons with Handel's *Messiah* and Gilbert and Sullivan's *H. M. S. Pinafore, Princess Ida*, and *The Pirates of Penzance*. 'The Campus Frolics' were revived, by an independent group, to be followed by 'The Golden Years'. A succession of aquacades attracted capacity audiences.

Downtown at the movie houses one could see Clark Gable and Rosalind Russell in *They Met in Bombay*, Abbott and Costello in *Hold That Ghost*, Douglas Fairbanks Sr. in *The Corsican Brothers*, and Nelson Eddy in *Chocolate Soldier*.

On campus, thanks to the generosity of the Rector, Dr. L. W. Brockington, who was also president of Odeon Theatres Canada Ltd., one could see, free, such classics as *Madonna of the Seven Moons*, *The Wicked Lady*, *Waterloo Road*, *Brief Encounter*, *Caravan*, and *Notorious Gentleman*.

The University Concert Series began in the early Forties and added much to the enjoyment of music lovers in both the University and the community. Top artists were brought in, including such outstanding attractions as the Baltimore Symphony Orchestra, the Toronto Symphony Orchestra and the Vienna Boys Choir.

LAUGH CAMPAIGN

The unlikely vehicle of an Arts Society election provided a humorous highlight when Bill O'Hara, Arts '49, ran for the presidency in the spring of 1949. For three days before the election O'Hara and his machine decorated the campus with upwards of 500 hand-made posters, allegedly prepared by 'The Anti-O'Hara WCTU League'. The posters consisted mainly of advertising pictures taken from magazines, fitted with new captions to give them a local slant. Students and staff eagerly awaited the posters as they were replaced, as O'Hara was depicted imaginatively in various vocations, from a dog-fancier to a Skid Row version of a gentleman of distinction. Abramsky's Department Store had a window display of a student's room which looked as if it should have been declared a disaster area and which bore a sign, 'O'Hara Slept Here'. The campaign paid off. A record 60 per cent vote was registered, and O'Hara was swept into office on an avalanche of votes. It would be fitting to be able to report that he became the best president the Arts Society ever had, but the truth is he never worked at it; by the time classes began in the fall he had transferred to Dalhousie to study Law.

INCIDENTAL INTELLIGENCE

In 1941 G. S. Bowell and R. S. Rettie were selected as the two Rhodes Scholars for Ontario, the first time Queen's had won both awards for the province. ... Queen's Radio Station CFRC dissolved a partnership of several years' standing with the Kingston *Whig-Standard*. From this point forward the University would run CFRC as an experimental station and the *Whig* would operate a commercial station. ... In 1942 the AMS adopted a new election plan whereby the president would be elected at the end of the term by a small electoral college consisting of representatives of the various faculty societies. ... Stew Webster, Arts '43, by a vote of Levana, was declared Kampus King, 'the most outstanding Queen's man of the year'. ... During the summer of 1945 Queen's Biological Station was established at Lake Opinicon near Chaffey's Locks, Ontario, with Dr. H. W. Curran as director. The School of Nursing opened the following year, and the School of Physical and Health Education the year after that, with Fred Bartlett as director. ... Raids on the women's residences by groups of men out for a little excitement became almost an annual affair until the AMS Court fined 20 final-year engineers $5 each and denied them the right to write their final examinations until the fall – a penalty which was subsequently rescinded.

Women students got into the news in other ways as well. A survey revealed there were only two telephones in Ban Righ Hall, both of the pay variety. Perhaps this was the reason Levana Society went into the lonely hearts business with the establishment of a Date Bureau in Ban Righ. ... Levana also offered a new service for the bachelors in their midst. A deposit box was located in the Douglas Library for hosiery in need of repair. One-hour service was available on request. 'Please refrain from sending along holes without sox,' cautioned the *Journal*. ... A missing co-ed made news when she became the object of a two-day search by hundreds of men and women students. She was finally found on an ice floe near Snake Island in Lake Ontario, a few miles from the campus. She had died of exposure. ... J. W. Bannister, Com.'47, joined the administrative staff, beginning a long career that was to include the post of Secretary of the University and Secretary of the Board of Trustees.

The yearbook *Tricolor* received a professional face-lift with the appointment of Wally Berry, Arts '42, as the official photographer. This move assured a uniform quality in the graduation portraits and upgraded the entire publication. It was a happy appointment. Wally was to continue in the post for 27 years, and for a period he doubled in brass as coach of Queen's water polo team.

Ten years after Franklin Delano Roosevelt, President of the United

States, received an honorary degree, Mrs. Eleanor Roosevelt came to Queen's to deliver an Alma Mater Society Lecture and to receive an LL.D. Grant Hall was packed, and hundreds who could not gain admittance were able to hear the ceremony and address over public address systems in two lecture rooms in the New Arts Building and on a broadcast over CFRC. Her address was a plea for an effort on the part of every individual to make the United Nations a success.

DEATHS AND RETIREMENTS

During the Forties death terminated the association of many members of staff who had made notable contributions over long periods of time. In this group were such as Prof. W. P. Wilgar, Dr. Thomas Gibson, Dr. L. F. Goodwin, Dr. L. J. Austin ('a strong and colourful character'), Prof. C. E. Walker, Dr. C. F. Gummer, Prof. A. E. Prince, Prof. L. T. Rutledge, Dr. G. S. Melvin, Dr. Gordon Sinclair, Dr. E. L. Bruce and Dr. Marcel Tirol.

Through retirement Queen's lost the services of Dr. W. T. Connell ('chief medical ornament of Queen's University'), Dr. A. C. Neish, Dean John Matheson, Dr. L. M. Arkley, Dr. Frederick Etherington, Dr. S. N. Graham, Dr. A. L. Clark, Dr. J. S. Delahaye, Dr. P. M. Macdonnell, Dr. P. G. C. Campbell, Dr. M. B. Baker, Prof. W. M. Conacher, Prof. J. M. Brovedani and E. C. Kyte, librarian. Dr. George Humphrey, Professor of Philosophy for 23 years, resigned in 1941 to accept appointment as the first Professor of Psychology at Oxford.

*

A news item in the Toronto Star *some years ago reported that a University of Toronto graduate, successful in business, advertised for an assistant. His notice read: 'Varsity grad preferred, or his equivalent.'*

Of all the applications that were received, one stood out. The applicant said: 'I am very much interested in what you consider as an equivalent. Do you mean two Western or one Queen's part-time?'

The Golden Anniversary of the Alumnae Association was celebrated in fitting fashion in the spring of 1950. Half a century had elapsed since a handful of women, under the chairmanship of Mrs. Adam Shortt, had banded together to form an organization that would further the interests of the alumnae, the women students, and the University. The list of its achievements was impressive, the most notable being the construction of Ban Righ Hall, the first women's residence – the first residence of any kind, for that matter – on campus. The Alumnae Association celebrated with a sod-turning ceremony for a new wing to Ban Righ Hall, a significant milestone in which all Queen's women could and did take pride.

The program included skits by alumnae groups from Toronto, Montreal, and Ottawa; a dinner with Dr. Wilhelmina Gordon, member of the Queen's faculty and daughter of former Principal Gordon, as guest of honour; and a church service.

WOMEN'S WEEK.

In 1952 the opening of a new women's residence, Adelaide Hall, named in honour of Mrs. R. S. McLaughlin, a generous donor, was marked with celebrations called Queen's Women's Week. Col. and Mrs. McLaughlin were guests of honour at a dinner, and four distinguished women were given honorary degrees at Convocation: Dr. Mary McCallum, Dr. Elizabeth MacCallum, and Dr. Dora Stock, all graduates of Queen's, and Dr. Muriel Roscoe, Dean of Women at McGill. Principal Wallace took advantage of the opportunity to pay tribute to all Queen's women, whether Queen's by graduation or association, particularly Dr. Agnes Craine, Mrs. McLaughlin, Mrs. James Richardson, Mrs. Frederick Etherington, Mrs. W. E. McNeill, Mrs. Daniel M. Gordon, and Dr. Charlotte Whitton.

This was the decade when senior co-eds living in residence were given their own house keys. If the keys were lost or the privilege abused, the offenders were put back on freshette regulations.

Official opening of Adelaide Hall. Left to right: Joan Hanson, President of Levana, Mrs. Adelaide McLaughlin and Chancellor C.A. Dunning

MISS MARY R. ANGLIN retired after 32 years of continuous service as private secretary to three Principals. A dinner was held in her honour, and among the many messages and tributes was a poem from former Principal W. H. Fyfe. One of the verses:

When roystering 'studes' went on a spree
Or Trustees kept on bothering me
Who soothed my nerves with cups of tea
*   When they were janglin'?*
Who gave me low-downs on the Deans
And told me what Na-Banrighinn means
And who were Grand Old Men of Queen's?
*   Miss Anglin*

RAMPAGING STUDENTS on campuses everywhere were guilty of vandalism, and the papers were full of accounts of their misdeeds. At Queen's the football train to Toronto was a continuing source of trouble, necessitating almost annual sessions of the AMS Court. The railway protected its own interests by providing old rolling stock, some of it dating back to the days before the turn of the century when it was used to transport immigrants to Western Canada, and the students failed to show veneration for its age. A 1952 decision in which a campus-wide fine of 25c per head was assessed to cover the damages precipitated a storm of protest, particularly from the stay-at-homes and those away on field trips at the time of the excursion.

There was considerable paint damage at home and abroad. In Montreal the McGill students went on a rampage and did $5,000 damage in street rioting. Drinking became a problem at football games, and all alcoholic beverages were banned in Richardson Stadium. Students were frisked at the gate by AMS constables, which led to all sorts of ingenious manoeuvres, such as hoisting beer cases into the stands by ropes suspended outside the walls, and the injection of vodka into oranges by hypodermic needles.

An Arts frosh weiner roast, climaxed by a snake dance up Princess St., ended in a raid on the police station after three students had been charged with property damage. A plate glass window was broken in the demonstration, and one belligerent student spent the night in the slammer.

ON THE CONSTRUCTIVE SIDE, a mission team headed by Rev. David Read, Chaplain to Edinburgh University, visited Queen's for a week for the purpose of making clear the relevance of Christianity and showing the relationship of Christianity to history. ... In a move designed to bring industry and academic engineering together, an Advisory Council on Engineering was formed, so that practising professionals, many of them Queen's alumni, could share ideas with professors and students in the Faculty of Applied Science. The moving spirit was Norman F. Tisdale, Sc. '17, then chief engineer of the Molybdenum Corporation of America.

ACCOMMODATION for students became an acute problem. The *Journal* of September 30, 1952, reported, 'The battle for rooms is on. Queen's students are clashing with Barriefield soldiers as both seek housing in overcrowded Kingston. Soldiers, allowed for the first time to live in town, have taken away many rooms normally held by students.'

A '53 Artsman found accommodation in a six-room house on Victoria St. with eight other students. There was a family of four living in the house, and all 12 shared a bathroom. 'You have to get up at 6.30 a.m. if you want to shave and make a 10 o'clock class,' he said.

The situation was worse for the co-eds. Most landlords took the position of the one who said he didn't have 'to put up with the numerous telephone calls, visitors and demands for laundry facilities that girls need.'

This advertisement ran in the *Journal:*

ROOM FOR STUDENTS TO RENT
One trunk, bound in genuine Algoma steel. Suitable for sleeping. No breakfast, $13.50 a week. Write Box Z, Journal.

No wonder that the University went into the residence business. Dr. John Orr, as head of the Residence Council and later Director of Residence Planning, and his committee made plans that culminated in the erection of three men's residences during the decade: McNeill House, Morris Hall and Leonard Hall. A third residence for women, Chown Hall, was also added, and in the idiom of the day was described as 'real George'.

AN EARLY STREAKER

Early one morning in the fall of 1954 the girls of Ban Righ Hall and Adelaide were greeted by the sight of a body hanging from a tree at the rear of the residences. It was a cadaver that had been liberated from the Anatomy Building, where it was used in the instruction of Medical students learning their trade.

The corpse, clad only in a loin cloth, was that of a tall, thin man, very red in the face, which showed that he must have been a person of some sensitivities. He was half-hanging, half-reclining, as if the mission to get him tree-borne had been interrupted or had proven beyond the strength or the stomach of his unknown companions. Dean Douglas had the body whisked out of sight, but not before most of the co-eds had an opportunity to view the mysterious visitor and even, in the case of some of the less squeamish, to have their picture taken with him. Such film was confiscated by the Dean, and every effort was made to suppress the story, but the *Whig-Standard* was able to publish a brief account. As Casey Stengel was wont to say, 'You could look it up.'

My memory of the incident is vague. Not so in the case of some of those who were there. Cathy Perkins Morton of Arts '58 told me without a moment's hesitation that it had happened on November 19, 1954, and when I looked in the *Whig-Standard* of that date I found that she was bang on. And this was after 20 years.

It is said that a highly respectable doctor now in the Toronto area could fill in the gaps in the narrative.

PROJECT HAPPY BIRTHDAY

It is not unusual for student pranks to hit the headlines of the daily newspapers, but it is out of the ordinary when they do so without unhappy vibrations being raised in someone's breast somewhere.

Three carloads of students managed to pull off this difficult feat when they invaded northern New York State on George Washington's birthday in 1956, and placed Union Jacks and plaques in Watertown, Clayton, Lefargeville and Alexandria Bay. The proclamations repossessed the territory and the inhabitants, together with personal effects, retroactive to July 4, 1776.

The natives, for the most part, took the invasion in the spirit in which it was intended. One community, however, was disturbed and called in the FBI to investigate the possibility of subversive elements in their midst. The City of Watertown sent a bill to Queen's for $40, the amount required to hire a steeplejack to remove the flags. The bill was paid, by some Engineering students, in pounds, shillings and pence.

The incident attracted widespread attention and was reported by news services in Canada and the United States. Mrs. S. B. Whitmore (Pops Vollmer) sent in a clipping from the New Orleans *Times-Picayune*, with the comment that 'it tickled me to no end.' The Watertown, N. Y., *Times*, said: 'The whole thing that surprises us now, as we reflect, is that some American college students, always seeking ways to "let off steam," didn't think of this and carry it out the other way, years ago.'

When the news reached Dr. W. H. Fyfe, former Principal and then resident in London, England, he wrote to his good friend Dr. W. E. McNeill that he would not be surprised if there were some Americans who thought that George III was still on the throne of England.

The incidents did not end at that point. A flying squadron of 'admirals' of the 'Thousand Island Navy' retaliated with a raid on Canadian soil in which they posted declarations at Kingston City Hall, the men's residence at Queen's, and Old Fort Henry, 'taking

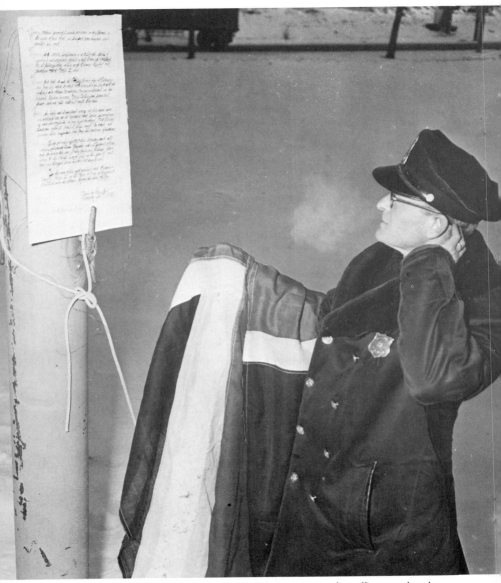

Project Happy Birthday, February 22, 1956: Watertown police officer ponders the retroactive reclamation of his state in the name of George III.
Watertown Daily Times photo

into possession the citadel of Upper Canada and land for miles around' and giving it back to the Indians and Eskimos. The invaders hoisted their own flag, a bedsheet with rotten fish rampant, a lighthouse, and the legend 'Thousand Islands Navy'.

The affair might easily have developed ugly proportions, but *détente* was effected by far-sighted statesmen on both sides of the border. A truce was signed at Alexandria Bay between the 'Roundheads', as the students were known, and representatives of the Thousand Islands Navy. Chief negotiaters for the Roundheads were Gordon Sedgwick, Arts '55, and Al Gretsinger, Theol. '58. Peace had been restored.

SIDELIGHTS

When the Kingston Community Chest threatened to fall short of its objective in 1954, Science sophomores and freshmen volunteered their services for a city-wide follow-up canvass. The sum of $4,700 was realized. On other occasions, as well, the students displayed a growing social consciousness. They collected $1,628 for the Hungary relief section of the Canadian Red Cross. More than 100 canvassers pitched in to raise funds for the victims of the Springhill, N.S., mine disaster, and Queen's contributions were reported to have topped those of all other Canadian universities. Queen's usually was among the top universities in sales for the World University Service caravan.

The personal library and private papers of author John Buchan, who as Lord Tweedsmuir served as Governor General of Canada from 1935 until his death in 1940, were given to Queen's as a gift from Col. and Mrs. R. S. McLaughlin, with Dr. L. W. Brockington, Rector, serving as intermediary.

The Queen's Journal won the Southam Trophy in 1956 as the best student newspaper in Canada. Frances Code, Arts '56, was the editor. ... Emancipation of women took another big step forward when ordinary telephones replaced the pay 'phones in the women's residences. ... The reception room of the Students' Memorial Union was named in honour of Dr. John Orr, Chairman of the Union Council, a tribute to his devotion and faithful service.

A new literary magazine, *Quarry*, made its debut, the product of the Writers' Workshop. ... Three undergraduates – Hale Trotter, Allan Reddoch and Richard Cowper – were awarded first prize in the 12th Putman Mathematical Competition, open to universities in

Canada and the United States. ... Pat Galasso, Arts '55, and Terry Anderson, Arts '56, were named to the all-Canadian track and field all-stars. ... The entire edition of the *Arts Journal* was stolen, but later returned, the copies marked, 'OK, Sc'.

Published by the Aesculapian Society, the first issue of the *Queen's Medical Review* was brought out under the editorship of J.B. Greenspan, Med. '54. ... Rev. Dr. S. M. Gilmour was installed as Principal of Queen's Theological College during the 61st annual conference of the Theological Alumni Association.

The Queen's Quarterly celebrated its 60th birthday with a special Jubilee number. ... As a graduation gift to the University, the Class of Arts '54 presented the Douglas Library with a complete Modern Library series of 270 volumes. ... The Skelton-Clark Memorial Foundation was established in honour of Dr. O. D. Skelton and Dr. W. C. Clark. Personal friends and others who appreciated the great contribution of these two men to the public service of Canada subscribed a fund of more than $300,000.

The University launched a campaign for funds, with a goal of $4,000,000. N. R. Crump, President of the Canadian Pacific Railway, served as campaign chairman. ... A movement to obtain a discount for students at Kingston stores was abandoned when it stirred up a lot of controversy. ... Some of the professors complained when students started to wear sweatshirts and T-shirts to classes. ... 'Don Curtis', a fictitious student, was elected to the Arts executive in a hoax designed to show how little interest students took in their elections. ... Grant Hall was filled to capacity for the annual AMS Lecture in 1957 by Sir Alan Herbert, humorist, author, and one-time member of the British Parliament. Sir Alan received an honorary LL.D. degree at a special Convocation which preceded the Lecture.

The Alma Mater Society celebrated 100 years of student self-government in 1957-58. R. W. 'Herb' Harmer, Sc. '58, was president in the centennial year. ... When householders along Stuart St. complained that the lids of about 20 garbage pails were missing after a men's residence party, an appeal for restoration brought in about 80 replacements. ... More than 100 members of second-year Science held a funeral service in front of the administration building to mark the passing of 29 classmates required to withdraw at midterm 1957. ... The AMS adopted an official Queen's blazer, complete with wire crest, in an effort to establish a standard quality garment. Whereupon half a dozen merchants brought out their own 'official' jackets.

Looking for $4,000,000 to build a better Queen's: Vice-Principal Corry, Principal Mackintosh and campaign chairman N.R. Crump, President of CPR

... Several successful Open Houses were held during the decade, drawing as many as 5,000 visitors. The programs were arranged by the students, with the full co-operation of the staff.

A FACULTY OF LAW opened in the fall of 1957, with Dr. J. A. Corry, Vice-Principal, as Acting Dean. It marked the third venture into this field, the earlier attempts having broken down because of finances and the ruling of the Law Society of Upper Canada that everyone who wanted to become a lawyer had to attend Osgoode Hall in Toronto. For the opening session there was a class of 24, with a staff of two in addition to Dr. Corry. The following year Prof. William R. Lederman of Dalhousie University was appointed Dean, and by 1960 the Faculty had quarters of its own, Sir John A. Macdonald Hall, 18 graduates, an enrolment of 59, and a teaching staff of ten.

COST OF LIVING

In 1951 student fees were increased 15 per cent – Arts to $230; Applied Science, $340; Medicine, $365. By the end of the decade fees were up to $330 for Arts and Science, $345-$500 for Applied Science, and $350-$500 for Medicine. Student interest fees to cover health insurance, athletics, faculty society dues and the like, went up to $36.75 from $30.50.

A new salary scale for staff put a lecturer in the $2,000-$3,500 range, with professors at $5,000-$6,000. The head of a department made up to $6,500 (more in some particular cases), and Deans knocked down an additional $1,000. The Principal was able to report that 'our salary scale is now fully competitive with the best scales in other Canadian universities.'

At the beginning of the decade, board cost $10-$11 at the Union, $8-$9 in boarding houses. At the end of the Fifties, board was up to $12-$14 a week and a room cost $6-$8. At the Co-ops, the charges were $15.50 a week for both board and room. A nickel would no longer pay for a cup of coffee at the Union. It went up to 7c and then 9c.

HISTORICAL

A plaque marking the first building to house Queen's, at 67 Colborne St., was unveiled in a colourful ceremony. ... Hon. J. M. Macdonnell resigned as Chairman of the Board of Trustees, a position he had graced since 1930. E. C. Gill, President of Canada Life Assurance Company, was elected as his successor. ... Graffiti discovered on an old rooming-house wall at 207 William St., dated March 10, 1854, indicated that the average student more than a century ago was shorter than those of the present period. The tallest mark of recorded measurements was five foot, six and one-half inches.

An arrangement of ten years' standing with the Ottawa Civic Hospital, whereby Queen's Medical students took half of their instruction in final year in Ottawa, was ended in 1958. ... C. A. Dunning died October 1 that same year, after having served as Chancellor since 1940 'with great dignity and charm'.

It was in 1958 that the first Quarathon (Queen's, plus marathon) was organized. This event involved a relay of runners starting from Queen's and ending up in Toronto for the annual Queen's-Toronto game. A football was used in place of a baton, and the honour of bringing the event to a successful conclusion went to Al Hyland, Sc. '61. This was the first of a number of successful Quarathons.

History was made when a male student in full drag invaded the privacy of the Levana Candlelighting ceremony and managed to pass undetected. ... Snoball made its debut in 1959, modelled on the highly successful McGill carnival. It was moderately successful for a number of years, but a succession of rainy seasons finally discouraged the promoters. ... There were 740 student cars registered in 1959. The parking problem was in full flower. No longer could a member of staff expect to park right outside his office.

Dr. Amasasp Aroutunian, Soviet Ambassador to Canada, gave the annual Alma Mater Society Lecture to a standing-room-only crowd in Grant Hall. ... Courses in opera were offered at Summer School for the first time, conducted by Luciano Della Pergola, formerly of La Scala Opera, Milan, and Edith Della Pergola, formerly of the Staats Opera in Vienna. ... The Computing Centre was organized in 1959 to provide a high-speed facility for researchers working in scientific areas.

Queen Elizabeth and Prince Philip paid a brief visit to the campus. They were greeted by Principal W. A. Mackintosh at a ceremony in Richardson Stadium. ... Under the auspices of the Alma Mater Society, a fund was started for a theatre to serve the needs of the Drama Guild, Glee Club, Faculty Players, and the University Concert Series. ... There was no shortage of employment. The bulk of the *Journal* advertising space was taken over by companies describing job opportunities.

ENTERTAINMENT was plentiful, on campus or off. Television made its official debut with the purchase of a set for the Union, available from 5 p.m. to 11 p.m. with provision for special events such as the World Series. ... Sir John Gielgud appeared before a capacity audience in Grant Hall in *The Seven Ages of Man*. The Drama Guild operated at a stepped-up tempo, with major productions in the fall and spring and in between, heavy on Shakespeare, leavened with such fare as *The Male Animal, Death Takes a Holiday, French Without Tears, The Crucible* and *Harvey*. Outstanding performances were given by Mike Humphries, Joyce Beggs, Art Todd, and Peter Macklem, among others. Not content with local appearances, the Guild took its productions to Belleville, Brockville, and Ottawa. The Guild also provided the Kingston TV station with its first live program, Robertson Davies' *Overlaid*. Downtown the International Players operated a pay-as-you-like theatre, the spark plug behind which was Arthur Sutherland, formerly a member of the Guild and a player with Broadway experience.

A series of highly successful musical revues, written and produced by students, was put on, starting with the smash hit *Dear Susie* and continuing with *Falling Leaves, Riot '54, The Painted Doll* and *Daddy-Oh!* The latter featured the Two Dots, Dorothy Desjardins and Dorothy Enright, who made a tremendous hit with their rendition of 'Mountain Dew', featuring new lyrics. They became the darlings of the campus, in demand at more functions than they could accommodate.

The Glee Club put on scintillating performances of Purcell's 17th century opera, *King Arthur* , and *Beggar's Opera* and *The Bartered Bride*. The annual aquacade attracted sell-out audiences to *Showboat, Evening in Paris* and *Cinderella*. And the students even tried their luck with an ice show or two, e.g. *Wing-Ding on Ice.*

The University Concert Series brought in a succession of outstanding artists, with such attractions as Glenn Gould, Lois Marshall, the Buffalo Symphony, and the Boyd Neel Orchestra.

Through the generosity of the Rector, Dr. L. W. Brockington, the students were able to enjoy, free of charge, such film classics as *Chiltern Hundreds, Hamlet, Genevieve*, and *Passport to Pimlico*. At the downtown theatres one could see Betty Grable in various light entertainments, Shirley Booth in *Come Back Little Sheba*, Gary Cooper in *High Noon*, Marilyn Monroe in *Niagara*, and Rita Hayworth, Stewart Granger, and Charles Laughton in *Salome*.

DEATHS AND RETIREMENTS

During the decade, retirements and deaths played their usual role in depleting the ranks of notable members of staff who made substantial contribution to life in the University and who had a remarkable impact on students with the good fortune to take classes under them. Those retiring: Dr. Wilhelmina Gordon, the first woman to become a member of the Arts teaching staff; Dr. J. A. Gray, Chown Research Professor of Physics and a one-man graduate school; Dr. H. A. Kent, Principal of Queen's Theological College; Dr. A. V. Douglas, Dean of Women; Prof. James A. Roy, Dr. J. A. McRae, Dr. N. E. Berry, Dr. R. O. Earl, former Dean of Arts, Dr. D. C. Matheson, Prof. H. Alexander, Prof. Arthur Jackson, Prof. T. V. Lord, Dr. A. R. M. Lower, Miss Mary L. Macdonnell, Dr. Norman Miller, Dr. C. H. McCuaig, Dr. R. R. MacGregor, Dr. F. A. Cays. Death claimed Dr. R. G. Trotter, head of the Department of History, Dr. G. B. Reed, Dean D. S. Ellis, and Dr. Frederick Etherington.

During the late Fifties, 'Club A', at the corner of Union St. and University Ave., the home of Miss Margaret Austin, who offered several rooms to fortunate students, was razed to make room for Dunning Hall. The University provided Miss Austin with a new home on Barrie St. It marked the end of an era, because Miss Austin, an eccentric but extremely warm-hearted woman, went out of the landlady business and with her went her visibility as one of the colourful characters associated with the University.

It was said of her that she was the only woman in the world who could walk down the street holding two dogs on a leash, knit a sweater, and read a book, all at the same time, and know all that was going on about her.

Many stories were told about Miss Austin. One, probably apocryphal, tells about a lad investigating a room to rent at the Club A. He saw what was available, liked it, and said he would take it.

'Just a minute,' cautioned Miss Austin. 'Do you drink?'

'No, Miss Austin.'

'Would you be bringing girls up to your room?'

'No, Miss Austin.'

'Then I think you should look somewhere else. You wouldn't like it here.'

Miss Austin was the sister of Dr. L. J. 'Blimey' Austin, who served as Professor of Surgery for 23 years and was himself a loveable character and a legend.

The Sixties

John Bertram Stirling was installed as Queen's eighth Chancellor in the fall of 1960 before a capacity audience in Grant Hall. An honours graduate of Queen's in Arts and Science, he was an engineer of national and international repute, and he brought to the office a graciousness, dignity and poise that were his hallmarks.

At the installation ceremony a number of outstanding Canadians were granted honorary degrees: John George Diefenbaker, Prime Minister; Hon. Mr. Justice Charles Abbott; Carlyle Smith Beals, Dominion Astronomer; James Ferris MacLaren, prominent consulting engineer; and Ray Edwin Powell, Chancellor of McGill.

After the ceremony, Prime Minister Diefenbaker and Chancellor Stirling formally opened Sir John A. Macdonald Hall, the new Faculty of Law building. Students of all political stripes were in attendance, and the Liberals among them took advantage of the opportunity to show where their particular loyalties lay.

WORLD RECORD

Queen's students pushed a hospital bed around the campus and through the city streets for 1,000 miles, with only one 20-minute pit stop for repairs, and claimed a world record. Protests were raised by purists at other universities who took the position that an urban course could not compare with the topography of a frozen countryside with natural hazards of hills, dogs and below-zero temperatures. The Queen's contenders made the rebuttal that they had to cope with icy rutted streets, women drivers, stoplights, children and parents.

The marathon started as a stunt to publicize the Heart Fund, and there was no argument about the success of that part of the venture – contributions were up 36 per cent over the previous year.

SNOBALL

The program of the winter carnival, Snoball, was a good thermometer for the changing political climate. In 1960 the prize-winning sculpture was a large Playboy Rabbit; the second-place winner was entitled 'Old Lang Syne', and featured a group seated around a piano. If the instrument looked realistic, there was good reason – members of Berry House, under the direction of Ken Takasaki, had sprayed a real piano with water and the effect was a show-stopper. The following year the prize-winning sculpture was labelled 'Cold War' and depicted Krushchev and Uncle Sam splitting the world

Snoball '64's version of the Playboy Rabbit. *R. Flynn Marr photo*

between them. From this point on the majority of the ice sculptures took on a distinctly political tinge.

CULTURE

To mark the opening of the new galleries and studios that had been added to the Agnes Etherington Art Centre, an Art and Music Festival was held in the fall of 1962. ... An honorary degree was given to Marian Anderson at a special Convocation. ... The movement for a student theatre and auditorium on campus, begun in 1959, got into full swing in the Sixties. An objective of $750,000 was set, with the students hoping to raise $100,000 to $150,000 through a levy and various fund-raising schemes. Despite a most promising start, the project was a dead issue by the end of the decade.

UNIVERSITY DAY

In 1962 the Alma Mater Society revived the tradition of University Day, commemorating the date the University Charter was signed: October 16, 1841. Its celebration had long been a day of observance and celebration, mostly of an athletic nature, but the practice had lapsed.

In rebirth it featured a special lecture, and the first was given by Dr. A. R. M. Lower, Emeritus Professor of History, entitled 'Queen's, Yesterday and Today'. The *Journal* also published special articles on the history of the University. As an effort to make the current crop of students aware of their heritage, the project met with only partial success, and after a few years it slipped back into limbo. Perhaps it was too much to expect youth to become interested in what went on long ago when there were so many interesting things closer to hand.

INTERNATIONAL HOUSE

To provide amenities for the rapidly growing numbers of students from outside Canada and the United States, an International House was established in 1962 in an old residence at 118 University Ave. The moving spirit behind this was E. C. Churchill, a Kingston businessman whose generosity made it possible. Five years later the House became a Centre located within the Students' Memorial Union complex. By this time the number of foreign students had increased to 300. A plaque in the Centre proclaims: 'This place of meeting for students from Canada and overseas, created by the

Wallace R. Berry photo

vision and purpose of the Rotary Club of Kingston and other Rotary Clubs in this area in co-operation with Queen's University, is dedicated to international understanding and friendship among peoples of every land.'

Dr. A. J. Coleman, Head of the Department of Mathematics, was the first Director of the Centre and E. C. Churchill was the first Council Chairman. D. G. Dewar served as Secretary, a full-time officer. He died in March 1967, but 'his selfless service to and friendship for overseas students was a valuable contribution to the formative years of the Centre.'

Col. R. D. Harkness was appointed chairman of the Board of Trustees in succession to E. C. Gill in 1963. ... A squad of 550 students raised $8,500 in a blitz for the Heart Fund, and more than $1,900 was collected for the Cystic Fibrosis Foundation by a group of first-year students. ... The statue of Sir John A. Macdonald in City Park welcomed the dawn one fall day with a face painted red, gold robes and blue pants, plus a sign 'Welcome Alumnae'. It was *not* part of the University's official program for Reunion Weekend. ... Harley S. Smythe was named a Rhodes Scholar. The following year Doug McCalla, an honours student in Arts, was chosen Rhodes Scholar for Alberta. Bruce Amos became a Rhodes Scholar in 1968.

A $25,500,000 building program was announced in 1964 by Dr. Corry, covering projects planned or already under way, and scheduled for completion by 1970. Of this amount, $15,500,000 was expected to come from government grants, foundations, and bequests, $4,950,000 from CMHC residence loans, and $5,000,000 from a financial campaign. W. Earle McLaughlin, President and Chairman of the Board of the Royal Bank of Canada, was appointed general chairman; Donald Gordon, President and Chairman of Canadian National Railway, chairman of the special gifts section; and Harvey Marshall, Past President of the Alumni Association, chairman of the national alumni committee.

STUDENT UNREST

Student governments everywhere became increasingly concerned with issues off campus, and at the same time wanted a bigger share in the guidance of their own destinies. On the Queen's campus there were some signs of the widespread unrest, but they were comparatively low-key. Dr. Corry and then Dr. Deutsch were readily available for discussion and thereby largely avoided confrontation.

Elsewhere students demonstrated in front of embassies, or did a million dollars' damage to the computer at Sir George Williams, but at Queen's the level of turbulence was relatively low.

The students demanded representation on the University Senate, and got it. They wanted full voting power on the Board of Trustees, and did not get it. They wanted complete control of their own financial affairs, and your humble servant, after 28 years as Secretary-Treasurer of the Alma Mater Society, and Dot Williams, with eight years' experience as business manager, managed to resign before the guillotine fell. This situation was not peculiar to Queen's; at the same time student governments elsewhere were restructuring their civil service.

The meetings of the AMS Executive showed more and more concern with local, national and international issues. A committee was set up to investigate and find reasons for poverty in the north end of Kingston, to the bewilderment of people who hadn't realized they were all that poor. Telegrams and letters were fired off to domestic and foreign governments expressing dissatisfaction with policy. At one AMS executive meeting, the president somewhat petulantly pointed out that 20 minutes had been spent in discussion of the apartheid policy of South Africa while there were any number of important questions still on the agenda, including the Royal Visit to Quebec, the war in Vietnam, and racial strife in the United States.

'Are we going to apply sanctions on South Africa or not?' queried the chairman, trying to bring the discussion to a head.

Queen's involvement with the National Federation of Canadian University Students (NFCUS) reached a high point of some sort when the Queen's delegates became recognized as the leaders and backbone of the national organization. This was a right-about-face from the earlier days when Queen's had refused to pay the per capita membership fee and had been persuaded, in the interests of national unity, to make a token payment of one dollar. On two occasions at least they had to be argued into paying the token fee. NFCUS always had trouble with its membership; at least one and sometimes several universities would withdraw for a period. As the conferences began to reflect the general unrest, the withdrawals proliferated, the organization finally dissolved, and was succeeded by the Canadian Union of Students, which in turn became fragmented into provincial organizations.

None of these vehicles was adequate for the 30-40 campus activists, who formed their own organizations, a new one almost every year, but with roughly the same membership: Fair Play for Cuba, Student Union for Peace Action, Seminars for Canada, Students for a New University, the Free Socialist Movement. They were concerned with the evils of private industry and American ownership, and pointed out that Dr. John J. Deutsch, who by this time was Principal, was a director of the Canadian Imperial Bank of Commerce. How about that!

DEANS GALORE

The year 1964 saw a great shuffling of Deans. Appointed were Dr. G. A. Harrower, Arts and Science, in succession to Prof. A. R. C. Duncan; Dr. James H. Brown, Applied Science, in succession to Prof. H. G. Conn – so that the latter could devote full time to his position as Vice-Principal (Administration); Dr. C. A. Curtis, Graduate Studies, in succession to Dr. J. M. R. Beveridge, who had accepted appointment as President of Acadia University. Two years later three more Deans were appointed: R. J. Hand, School of Business, in succession to L. G. Macpherson, who became Vice-Principal (Finance); T. Stewart Webster, to the new post of Dean of Student Affairs; and Vernon S. Ready, to the new post of Dean of McArthur College of Education. In 1969, Ronald L. Watts was appointed Dean of the Faculty of Arts and Science.

Queen's students invaded RMC grounds and spread some paint around, including the cannon in the parade square. In a move designed to head off retaliation, Air Commodore L. J. Birchall, Commandant, arranged a little ceremony at RMC in which representatives of the cadets and Queen's students symbolically and literally buried the hatchet. ... Model Parliament, a student activity since the Twenties, threw in the sponge in 1964 because of the general feeling that the proceedings were a farce. 'Pseudo parliamentarians demonstrated their ignorance of current affairs and disregard for parliamentary procedure,' was one appraisal in the *Journal*. ... Closed-circuit television made its appearance with a trial run in the new Biology Building. ... For the first time the number of graduates at Spring Convocation numbered more than a thousand, when 1,027 received their degrees in five ceremonies in the spring of 1965. ... There was considerable unrest in the men's residences, with three main gripes: a proposed fee increase, restrictions on women visitors in the men's rooms, and that perennial *bête noire,* the food. After prolonged negotiations it was finally agreed that girls would be admitted to the men's residences between 7.00 p.m. and midnight on Fridays, and from 5.00 p.m. to midnight on Saturdays. Guests had to be registered, and the room doors were to be left open.

STIRLING HALL

Named in honour of Chancellor J. B. Stirling, the $3,500,000 Physics building was officially opened by the Chancellor himself in May 1965. The ceremony was followed by a symposium on Science, Engineering, and the Canadian Economy, and the speakers were Dr. K. W. Taylor, Skelton-Clark Fellow at Queen's and former Deputy Minister of Finance and Receiver-General of Canada; Dr. Gerhard Hertzberg, Director of the Division of Pure Physics, National Research Council; Dr. G. C. Laurence, President of Atomic Energy Control Board; and Major-General R. H. Keefler, President and Chairman of the Board of Northern Electric Company, Ltd. The site of Stirling Hall was on Queen's Crescent, selected after an earlier choice to build on the Lower Campus met with howls of protest from students, staff, and alumni.

Golden Words, an Engineering Society competitor for the *Queen's Journal,* was born. Extra copies were available for interested students in other faculties.

In the spring of 1967 the Arts and Science Undergraduate Society and the Levana Society amalgamated when 80 per cent of the students voted in favour of the merger. The decision was arrived at after years of study and negotiation. The *Review* commented: 'In recent years the intransigent and belligerent Levana yell, *Women's Rights or War,* was no longer heard around the halls of Queen's. Presumably the objectives had long since been gained and the battle was over.'

It was somewhere about this time that the male students began to sprout longer and longer hair. There was a *Journal* comment in reference to the switching of sexual roles: 'The male trend is to long locks, tight pants, pointed-toe high-heeled shoes.' A new era in sartorial inelegance had been introduced.

71

McKenzie Porter, writing in the *Toronto Telegram*, said:

I happened to see scores of students from Queen's University in the Lord Simcoe Hotel the other night. They looked like a horde of ragamuffins. Dirty jeans, soiled T-shirts, sweaty running shoes and tatty windbreakers predominated in the dress of the men. Most of the women wore cheap and shapeless slacks and a variety of upper garments that came presumably from the stocks of the Salvation Army.

The number of unwashed faces and uncombed heads displayed by both sexes was repulsive. Many of the students were lugging about huge pieces of that inane electronic equipment with which they amplify their teeny ukelele music.

On the other hand the *Whig-Standard* found the co-eds highly attractive. In 1968 a feature story depicted the girls in the popular dress of the day, mini-skirts, with only one in jeans.

Long legs flashing, for it seems they are all long-legged in those brief skirts. ... shorts, jeans and culottes are the order of dress – but a hint of the cooler days ahead appears from time to time in dark cottons with demure lace trims, chunky shoes, and chain belts. ... And how do they look to the seasoned eye? Well, as one discriminating girl watcher put it from his vantage point as a staff member, 'better than ever.'

125TH ANNIVERSARY

The 125th anniversary of the University was observed in 1967 with a Convocation, a dinner, and the publication of a history.

Queen's University first opened its doors in rented quarters, a frame house at 67 Colborne St., on March 7, 1842, with an enrolment of 12 students, a staff of two, and a library of 52 books. In 1967-68, Queen's had a registration of 5,792, a full-time teaching staff of 507, and a library of 544,060. There were now four faculties and five schools: the Faculty of Arts and Science, the Faculty of Medicine (1854), the Faculty of Applied Science, which began as the School of Mining in 1893, the Faculty of Law (1957), the School of Nursing (1946), the School of Physical and Health Education (1947), the School of Business (1963), the School of Graduate Studies and Research (1963), and the School of Rehabilitation Medicine (1967). Duncan McArthur College of Education opened for classes in 1968.

At the Anniversary Convocation, held in Grant Hall on October 20, 1967, honorary degrees were conferred on 12 distinguished persons: a D.D. to Rev. Mathew Black; LL.D.'S to John Douglas

Arnup, Dr. George Harold Ettinger, John Kenneth Galbraith, William Archibald Mackintosh, Harvey Reginald MacMillan, John Russell McCarthy, Louis Rasminsky, Godfrey Ridout, Pauline Vanier and Charles Haynes Wilson; and a D.Sc. to Henry George Thode.

A commemorative history written by H. P. Gundy, University Librarian, was described as 'one of the better university histories ever produced in Canada. It combines graphic excellence, superbly handled copy that never bogs the reader in a mess of detail, and large number of photographs, both old and new, of the campus and university personalities.'

NEWMAN CLUB

Queen's Newman Club observed its 50th anniversary in the fall of 1967. The program consisted of an Open House at Newman House, recently moved from downtown to 164 University Ave., a mass in Dunning Hall, and a luncheon in Leonard Hall.

Of the 59 Catholic students at Queen's in 1917-18, 30 joined the new organization named for John Henry Cardinal Newman. Because of the small numbers it might not have survived but for the generous help of a few devoted friends, especially Dr. William Gibson, Dr. Fergus J. O'Connor, Sr., and Miss Florence O'Donnell.

During its 50 years the Newman Club had seven chaplains, with the Rt. Rev. Msgr. J. G. Hanley serving the longest term, 1941-58, and still taking a fatherly interest, if you will pardon the expression, at the time of writing. The Queen's Club was one of the founding members of the Canadian Newman Federation. It has taken an active part in the Newman movement on a national basis, and has been host to the national convention on several occasions.

ARMED FORCES UNITS

An association of more than half a century between the Canadian Officers Training Corps (COTC) and the University came to an end in 1968 with the closing of the armed forces units on campus as a matter of government policy.

Formal closure took place on May 31, preceded by a ceremonial parade at HMCS Cataraqui. The three units, Queen's Contingent COTC, the Queen's University Naval Training Division, and the Queen's University Training Squadron RCAF paraded before the Reviewing Officer, Brigadier D. G. Cunningham, CBE, DSO, ED, CD. It was a particularly appropriate manoeuvre since the Brigadier, who

74

was also the University solicitor, was the son of the late A. B. Cunningham, B.A. '91, the first Commanding Officer of Queen's COTC.

PROTESTS

Protests became a way of life, although the number of participants was usually small. The war in Vietnam was a favorite target, particularly on Remembrance Day, with the students bearing such signs as 'Lest We Forget. VIETNAM. How Many More Must Die?' The faculty got into the act, too. In 1967, 25 per cent signed a letter to the Prime Minister asking for a prohibition of the sale of Canadian military equipment for use in Vietnam and the provision of medical supplies for all Vietnamese, both North and South. Students participated in a demonstration at the Ivy Lea border crossing in 1969 with placards condemning a planned U.S. nuclear blast in the Aleutian Islands.

ENTERTAINMENT

As student society became more and more affluent, the choice of entertainment became more and more varied. The Drama Guild program stepped up in tempo, with the usual Shakespearean and Shavian fare, leavened with plays by Chekov and such offerings as *Tis Pity She's A Whore* and John Osborne's *Look Back in Anger*. The Glee Club put on ambitious performances of Gilbert and Sullivan operas. The Revue Guild continued to produce shows featuring student talent that drew packed houses, and there were ice revues, as well. The University Concert Series brought in, among others, Marian Anderson, Grace Bumby, and the Prague Chamber Orchestra.

Folksingers and rock groups made the scene. Gordon Lightfoot filled Grant Hall. Ian and Sylvia were a great success. Other artists appeared in coffee houses, including Bitter Grounds in the Union. Discothèque coffee houses, such as the First Church of Alice, operated downtown and attracted their own following.

At the local movie houses one could see Sandy Dennis in *The Fox*, Sidney Poitier in *For Love of Ivy*, Julie Andrews in *Thoroughly Modern Millie*, and such classics as *West Side Story* and *Dr. Zhivago*. On campus, free movies were available through the good offices of Dr. L. W. Brockington, and other movies were shown at reduced rates under the auspices of the Alma Mater Society.

Visitors to the campus included Irving Layton, Odetta, and Barry Morse. The Arts and Science Undergraduate Society sponsored the

Queen's Folk Festival in Richardson Stadium.

Kingston began to lose its image as a quiet little town when a co-ed was attacked on Lower Alfred St. This one managed to fight off her assailant. In later years others were not so lucky. ... Twenty-one parking meters newly installed along University Ave., south of Union, were twisted out of shape, painted red, and stripped of their heads, whereupon the City officials banned all parking along the blocks between Union and Stuart streets.

Despite such acts of vandalism the students showed an ever-increasing social awareness, and for summer employment sought jobs with Operation Crossroads Africa, on Indian reservations, and with the Grenville Mission in Newfoundland, for example. The AMS started a Student Volunteer Bureau to provide workers for a wide variety of charitable projects within the community. In its first year of operation 150 students were involved in serving area hospitals, prisons, and youth groups. ... Enrolment passed 6,000 for the first time. ... Draft dodgers began to show up from the U.S. ... The Nursing Science course was changed to a four-year integrated program. ... Chuck Edwards and Jan Lichty resigned as president and vice-president of the Alma Mater Society over issues arising out of their membership in the radical Students for a New University (SNU). They sought a vote of confidence, lost, and in the special elections that followed, Dave Pakrul was elected president and Andy Pipe vice-president.

Students were elected to the University Senate for the first time: John Buttars, John Gray, Barry LeRoy and Craig Aitkins. Students were also appointed to all Senate Committees. ... About 35 members of the SNU demonstrated in front of Richardson Hall prior to a Senate meeting, which they wanted open to the public. ... One of the activists writing in the *Journal* said: 'Queen's society is one of the most class-oriented I have ever encountered. And, given that Queen's is largely supported by public funds, it seems to be oriented towards the wrong classes.' ... Students in Toronto for the Varsity game did nearly $5,000 damage to the Lord Simcoe Hotel. ... The *Journal* brought out a bogus issue of the *McGill Daily* which was anti-semitic and which fluttered the dove-cots more than somewhat. There were threats of lawsuits, but the issue was ultimately resolved by a note of apology from the AMS executive.

Prime Minister Trudeau met with an audience of students that packed Grant Hall. There was a lively exchange of ideas. ... Queen's

Prime Minister Pierre Trudeau, LL.D., addresses Convocation at the installation of Principal Deutsch, November 1968. *Wallace R. Berry photo*

opted out of membership in the Canadian Union of Students, which they found to be too radical for the tastes of the majority. ... Members of the track team did well in Intercollegiate competition. Brian Donnelly, Dave Ellis, and Tim Baker won upwards of 50 gold medals in invitational meets from Edmonton to Halifax before they graduated in 1969.

R. M. Burns, with a background of distinguished work with provincial governments in Manitoba and British Columbia and with the federal Department of Finance, was appointed the first Director of the Institute of Intergovernmental Relations. The program was launched with a study of federal-provincial machinery on fiscal and economic matters for the purpose of harmonizing policy and programs.

Although the Levana Society was no longer in existence, one of the rituals survived – the candlelighting ceremony, with all its traditions and prophecies. Two women members of the AMS executive proposed a motion condemning the ceremony 'as a dehumanizing fertility rite which perpetuates the concept of university women as charming cultured accessories who are being prepared for careers as wives and mothers of university men, without consideration of their development and value as human beings.' The motion was defeated.

Queen's joined the Universities of British Columbia, Victoria, and an Alberta threesome (Edmonton, Calgary, and Lethbridge) in WESTAR (Western Telescopes for Astronomical Research). The consortium was set up to complete a telescope project on Mount Kobau, in British Columbia. ... The first student pub, The House of Commons, was opened in a rejuvenated second-floor lounge of the Students' Memorial Union, thereby implementing a student plan that had been on a back burner for a long time. ... Queen's joined with McGill in the formation of the McGill-Queen's University Press, with both institutions sharing equally in ownership, management and financing, for the purpose of stimulating and publishing scholarly research and such other material as the editorial committee considered suitable. ... Jerry Rubin, notorious American Yippie, addressed an open meeting in Grant Hall. He attracted a small audience, mostly apathetic.

The housing shortage grew worse. In the fall of 1968, the University provided temporary beds in the Gymnasium and the Students' Union and accommodation for 100 students, mostly women, in the

LaSalle Hotel. The students publicized their plight with a tent-in on the lawn in front of Summerhill, where they were visited by Dr. Deutsch, their landlord-in-residence. Science '44 Co-Op, reorganized and revitalized, purchased seven houses in Sydenham Ward. Dining facilities were centered in a house on Earl St., near Bagot. Plans were made by the AMS for a high-rise building on Princess St. to be known as Elrond College.

As the decade came to a close, one of the liveliest student issues was Orientation, or the lack of it. Opinion was sharply divided as to whether hazing and outlandish costumes should be included for first-year students. No clear-cut policy emerged.

COST OF LIVING

In 1960 a steak dinner cost $1.95 at Aunt Lucy's and by 1965 it was up to $2.99 (for a 14-ounce T-bone). When Prokop's Steak House opened it quickly became *the* place to eat; a small filet cost $2.95, a large filet $3.75, and a 'man-killer' $3.95. The Colonel's bucket of fried chicken could be had for $3.75. At the grocery stores white

Tent-in outside Summerhill, Fall 1968

79

sugar went at 69c for 10 pounds; sliced bread, two loaves for 35c; coffee, 79c a pound; butter, 49c; turkeys, 39c a pound. The butchers asked $1.00 for three pounds of hamburg or three pounds of weiners; breakfast bacon cost $1 for two pounds; T-bone steaks or roasts, 59c a pound; sausages, five pounds for a $1. A good TV set was worth $250 to $300, custom-tailored suits ranged from $70 to $115, and ready-to-wear, $60 to $90. At the February sales, these prices were cut in half. Ladies' coats, fur-trimmed and untrimmed, cost from $40 to $125; a man's harris tweed topcoat was $75. Beer was available in the beverage rooms for 15c a glass, or 18c to 23c a bottle. Ski boots sold for $11-$19. By the end of the Sixties, fees in Arts and Science were $500, Applied Science $575-$625, and Medicine $500-$625. Student interests fees were $62, up from $45.25.

MILESTONES

Death claimed several faithful servants of the University: Anne Corrigan of the Alumni Office, M. C. Tillotson, Dr. Gleb Krotkov, Dr. Glen Shortliffe and Rector L. W. Brockington. Retirements: Dr. G. B. Frost, Dr. J. E. Hawley, Prof. C. J. Vincent, André Bieler, Prof. J. C. Cameron. Dr. G. H. Ettinger, Dr. R. G. H. Smails, Dr. William Angus, Dr. O. A. Carson, Dr. W. A. Jones, Dr. F. M. Wood, Dr. H. L. Tracy, Dr. H. W. Harkness, Dr. R. L. Jeffery, Dr. D. M. Jemmett, Dr. B. N. Kropp, Prof. A. V. Corlett, Dr. L. A. Munro, Prof. F. L. Bartlett, A. H. W. (Sarge) Plumb of the Union, Prof. H. P. Gundy, Stew Langdon, Dr. F. A. Knox, Dr. W. A. Campbell, Dr. John Wyllie, Dr. E. M. Robertson, Dr. P. A. McLeod, Dr. Hilda Laird, Dr. S. W. Houston, Dr. C. A. Curtis, Dr. H. M. Cave, Dr. G. L. Edgett, Registrar Jean Royce, Dr. D. W. Boucher, Dr. W. D. Hay, Ralph Hinton, Mrs. Eleanor Tett Robertson Bolton, Miss Melva Eagleson, Prof. J.L. McDougall, and Dr. John Tweddell.

*

At the end of the first University Day of the modern era, Oct. 16, 1962, two students walking across campus were overheard discussing the University.

'No graduate of this place ever amounted to anything,' one said, 'with the exception of Lorne Greene, of course. You know, the fellow on television.'
'Oh, I don't know,' objected his companion. 'How about Ron Stewart?'

THE EDWARDS CASE

The decade was ushered in by what came to be known as the Edwards Case, an enquiry into charges made by a student, Charles Edwards, that he had been ousted from his Ph.D. studies in Chemical Engineering because of his Marxist views and his political activities with the Free Socialist Movement (FSM).

A committee of enquiry was established with Bernard L. Adell, Associate Dean of Law, as chairman; Valmore E. Traversy, a fourth-year Arts and Science student, appointed by the AMS President; Prof. Gordon Simmons of the Faculty of Law, appointed by the Principal; Dr. David Canvin, President of the Faculty Association, appointed by the Chemical Engineering Department; and Terry O'Hara, a student and a member of the Free Socialist Movement, appointed by Mr. Edwards. Legal counsel was provided by Prof. Morley Gorski, and later by Prof. L. S. Willoughby, representing the Chemical Engineering Department, and Donald Kuyek, a recent graduate in Law, representing Mr. Edwards.

A public hearing was conducted during most of the month of January and well into February, mostly in the auditorium in Macdonald Hall. Ninety hours were spent in 28 sessions, questioning 17 witnesses. The hearings attracted as many as 400 students and members of staff.

Mr. Edwards was on the stand for 20 hours, and the supervisor of his doctoral thesis, Dr. Henry Becker, was also on a long time. The burden of the Edwards side was the claim that Mr. Edwards had been told by Dr. Becker he must choose between political activities and his Ph.D. research, an ultimatum that followed an alleged campus investigation into his politics by the RCMP. The Chemical Engineering Department claimed, through Dr. Becker and others, that Mr. Edwards' work as a student had deteriorated and he had been asked to drop his course for academic reasons only.

In a report eventually submitted to the University Senate, the investigating committee found Dr. Becker 'utterly innocent' of any attempt to dismiss Edwards because of his political views. The treatment of Dr. Becker by Edwards and the FSM was labelled 'a paradox of social concern and individual callousness'.

On March 11 the Senate met in the Collins Room in Richardson Hall to implement the findings of the report, but the meeting was invaded by members of the FSM and had to be adjourned. The next meeting, held on April 3, moved to Wallace Hall in the Students' Union, with spectator accommodation for 140 students and 35 members of faculty. The proceedings were broadcast over CFRC.

A motion was passed unanimously, with one abstention, which read, in part:

That Mr. Edwards be strongly censured for his actions in this case, that as recommended in the report of the Special Committee he be permitted the opportunity of formulating and having accepted by the ordinary academic processes, an alternate plan of academic study within Queen's University, and that if Mr. Edwards is unable to arrange for an alternative plan of academic study by the 31st of May, 1970, he is permitted to apply for re-admission as a student at Queen's University with the assurance that his application will receive the normal serious consideration accorded to all other applications.

Also censured were Tom Good and Glenn MacDonell, members of the Alma Mater Society executive, who, making unauthorized use of AMS letterhead, had sent out to newspapers and student governments across the country the message that precipitated the enquiry.

Chuck Edwards' career as a radical was brief, but turbulent. A member of the University Council, he had been an unsuccessful candidate for the position of Rector when it opened for the first time to a student. He was, however, elected President of the AMS in the spring of 1968. By the time fall rolled round, his radical views placed him at loggerheads with the executive and he resigned, seeking a vote of confidence in the ensuing elections.

The special Senate committee constituted to investigate allegations relating to Mr. Edwards reported on his conversion to radicalism as follows:

The period between Mr. Edwards' election as AMS President in the spring of 1968 and his resignation from that position in October 1968 was politically and ideologically a heady time for him. He and Miss Jan Lichty, his vice-presidential running mate, successfully campaigned on an activist

'The Edwards Case' – historic open session of Senate in Wallace Hall, April 2, 1970.
George O. Lilley photo

platform which included increased student participation in university government and an accelerated attack on the student housing shortage. While he was in France, Mr. Edwards met students who had very recently taken part in the May Revolution, and was himself chased by a riot policeman in Paris. The cumulative effect of events at the Democratic National Convention in Chicago, student unrest at other Canadian universities, and the Marxist stand taken by the Canadian Union of Students at its 1968 Congress was to hasten Mr. Edwards' developing commitment to revolutionary ideology. In the fall he took an active part in the Emergency Committee for Student Housing at Queen's. As a result of his experiences on that Committee and in other matters, he came to the conclusion, which on cross-examination he completely failed to support, that the administration of Queen's University was incorrigibly 'reactionary and manipulative'. Opinion on the AMS executive began to harden against Mr. Edwards' attitudes and actions. In the face of a move to impeach them in October 1968, Mr. Edwards and Miss Lichty resigned their positions and were unsuccessful in their attempt to win them back in the ensuing election.

After the Senate handed down its decision, he was free to make application for re-admission as a student, but he did not do so. He stayed around Kingston for a while, then faded from the scene. Ultimately he surfaced again as a research chemist in the Toronto area.

THE FREE SOCIALIST MOVEMENT

Who were the members of the Free Socialist Movement? The actual number was small. They wore red armbands on which were emblazened the initials FSM. An indeterminate number of other students gave the group some degree of moral support, at least to the extent of publicly enjoying the harassment and embarrassment of the administration.

The *Journal* listed the membership at 25-30 students, two professors, five secondary school students, several St. Lawrence College students, and a few workers from the City. The members were not overly optimistic about the amount of support their movement could expect. In January 1970, they ordered 300 red and black buttons with the message: 'Stop RCMP. Stop Repression. Start a Free Society.' It was a collective organization with no president, secretary or treasurer. It started with the avowed purpose of democratizing the University and soon expanded its horizons to the building of a socialist Canada.

The Edwards Case gave the FSM its maximum exposure in the spotlight. It acted as a group in defending its star member. Many observers were of the opinion that Edwards was a pawn and that the movement had little real interest in him as a person.

When the Senate first met to consider the report on the Edwards Case, the FSM and sympathizers picketed Richardson Hall, and the Senators had to run a gauntlet in order to get to the Collins Room. Members of Science '73 on their way to a 3:30 class bombarded the picketers with snowballs. Finally the demonstrators, hooting and chanting, forced their way into the Senate meeting through the AMS constables on duty and the chairman, Dr. Deutsch, adjourned the meeting.

The group tried to enlist high school students in their cause, and put on demonstrations at some of the high schools, without much success. By the fall of 1970, the movement was dead. Most of the leaders had not returned. Some had graduated. Some were drop-outs.

While the disturbances were at their height, particularly in the invasion of the Senate meeting, there was widespread disbelief that this could be happening at 'good old Queen's'. Among the graduates there was considerable head-shaking and expressions of opinion that 'it couldn't have happened in our day.' There was a tendency on the part of the alumni, the older ones at least, to regard the incident on a par with the break-up of the British Empire. Ultimately the unrest subsided and comparative calm was restored.

Student government leaders later were quoted: 'Queen's was the last to get radicalism and the first to lose it.' An article on 'Activism at Queen's' in the 1975-76 *Who's Where* said: 'In spite of these events [the Edwards Case, FSM, demonstrations] Queen's was never a hotbed of political activity. Bloodshed was strictly confined to Blood Donor clinics. What about Queen's today? Will reductions in government aid to universities and students force us to politicize?' To this a current left-wing leader in Kingston commented: 'On a campus of students from the second highest income bracket in Canada!?'

There has indeed been a change from the days when Queen's was known as a poor man's university.

GRIEVANCE AND DISCIPLINE

A valuable by-product of the Edwards Case was the provision of channels for serious matters of grievance and discipline. The Edwards affair had been played by ear, and it was generally agreed that it had been handled in exemplary fashion. At the same time there was recognition of the danger inherent in a lack of well-developed policies.

While the Edwards hearings were still in progress, indeed hardly started, a Senate Committee on Grievance, Discipline and Related Matters was formed under the direction of R. L. Watts, then Dean of the Faculty of Arts and Science. The 11-member committee included one postgraduate student and four undergraduates.

After receiving briefs and oral representations from a wide range of individuals and groups within and outside the University community, and reviewing numerous documents from other universities, the final report was approved in May 1971. Heavy reliance was urged upon the existing informality and multiple channels for handling cases of grievance and discipline, but it was recommended that present procedures be augmented by an explicit statement of the rights and responsibilities of the members of the University community and by the addition of more visible formal procedures with clear channels of appeal.

The first definition of rights and responsibilities within the University rejected outright the notion that the University administration should act *in loco parentis*, or with parental responsibility for the student before the law.

In the section on External Rights and Responsibilities it was recommended and approved that 'There is no privileged status accorded to University members under our public law and none should be accorded in practice. Violations of civil or criminal law should be dealt with principally through the legal system of the country and not through a University system.' At the same time the report emphasized the function of AMS constables in crowd control at games and social functions.

The report also recommended there should be, first, no general continuous, permanently authorized RCMP surveillance on the campus; second, the appointment of a Faculty-Student Adviser for necessary investigations; and third, a system for handling grievances and discipline within the University. Altogether there were 56 recommendations approved. In the few instances in which it has since been found necessary to follow the system, the procedures have proven effective and adequate. The system is reviewed periodically, and only minor changes have been found necessary.

A visual revolution was introduced to the campus in 1971 with the appointment of Peter Dorn, RCA, as Co-Ordinating Director of Graphic Design. Under his direction a distinctive logotype was designed and a house style developed for all University publications. With two score national and international awards for typographic excellence already to his credit, Mr. Dorn soon established himself firmly by consistently winning many more awards for his efforts on behalf of Queen's.

In 1970, under the leadership of L. G. Greenwood, Vice-Chairman of the Canadian Imperial Bank of Commerce, a capital campaign was launched with a target of $6,500,000. The alumni accepted their largest objective of all time, $1,000,000 to be directed toward the construction of a University Centre. Doug Annan, Vice-President of DeHavilland Aircraft, was chairman of the alumni division; Dave Rigsby, Chief of the Fabrications Department, Alcan Research Development Ltd., was deputy national chairman. The students pledged a record $500,000 toward the cost of the University Centre. All objectives were realized.

H. G. Conn retired as Vice-Principal (Administration), returned to teaching, and was succeeded by Russell J. Kennedy; Dr. D. O. Waugh succeeded Dr. E. H. Botterell as Dean of Medicine, but Dr. Botterell continued as Vice-Principal (Health Sciences) until the following year; James M. Courtright left a vice-presidency at Shell Oil to fill the new post of Vice-Principal in charge of development and information.

The School of Business marked its 50th anniversary with a special alumni reunion which featured a symposium, smoker, dance, wine and cheese party, and informal get-togethers. There were 250 in attendance. ... Two new schools opened in the fall of 1970 – the School of Urban and Regional Planning, with Dr. S. D. Lash as Chairman, and the School of Public Administration, with Dr. Donald Gow as Director. ... The Canadian Institute of Guided Ground Transport also made its debut, a partnership of the University, Canadian National, Canadian Pacific, and the Canadian Transport Commission, with one of the major purposes being to find solutions for the problems that face Canada's railway industry. ...A new Centre for Resource Studies was established to carry out research and analysis on important questions of Canadian resource policy – such as the role of Canadian mining in the domestic economy and in the country's export trade. Basic funding was provided by the federal

Dedication of George Richardson Memorial Stadium, October 18, 1921

Closing ceremonies before move to the new Richardson Stadium, September 18, 1971, with the Richardson family and past football captains as special guests

government; Queen's supplies the academic and physical facilities.

The George Richardson Stadium was moved to the West Campus. In a public ceremony preceding the first game, a sod was taken from the old stadium to the new location in a colourful parade, with members of the Richardson family in attendance. ... Dr. R. J. Uffen, Chief Science Adviser to the Federal Cabinet, was appointed Dean of the Faculty of Applied Science. ... The Engineering Drawing building, formerly the Old Gymnasium, was named in honour of Arthur Jackson, Emeritus Professor of Engineering Drawing. ... The Senate established a Student Counselling Service under the direction of Prof. David Clarke, a psychologist, to offer assistance for a variety of problems facing students in a university environment. There was a staff of 15 volunteer psychologists.

Lorne Greene, the one-time Drama Guild star who became an internationally prominent stage, screen, and television performer, returned to Queen's for an honorary LL.D. degree. The visit was a tremendous success. Subsequently he established a scholarship in Drama worth $1,000 a year. ...The Douglas Library automated its circulation system. ... Evelyn Reid was appointed Dean of Women in succession to Beatrice Bryce, who had served with distinction in the demanding post during a period marked by fast-changing numbers, roles and mores.

After three years of negotiations, proposals, and counter-proposals, the first co-ed residence was opened during the 1972-73 session. Morris Hall was renovated to accommodate 91 men and 91 women, housed on alternate floors and sharing only common rooms and lounges. Within a few weeks the *Journal* reported: 'There is a terrific spirit. Life in a co-ed residence is calmer, easier, and more civilized than life in a men's residence.'

Queen's students received a high proportion of the federal Opportunities for Youth grants. About 350 were involved in 12 summer work programs accounting for total wages of $350,000. Students also found work for themselves through a Job Bank which they had set up to supplement the efforts of the University's Employment Service. ... Student aid amounting to $3,163,000 was distributed among 2,700 Queen's students from the Ontario Student Awards Program. Another 600 received help through the University Student Loan funds and bursaries. ... A Co-operative Day Care Centre was established. It eventually settled at 169 Union Street, providing care for children from ten months to kindergarten age for families of students, faculty and staff. The West Campus Nursery School, for children upwards of two-and-a-half years old, was located in the Married Students Housing Complex on Van Order Drive.

An ambitious program to help delinquent and potentially delinquent teenagers was conceived and developed by a first-year Medical student, Ronald Kimberley of Beamsville, Ont. Known as Camp Outlook, the venture was an instantaneous success. Most of the equipment and gear were scrounged, all the help was voluntary, and the necessary money was raised by a number of fund-raising projects and by subscription. The underprivileged teens were taken on self-challenging canoe trips in Algonquin Park. The program is still in healthy existence, a well-organized effort.

Anniversaries were much in evidence. The Queen's Alumnae Association celebrated its diamond jubilee with a residence weekend in Chown Hall. In 1972 Radio Station CFRC marked 50 years of

campus activity. It was now two stations in one: Queen's Radio AM and Fine Arts FM. *The Queen's Journal* celebrated 100 years of publication and brought out a centennial edition in February 1974. Queen's Drama Guild marked its 75th continuous year with a weekend for past and present Guilders in March 1975. Actor-writer Sandy Webster of Arts '49 was guest speaker at the anniversary banquet.

After losing $1,000 a month, the AMS-operated downtown outlet for student craftsmen, Heffalump, was closed. ... Gary Gannage was elected student Rector. ... Hare Krishna units visited the campus, and Transcendental Meditation also made its first appearance. ... Students took part in a province-wide movement to withhold second-term fees in protest against an increase in tuition fees imposed by the provincial government. After their point was made, with the Trustees' co-operation, they paid their fees. ... The AMS made an arrangement with the City for unlimited use of the bus service operated by the Public Utilities. Known as Bus-it, the service was provided by a $3.00 fee from each participating student and $2.00 from the University. The tariff was increased in subsequent years.

Kingston celebrated its Tercentenary in 1973 and the University provided many of the facilities and resources. Seventeen major events took place on campus. The Queen visited the City, attending a formal reception in Richardson Stadium and a civil banquet in Leonard Hall.

Open visiting hours in the women's residences were extended to 24 hours a day. ... Elrond College, a student-operated high-rise housing co-operative on Princess St., was finally opened after many frustrations and delays. ... *Golden Words* editor Kevin Van Koughnett, Sc. '75, was elected Male Chauvinist Pig of the year. ... Queen's Law students opened a Legal Aid office in the city's North End. ... On April Fool's Day, Engineering students gave the clock in the Grant Hall tower a Mickey Mouse dial face. Dr. Deutsch described the caper as 'the Queen's engineer at his playful, creative best'.

Dr. H. Garfield Kelly was appointed Vice-Principal (Health Sciences), succeeding Dr. Douglas O. Waugh, who continued as Dean of the Faculty of Medicine. ... The Rt. Hon. Roland Michener, C.C., C.M.M., C.D., LL.D., was named the ninth Chancellor of Queen's, which post he assumed a year later on the completion of his duties as Governor-General of Canada. The incumbent, Dr. J. B. Stirling,

Royal Visitors at Leonard Hall during Kingston's Tercentenary, 1973. Left to right, Mrs. Stirling, Chancellor J.B. Stirling, Queen Elizabeth, Mrs. Speal, Mayor George Speal and Prince Philip. *Toronto Star photo*

agreed to carry on in the interim, and in the fall of 1973 he capped his 20,000th graduate.

The books in the Douglas Library passed the million mark, joining the university libraries at Toronto and Western in this category. ... Tech Supplies, renovated and enlarged, became the Campus Bookstore again, a name it had borne for 21 years after business began in 1909. The manager is Frank Gauchie, who succeeded A. M. 'Brad' Bradburn in 1970. ... Associated Medical Services Inc. presented the University with $250,000 to endow the Jason A. Hannah Chair in the History of Medical and Related Sciences. The chair was named for the pioneering founder of Associated Medical Services, a distinguished graduate, and a member of both the Board of Trustees and the University Council.

Prof. C. H. R. (Chuck) Campling, Professor and Head of the Department of Electrical Engineering, ran and completed the Boston Marathon within the prescribed time. It was a remarkable accomplishment for a man 51 years of age and a former smoker with a history of high blood pressure. ... The Rev. Dr. Robert Bater was installed as Principal of Queen's Theological College. Dr. Bater was a former Rhodes Scholar from Saskatchewan, an author, and a specialist in the field of Biblical literature. He succeeded Dr. Donald M. Mathers, who had died of leukemia at the age of 51.

STREAKING

The spring season brings on all sorts of madness in campuses across the land, fads such as gold-fish swallowing, students cramming into telephone booths, and other forms of nonsense. These fads usually start in the United States and take a year or two to cross the border, but the streaking craze of 1974 seemed to erupt by spontaneous combustion at all points of the compass and regardless of weather conditions. The record number of participants seemed to have been reached at the University of Colorado when 1,200 naked students dashed around the campus cheered on by 6,000 onlookers. In Canada the numbers were considerably fewer, probably as a concession to lower temperatures.

At Queen's the craze lasted two nights in the month of March. First, a couple of dozen, some on bicycles, others on car tops, braved the chill breezes; as a follow-up, 75 Queen's men wearing only sneakers held a pep rally on the lower campus and proceeded to serenade the co-eds in Victoria Hall. They achieved a fleeting sort of fame when a group picture was printed in the *Whig-Standard* and the *Journal* of March 12 bore on the front page the picture of a male streaker wearing only a President Nixon mask. The issue became an instant collectors' item. At the Royal Military College, across Kingston harbour, two cadets streaked across the parade square. They were charged with being improperly dressed for parade and given extra guard duty as punishment.

Said the *Journal*, prophetically, 'The novelty of streaking will wear off. As it is, it may be suffering from a case of overkill.'

The home on Queen's Crescent built by Dr. W. E. McNeill and later occupied by Dr. John Orr was made the headquarters in 1974 for the Ban Righ Foundation for Continuing University Education for Women. Financed by funds accumulated over the years through the work of the Ban Righ Board, the Foundation was established to serve as a resource centre for the academic and social interests of mature women students. Mrs. Helen Mathers was the first director. ... Finn O. Bogstad was appointed as the new Co-ordinator of Student Services. ... Dr. Duncan G. Sinclair became Dean of the Faculty of Arts and Science in succession to Dr. Ronald L. Watts, Principal-elect. ... Bruce Trotter was elected Rector, the third student in succession in the post. ... There were official openings for the latest building additions: Mackintosh/Corry Hall, the Arts/Social Sciences complex; Jean Royce Hall, the West Campus residence complex; the Donald Gordon Centre for Continuing Education, built around the elegant Roselawn at Union and College Sts. and financed privately; and Harrison-LeCaine Hall, the new Music building on Queen's Crescent, named for the first resident musician at Queen's and a graduate who has had a distinguished career in the field of electronic music.

The limestone building on Arch St. which houses the Physiology Department was named Abramsky Hall in recognition of the funds pledged by Harry and Ethel Abramsky. ... As their traditional April Fool's Day prank, the Engineering students winched a Volkswagen into a tree on University Ave. One member of staff commented, 'I know there is a shortage of parking space at Queen's, but this is ridiculous.' ... Science '44 Co-op staged a Bike-a-thon to support the Rotary Club's work with crippled children. ... Total registration surpassed 10,000 in the fall of 1975, made up of 9,108 undergraduates

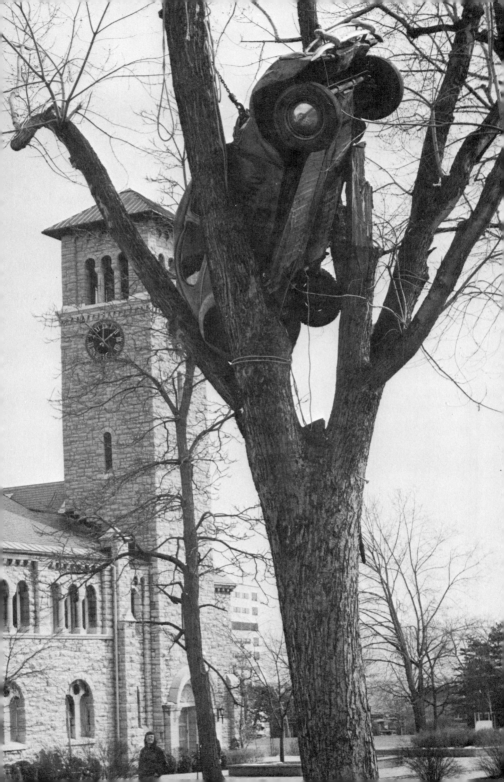

and 1,085 graduates. This was the level at which the University administration had vowed to hold the line until 1980.

Dr. Thomas J. Boag, Head of the Department of Psychiatry, succeeded Dr. D. O. Waugh, who resigned as Dean of the Faculty of Medicine. Prof. H. Morris Love was appointed Vice-Principal (Services), streamlining the functions of two retiring Vice-Principals – Prof. R. J. Kennedy (Administration) and Dr. George A. Harrower (Academic). It was all part of the program for financial restraint urged by a special Principal's committee in 1975.

Two students in Arts and Science were named Rhodes Scholars for the same year (1976): Chesley Crosbie, St. John's, Nfld., and Douglas Hutchinson, Vancouver, B.C.. ... The Engineering Society introduced the Golden Apple awards in recognition of teaching ability and outstanding interest in engineering activities, for presentation to professors nominated by their students. ... R. W. Southam of Ottawa was appointed Chairman of the Board of Trustees, in succession to J. D. Gibson. Mrs. Agnes Benidickson and Norman Rogers were named Vice-Chairmen.

LIFESTYLES

The student of the Seventies, like the month of March, came in like a lion, and judging from the transformation by mid-decade, would go out, if not like a lamb, at least considerably subdued. Jeans, new and used, were the popular dress for men and women alike, and sometimes the only distinguishing feature was that the boys had longer hair. Beards and whiskers became commonplace – wild, untrimmed, uncombed hirsute appendages; so did mustaches – undisciplined, unruly, untidy, for the most part, ranging from Fu Manchus to British army; and long, long sideburns. When the girls wore skirts they were mini-skirts which were the maximum of minimums – there was never a more fertile era for girl-watchers. All sorts of headgear were worn – leather hats, German helmets, Sherlock Holmes deerstalkers, woollen toques, railway engineers' caps. Every day was Hallowe'en. Old commonplace courtesies between the sexes, such as men holding the door open for women and walking on the outside when escorting female companions, disappeared.

A 1970 editorial in the *Journal* depicted the Queen's archetype as one who would 'make your common garden slug look independent.'

Whatever is 'in' is done; but at Queen's it's done a year after everybody else did it. The most amazing thing about the typical Queen's student is that each believes he is the most atypical person here. None of this would bother me, except that everybody acts so smart and independent about their sameness. If we have 10,000 different minds here, why haven't we got 10,000 different topics of conversation, 10,000 different personalities?

The truth of the matter, as some of the students were quick to point out themselves, was that conformity rather than independence was the order of the day.

Gradually the scene changed. Hair styles became tamed, shaped and combed. Jeans and denims looked laundered. Bare feet gave way to high-heeled boots, sandals, running shoes and, in the winter, sturdy workboots. Students still went most places in shirts and sweaters, but formal suits, even vests, began to make a comeback.

Perhaps one of the greatest changes was in height. The campus looked as if it were populated with basketball players, with six feet the apparent minimum for men, and with many girls in the five-foot-eight to six-foot range. There were still some smaller personnel around, but they were in the minority.

Nearly everyone drove a car or had access to one. Parking became a highly competitive game. The City Parking Authority meter men and the tow trucks reaped a fortune.

When Reading Week came along, a surprising number of students were able to afford a ski trip, or a trip to sunnier climes. There were those who couldn't afford either, or who preferred to study, but they weren't so noticeable. All the same, students of the Seventies studied longer and harder. They had to, to survive.

And what has this metamorphosis done to that intangible but very real element known as the 'Queen's spirit'? It is a pleasure to report that the sophisticated young men and women who populate the campus today are just as enthusiastic about the old school as they were in your day and mine. 'This place is just fabulous,' one young man confided to me after he had been on campus one week.

Chris Redmond writing in the *Journal* in 1971 said: 'Queen's is to love: to walk night-shivering past Leonard Field to the lake, to devour history readings in a three-hour reserve-room loan period, to fling hoarse *Oil Thighs* to the wind at a football game in which Queen's is not even playing, because Queen's is the only university and all the world must know it!'

What of the future? Redmond concluded:

Never again will Queen's be a homogeneous college as it was 40 or even ten years ago. Never again, quite possibly, will the limestone loyalty of the last few years exist. Never again, probably, will an *Oil Thigh* be sung as big as it was sung last November. But a loyalty to Queen's can continue. It will only come from a recognition that there is no value in 'loyalty' to walls and a name, but to people and to the four years spent among them.

Queen's is a people place.

A CULTURAL EXPLOSION

As *Tricolor '74* pointed out, 'entertainment no longer means the occasional concert and the once-a-week wild dance in Grant Hall.' The arts could not be visualized as a separate compartment of Queen's; on the contrary, music, art, film, dance and drama were carefully integrated into the academic and social life of the students and members of staff.

For the long-hairs there was a wealth of attractions offered through the Dunning Hall and Grant Hall concert series which brought in such outstanding attractions as the New York Pro Musica, the Prague Orchestra and the Moscow Chamber Orchestra; every season offered a musical feast, featuring internationally renowned groups, chamber ensembles, and soloists. The Vaghy Quartet, artists-in-residence, played on campus and on tour, spreading the name of Queen's far and wide and making a fine subject for a National Film Board movie.

The Music Department produced its first Bachelors of Music in 1973 and had an important impact on the campus. Gone were the days of uncertain music at Convocations and other important functions; there was now a professional touch that brought quiet contentment to the ears of music lovers. The Department offered a wealth of opportunities to students and staff to join various performing groups such as the Chamber Singers, Collegium Musicum, Choral Ensemble, Jazz Ensemble, Wind Ensemble, and Improvisation Group.

The Ban Righ Fireside programs helped to bring music to the students and to encourage their appreciation. In the spring of 1974, one ambitious project was a concert performance of Monteverdi's opera *L'Incoronazione de Poppea*. Downtown one could attend concerts by the Kingston Symphony Orchestra and the Kingston Choral Society.

The Agnes Etherington Art Centre, named after the generous benefactor whose vision had provided the first break-through, expanded more and more into a pivotal point for all things cultural on campus and in the community. In no areas were the efforts to promote town-gown relationships more effective than in the work of the Music Department and the Art Centre, or Art's Place, as it was referred to by its friends, who were legion. There was a procession of exhibitions, displays, art classes, concerts, visits and talks by prominent artists, brown bag luncheons, poetry readings, dancing – you name it, there was something for nearly everyone almost all of the time. The Heritage Kingston exhibition mounted during Kingston's Tercentennial celebrations was a classic, and so was the book *Heritage Kingston.*

The Modern Dance Company, under the direction of Sandra Aitken, a Drama graduate who taught modern dance as part of the School of Physical and Health Education curriculum, was formed in the early Seventies and offers a new dimension to Queen's world of entertainment. New art forms are developed, combining elements of dance and theatre and involving the talent of actors, acrobats, poets, writers, musicians, and artists in all media.

Dancing as a social pastime had undergone a dramatic transformation over a period of years. Music was provided by small combos dispensing various versions of rock, country, jazz, boogie, blues and bluegrass, most of it strident and all of it loud. Each had its own cult among the students, who seemed to be as content to listen as to join in the dancing, which perhaps was understandable with couples going their separate ways in convulsive, writhing, epileptic movements. Music was dispensed by such esoteric groups or individuals as Greaseball Boogie Band, Downchild Blues Band, Boojum, Streetnoise, Crowbar, Mother Nature, Slewfoot, and the Greasers, to mention a few. Gordon Lightfoot was a popular entertainer and played to packed houses. Ditto the group Lighthouse. Off campus one could go to discothèques downtown or such quaint spots as the Scarecrow, a natural foods restaurant and coffee bar. When ballroom dancing showed some signs of resurgence, it was found necessary to provide lessons, since the current crop had no experience with this cheek-to-cheek business. They caught on quickly and enthusiastically.

The Drama Guild continued to provide ambitious fare, ranging from Shakespeare to Chekhov to *The Ecstasy of Rita Joe*. The Musical Theatre launched such vehicles as *Bye, Bye, Birdie!*, *Cabaret*, and *The Boy Friend*. The Medical students had their own variety night, which one year was titled 'Thanks for the Mammaries'. There were Snoballs, with the students trying their hands at ice sculpture even if they had to import the snow, as was necessary more than one 'green' January.

Movies were shown on campus almost every night of the school year, including documentaries, classics, foreign, underground and *avant garde* varieties. A new Department of Film Studies heightened interest and appreciation. Students made their own films, some of high calibre. Downtown one could see such fare as *Alice's Restaurant*, *Last Tango in Paris*, *The Prime of Miss Jean Brodie*, *The Sting*, *Jesus Christ Superstar*, and *One Flew Over the Cuckoo's Nest*. There were annual Arts Festivals in which students were given an opportunity to express themselves through singing, writing, painting, films, photography, and puppet theatres.

The Students' Union had its own coffee house, Bitter Grounds, and two pubs, the House of Commons and Wallace Hall, which had the desirable effect of keeping the kiddies off the street. Popular off-campus bistros and watering-holes were Beaup's, the Lakeview Manor, the Commodore, the Pub, the Shamrock, Finnigan's and Muldoon's. The sweet smell of maryjane was still pervasive, but not as much in evidence, by the mid-Seventies; the drug scene was never big at Queen's.

And speakers, speakers, speakers. Never a school week went by without some authority, or expert, or politician, or person in the news for some reason or another, mounting a platform to discuss, declaim, orate – Dr. R. O. Balfour, for example, and Buckminster Fuller, Premier William Davis, Sir Bernard Lovell, Kahn-Tineta Horn, Dr. Gunnar Myrdal, Lord Bowden of Chesterfield and Dr. Jean Vanier.

SIGNS OF THE TIMES

A Women's Office was opened under the auspices of the AMS External Affairs Commission, pledged 'to initiate a higher level of consciousness on the part of the student body with regard to feminist issues on campus.' ... The *Journal* published a weekly series of menus, designed for those who cooked their own meals, as a change of pace from hot dogs, fried chicken, hamburgs, Chinese food, and pizzas. They included steak and kidney pie, roast beef with all the trimmings, and cherry cobbler. ... The AMS brought out a booklet, 'You and the Law', about legal rights of students who might be hassled by the fuzz, and giving information on such topics of the day as bail, police questioning, arrest, search, vagrancy, causing a disturbance, riots, drugs and alcohol.

A phenomenon of the Seventies was the annual *Golden Words* beer brewing contest in which a panel of judges selected from among student leaders, members of staff, and Molson's brewery representatives passed judgment on a variety of home brews. Competition was keen, and to the Brewmaster First Class went a suitably engraved tray and a monetary award. ... Football pubs became an adjunct of the football scene. Students could meet in the Jean Royce Hall dining room on the West Campus and drink beer before, during, and after, or instead of, the game. A radio broadcast helped to keep the customers informed as to what was taking place on the field.

Dance marathons were held to raise funds for the Camp Outlook project. Twelve hours of music were provided by such groups as Fallen Angel and the Queen's Jazz Ensemble, $400 in prizes were offered, and admission was a commitment of at least 25c per half-hour in pledges. ... Horse-drawn sleigh rides on Wolfe Island made a return to popularity with a 'stop at General Wolfe Hotel if requested'. ... A Ban Right Foundation lecture was offered on Contract Co-habitation – an Alternative to Marriage.

The Journal was a popular medium for a wide assortment of invitations, announcements and proclamations. For example, '219 Stuart announces a Homecoming Party. The sordid guest list includes friends and lovers from Morris, 123 Beverley, Ferenci and crew, Tweedledee and Tweedledum, and Crystal, the Happy Pervert, the Cornishes, Gael groups 51 and 56, and other assorted ragtags and street urchins. Curtain time 8:00 p.m., Saturday.' ... '2nd Gordon – We love you. You're the best. Love from the chicks on 2D.' ... 'Queen's Homophile Association. Information and counselling on matters concerning sexual identity 547-2836.' ... Notice for a hockey game with the University of Toronto: 'No cans or bottles of any sort will be allowed inside the arena proper. Wineskins only. Constables checking at the door.'

The *Journal* classifieds were also a popular place to advertise for accommodation:

It's not your body we are after – it's where you keep it. You might have what we're looking for: a five-man house that could be turned into a den of iniquity! If you can fill this order (wink, wink, nudge, nudge, say no more), please call John (544-7505), Anne (544-8342), or Cathy (544-8359). P.S. If you can find us a house we'll sell you our seester for five pesos or treat you to a night at the pub!

ORIENTATION

The problems of a physical initiation which had plagued the authorities for more than half the life of the University were gradually phased out by the emergence of what came to be known as Orientation Week. Prior to the start of classes in September, a variety of activities are planned each year to familiarize the freshmen, freshettes and transfer students with the social, cultural and academic opportunities available to them. The emphasis is on academic counselling and introduction to Queen's and Kingston rather than physical initiation rites.

The University Senate took advantage of this development to pass the following resolution: 'The Senate forbids the use of physical violence on any person as part of initiation activities at Queen's University. The consent of the victim does not make such violence permissible or justifiable.' This was the party line which had been paid lip-service from time to time over the years, but now it became a way of life because the students themselves were in agreement. It might be argued that the annual greasepole ritual conducted by the Engineering students is not exactly a daisy-chain ceremony, but nothing in life is perfect.

COST OF LIVING

The cost of being a student continued to rise during the Seventies and, indeed, increased by leaps and bounds. Tuition fees in Arts and Science were $600, plus another $70.15 in student interest fees; Applied Science tuition, $675 to $725 and student interests, $76.15; Medicine tuition, $725, student interests, $84.15. Room and board was in the $950 to $1150 range for the academic year, although these costs could be reduced by joining one of the Science '44 Co-ops or being one's own chief cook and bottlewasher. When OSAP (Ontario Student Aid Program) announced in 1974 that a student could live on $32 a week for room and board, there was a barrage of protests that the figure was much too low, indeed below the poverty line. Meals downtown cost from $1.75 for spaghetti and

Veteran of the Engineers' Toilet Bowl, 1976. *Fred Van Driel photo*

meatballs to $4.95 for a T-bone steak at Lino's, $7.75 for a filet mignon at the Continental, $4.50 for Sunday smorgasbord at Chimo, $6.75 for roast spring chicken at the Buttery, $5.95 for roast beef at Aunt Lucy's, or 99c for a spaghetti special at Mother's. Christmas dinner at the Students' Union was $2.75.

At the stores, hamburg averaged 61c a pound, round steak, $1.27, wieners, $1.01, chicken, 92c a pound, salmon, $1.34, eggs, 95c a dozen, margarine, 74c, coffee, $1.43, flour, 72c, tomatoes, 67c, corn flakes, 49c, soda crackers, 72c. In the clothing area, denim suits ranged from $40 to $125; woollen suits, $90 to $225; women's all-weather coats, $32.99; blouses, $12 up; panty hose, 69c, leather sandals, $18 to $25; spring coats, $55; leather coats $150; shoes, thick soles, high heels, on sale at the Adam's Apple Boutique, $21.99; Dack's shoes, $50. The most overworked word in the advertisements was 'only', as in 'only $143'.

All sorts of skiing weekends were available from a modest few dollars to packages costing hundreds. Ambitious and well-heeled skiers could try their skills in Austria and Switzerland at special rates, and some did. Or one could go to Cocoa Beach in Florida in Reading Week for $180.

The formals cost more. The charges for the Science Formal with a D'Artagnan theme were $30; dress, white tie. Since few own formal clothes in the Seventies, the rental agencies do a land-office business. The Arts Formal at the Holiday Inn cost $20, with all-night music by Charity Brown and Bill Baker, cocktails at 7 p.m., hot and cold buffet, black tie optional. Commerce '76 put on a dinner dance for $21 a couple at the Austrian Club, with music by Major Hoople's Boarding House, a roast beef dinner with wine, semi-formal attire.

The Alumni Association established an annual Alumni Award for Excellence in Teaching to recognize faculty members whose knowledge of their field and whose concern for students are exemplary. The award consists of a certificate and $1,000. The first winner was Prof. William D. Gilbert of the Department of Mechanical Engineering, in 1975. Prof. H. R. Stuart Ryan of the Faculty of Law won in 1976.

The number of women enrolled in professional faculties continued to increase, most notably in the Faculty of Applied Science, where there were 115 in 1975-76 compared with 40 two years previously. At mid-decade women accounted for about one-third of the enrolment in Medicine, one-quarter in Law, and one-fifth in Business. Of the total enrolment in first-year undergraduate programs for all faculties, the proportion of women reached 50 per cent in September 1975.

When the Olympic sailing events were held in Kingston in the summer of 1976, Queen's facilities and personnel played an important role. The men's residences on Leonard Field were made the official Olympic Village, housing the competing crews of many nations. Regatta officials and security staff were housed in the women's residences, the international press on the West Campus, and special visitors in the Donald Gordon Centre. The Computing Centre processed the race results. Photographers from Queen's Television were official recorders. Scores of staff members were involved in the arrangements, with George Wattsford, Director of University Services, as chairman of the Queen's co-ordinating committee. Principal Watts was a member of the organizing committee and served as Chief Class Officer, co-ordinating competitors in the six Olympic classes; Col. 'Cam' Jones, Director of Physical Plant, was Director-General of Yachting; Prof. S. S. Lazier was in charge of testing the boats to ensure that they met Olympic measurement requirements. Also involved were Bob Partridge, Arts '35, Commodore of the Kingston Yacht Club, in charge of finances for the sailing events, and Mayor George Speal, Q.C., Com. '54. Many students found employment as guides, hostesses, clerks, etc.

A new formula to preserve the colour and shape of flowers and leaves, perhaps forever, was developed by technician Jack Webb of the Biology Department, and the news was greeted with widespread enthusiasm. The University entered into a contract with Boreal Laboratories of Cooksville to market the product and method for universities and other educational institutions. It was also planned to have the product available to the general public. Mr. Webb pledged any and all profits to Queen's.

MILESTONES

Death ended long and distinguished careers: Rev. Dr. Donald Mathers, Principal of Queen's Theological College, Dr. J. W. Ambrose, Prof. K. G. Crawford ('probably the outstanding authority in Canada on local government'), librarian Diana Blake, and Gordon J. Smith, former Alumni Secretary, Director of Endowment and Treasurer of the University.

And there were many retirements: the popular Dean of Women, Beatrice Bryce; Dr. H. Wesley Curran, twice voted Kingston's Man of the Year; L. G. Macpherson, Vice-Principal (Finance), who commenced his retirement by heading the Principal's Committee on Financial Constraint; Misses Melva Eagleson, Kathleen Healey, Hon. M.A. and Jean Richardson; A. M. 'Brad' Bradburn; Doctors E. M. Boyd, G. W. Mylks and R. C. Burr; Professors Marion Ross, A. W. Jolliffe, B. W. Sargent (called one of the western world's top scientists), H. M. Estall, H. H. Stewart, E. E. Watson, Harold Pollock, R. W. Thompkins, S. D. Lash, W. D. Gilbert, W. H. Poole, J. Lorne McDougall, C. H. Curtis, W. H. Evans, W. E. C. Harrison, B. H. Hopkins, B. M. Koster, E. A. Walker, and the Rev. Dr. Elias Andrews. R. D. Bradfield, Hon. M.Sc., the instrument maker for the Physics Department, also retired.

Several who had served in senior posts for specified terms stepped down to return to teaching: Dr. T. S. Webster, Dean of Student Affairs, Prof. H. G. Conn, Vice-Principal (Administration), and Dr. James H. Brown, Dean of Applied Science. Professor Conn retired in 1976 after a career that had begun in 1937, interrupted only by a distinguished war career.

*

Prof. Arthur Jackson possessed a fabulous memory. He was usually able to identify each student who had ever registered in Engineering at Queen's, years after the event, and even if the lad had been in attendance only one year. Whenever the Alumni Office had difficulty in identifying engineers in a picture, Professor Jackson was one of the first ports of call.

Another with an excellent memory is the University Chaplain, Rev. Dr. A. M. Laverty. He not only can call by name most of the students who have been at Queen's in his time, but, in a remarkable number of cases, the names of their parents, relatives, friends and paper boy, as well.

He is rarely stumped. I recall one such occasion, however, after a football game, when a group of recent graduates was streaming into the Gymnasium. Marsh was at the door, and as they passed him, at the double, he returned their Hiya, Padre's by calling each one by name. All but one, that is. The last to file by was left ungreeted. The Padre stood there, obviously discomfited, trying in vain to dredge up from his memory the name of that lad, and the strain was deeply etched on his face. Finally one of the group, a good Samaritan, returned.

'It's okay, Padre,' he said. 'You never saw that guy before. He's a friend of ours from the University of Toronto.'

III
Among
those present...

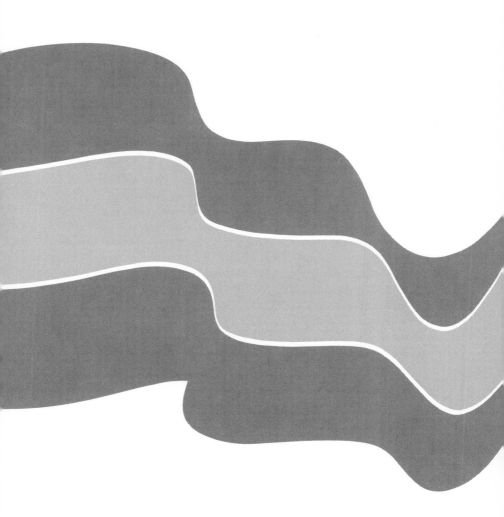

D.G. Dewar photo

William Everett McNeill

All he ever aspired to be was a teacher of English, which goal he attained early in life. However, in the process, he had also displayed executive and administrative talent to such a degree that he was pressed into service as a businessman, and he conducted the financial affairs of Queen's University with such efficiency and effectiveness that his name will long be remembered as a financial genius.

William Everett McNeill served Queen's University for 38 years. Principal after Principal paid tribute to his acumen. His colleagues, frustrated by the Draconian economic measures adopted because money was scarce, a condition that was intensified during the Depression, nevertheless valued his singular talents. To the students he was a remote figure, a monster and an ogre who did not allow the heat to be turned on until 9.00 a.m. And yet all who came in contact with him found him to be, if stern and formidable, actually humane and understanding. He had a magnificent sense of humour which he held firmly in check until he felt the time was opportune. As a one-man financial bulwark, he always had a plateful of problems and not nearly enough time to deal with them, and so he probably felt restrained.

He always had a nagging regret that his skills as a scholar had not been allowed wider scope. He told of a friend who, when shown his Harvard graduation photograph, exclaimed: 'Why, you used to look like a scholar!' 'What do I look like now?' asked Dr. McNeill. 'A business man,' was the reply.

On another occasion he told of being asked to speak at an out-of-town school. 'I was told I would be met at the station. I stood on the platform until every other passenger had disappeared. Then a seedy-looking taxi-man approached me and asked, "Would you be the professor from Kingston?"

"Yes," I said.

"Well, I'll be damned," he exclaimed, and added, Do you see that fellow over there?", pointing to an even seedier taxi-man. "I

109

said to him, Do you see anyone who looks like a professor? Not a damned one, he said." '

Said Dr. McNeill, 'I've always wanted to look like a professor, but the Trustees of Queen's, like the two taxi-men, could see no resemblance. That was the greatest disappointment of my life.'

In his view the teacher was the great man in a university. 'Trustees, Chancellors, Principals, Deans, Registrars, and Librarians exist only that the teacher may enrich the lives of students. In my judgment the greatest teacher this University has had was James Cappon. I suggested the epitaph on his tomb in Cataraqui Cemetery. It is the last line of Chaucer's description of the Oxford scholar: "And gladly would he learn and gladly teach." I wish that could have been said of me as a final tribute.'

There was a parallel to his career and that of Sir Edward Peacock, an M.A. of 1894 and one of Queen's most distinguished graduates. Sir Edward had specialized in English and Political Science, taught English at Upper Canada College, and then developed into a great financier, a director of the Bank of England, Receiver General of the Duchy of Cornwall, and financial adviser and confidant of the Royal Family. It is interesting to note that when Dr. McNeill retired he was elected to the University's Board of Trustees to fill out the unexpired term of Sir Edward, who had resigned after 33 years of service.

Dr. McNeill was born at Lower Montague, Prince Edward Island, on November 29, 1876. His preliminary education was obtained at Prince of Wales College, Charlottetown, where he held a government scholarship. In 1900 he graduated from Acadia University with a B.A. and the Governor-General's Medal. In 1902 he obtained his B.A. from Harvard. He taught at Bates College for three years, and there he met his future wife, Caroline Emily Libby, Professor of Romance Languages and Dean of Women. He returned to Harvard for graduate studies, at the same time being an assistant in English. A James Savage Scholar, he was awarded his M.A. in 1907 and his Ph.D. two years later.

At Harvard, Dr. McNeill studied under some of the outstanding English scholars of the day. He had Kittredge in Shakespeare, Neilson in Romantic Revival, Bliss Perry of the *Atlantic* in 19th Century, Baker in Drama, Robinson in Chaucer, and Copeland in great poetry and prose. Years later, at his retirement dinner, he told his audience that up to that point the highlight of his career had been the time that Kittredge, rated one of the top three English scholars of the world, had chosen him to read his examination papers. He assisted Kittredge for two years. Later he was to study at Oxford under such noted scholars as Sir Walter Raleigh, D. Nichols Smith, and Professor Napier.

But he longed to return to Canada. He chose Queen's at $1,350 a year, although he had been told the University had no future, instead of an American college at $3,000. He was influenced in his decision by two colleagues from Bates who preceded him at Queen's, Dr. A. L. Clark and Dr. Cecil Lavell. His credentials carried no weight with James Cappon, Dean of the Faculty of Arts and Head of the Department of English. As a new man he was assigned a heterogeneous assortment of subjects: Junior English Composition, Senior English Argumentation and History of the Language, Honours Anglo-Saxon, and Romance Philology, and, what seemed to be the crowning indignity, Public Speaking in Queen's Theological College. When Dr. McNeill pleaded that he might have an hour or more in Shakespeare, 'Cappon looked at me over his glasses in resistant surprise and sternly demanded: "How can you teach literature? You are American trained. There are not two men in Boston who do not think James Whitcomb Riley the greatest poet who ever lived." '

It was one of Dr. McNeill's proudest memories that he soon won Cappon's favour, because the Dean was 'notwithstanding formidable prejudices, one of the greatest men I have ever met.' During Cappon's sabbatical leave in 1913-14 Dr. McNeill was Acting Head of the Department. When Cappon resigned in 1919, he was again appointed Acting Head. In the summer of 1920 he was made Head, but he functioned only two weeks in this capacity. G. Y. Chown, Registrar and Treasurer since before the turn of the century, resigned. He was one of Grant's men, one of the Makers of Queen's, as great in planning and execution as others in scholarship and teaching. When Chown urged the appointment of McNeill as his successor as Registrar and Treasurer and also as Secretary to the Board of Trustees, the Trustees acted on the suggestion without hesitation.

McNeill always felt the appointment was a mad one. He had no business experience. He felt it was in retribution for his sins in attending faculty meetings regularly and taking an active part in discussions. He always came to a meeting well prepared, having made a careful study of the points at issue, his thoughts marshalled logically. He had particularly distinguished himself as chairman of the

University Board of Studies in Arts, responsible for the modernization of undergraduate and graduate studies in Arts.

At all events he embarked upon his new career with misgivings that were not shared by those in authority and soon justified the confidence that had been shown in him. His horizons broadened from a department to an entire university. The welfare of Queen's became his all-encompassing concern. Those were not easy times. Money was scarce, and when the Depression came along the balancing of the budget became even more formidable. It gave Dr. McNeill the greatest of pleasure to be able to present a balanced budget year after year, managed without reducing salaries.

Upon retirement in 1947 he was able to say:

In the last 25 years there has been a greater development than in the previous 80, and I have sat with the Chancellor, Principal, and Trustees in the planning. Queen's has changed from a small institution of three excellent but somewhat conventional faculties to a large modern university with a great variety of courses and facilities. Its revenues in that time have increased from $300,000 to $1,500,000 a year.

His financial genius was widely acclaimed. H. B. Muir, co-owner of the *Kingston Whig-Standard*, told me that Dr. McNeill was as astute a businessman as he had ever encountered and that he could have been an outstanding success in the financial world. Dr. R. Bruce Taylor, in his last annual report, said: 'He was the great discovery of my time. ... He has, by exercising care, made the financial situation easier for everyone and has produced budgets which have provided for everything by insisting on care on the part of all.'

Principal Fyfe said: 'Not only does he jealously watch our dwindling resources and devise those ingenious, small economies by which alone the University is kept out of bankruptcy, but in the decision of every question that arises his experience and wisdom are factors of dominant weight.'

Tricolor praised him for 'the tireless fidelity with which [he] has borne – and bears – heavy burdens. ... Queen's is proud of William Everett McNeill as administrator and as man.'

A *Review* editorial said:

In the short space of 12 years Dr. McNeill has come to be regarded as the tutelary genius of the institution. ... It is his very watchword that Queen's shall live within her means. In taking this stand against any mushroom growth that cannot be justified in the light of available funds and actual requirements, he personifies the very development of the University. To the financial world and in the eyes of Queen's he stands as the palladium on which the security of the institution depends.

His fame was not merely a local phenomenon. He was recognized as an academic power all across the country.

In 1930 Dr. McNeill was appointed Vice-Principal, the first since Dr. John Watson had resigned in 1924. He relinquished the duties of Registrar, but in his new responsibilities became even more important in the government of the University. As Treasurer he kept a tight control of the purse strings. He knew his own worth. 'It is doubtful whether there is a better system anywhere,' he said in describing his administration of the finances. There was no indication of any personal responsibility for that system – but everyone knew where credit was due.

He was always a meticulously careful administrator, but it was during the Depression that he really earned his reputation for cheese-paring, and many are the stories told of his penuriousness. Electricity was rationed, the buildings were not opened at night, and supplies were carefully husbanded. Trained as I was at the feet of the master, I find myself still saving stubs of pencils, using old envelopes for interdepartmental correspondence, and raiding the bulletin board for thumb tacks. Dr. McNeill scolded a member of staff who had requested the purchase of a pencil sharpener. He decried the temerity of such a request in view of the perilous economic situation, particularly when there already was a pencil sharpener on another floor in the same building.

He once confirmed his worst suspicions that a local supplier was short-changing on the quantity of letterheads and envelopes. Sceptical that not every package contained 1,000 as labelled, he painstakingly counted several bundles and sure enough discovered that never, never, did the tally come to 1,000 exactly, and was more apt to be a few short than any over. It seems that in those days before mechanical counters the supplier was packing by weight, a fast and fairly accurate method, but by no means accurate enough for Dr. McNeill. The system was changed.

He not only did not believe in equal pay for men and women doing equal work; he did not believe in equal pay for women. If a Queen's graduate, resident in Kingston, worked for the University, he felt that she did not need as much salary as one who wasn't living at home. Evelina Thompson, Head of the Department of Secretarial Science at Ryerson Polytechnical Institute, has told me that when she sought an increase from the $10 a week she was making as a secretary in the Department of Extension, Dr. McNeill demurred, but finally offered her an additional dollar on condition that she did not tell the other girls. She turned the proposition down, perhaps because she felt she would never be able to keep all that good news to herself.

Prof. H. H. Stewart tells a story about the university radio station CFRC. He remembers when there was only one person to do all the jobs, from answering the telephone to spinning the discs. 'It occurred to me that it would be a tremendous help to this person if he had the use of one of the new cradle telephones, one you could use with just one hand. There was a catch, however; it cost 25c more a month.

'I asked Dr. McNeill if we could get one, and he said, "No, sir. That is a prestige item and the first one will be for the Principal, the next for me, and after that I'll think about it." '

Even though Professor Stewart offered to pay for it out of his own pocket, the answer was still No.

I remember once driving Dr. McNeill and Gerry Graham, then a junior member of faculty and now a top world historian whose abilities have been recognized by an honorary degree from Queen's, home from a meeting at the home of Ross Winter on Collingwood St. When we reached the Graham house on Queen's Cres., Dr. McNeill started to get out, and it was only with difficulty that I persuaded him to stay with me so that I could drop him off at his own place, about a block further along. Dr. McNeill was grateful and said so, but could not resist drawing my attention to the fact that it took an extra teaspoonful of gasoline to start a car up again after a stop.

Such stories about Dr. McNeill are innumerable. Colleagues and graduates of his period vie with one another in competition with tales of his economies. Complaints were many, but seldom made to his face. In fact, most beneficiaries of his niggardliness seemed to take a perverted pleasure in the restrictions, but others chafed. A student, writing from the safe distance of the letters-to-the-editor column of the *Journal*, asked, 'Why do the students fear Dr. McNeill? He is only a clerk hired by the Trustees.'

The assessment was patently wide of the mark. This particular student may have misjudged Dr. McNeill's position in the pecking order, but this was not true of the majority. They recognized authority when they saw it, and they respected Dr. McNeill's interpretation, even if they did not always agree. Students who had occasion to seek his advice or assistance found him helpful, humane, and understanding. And so did the members of staff. Said Dr. Taylor: 'His door has never been closed to professor or student. Men who have gone to him with a grievance have come out feeling that they had had every kind of consideration. The student has understood that a curriculum was no soulless piece of machinery, but a necessary device for securing a broad education.'

I myself had many occasions to feel gratitude to the good Doctor. The Alumni Office was located in the Douglas Library, as were all the administration offices (which made it convenient for executives, but did little or nothing for the librarians) and so I was in frequent contact with Dr. McNeill. He was always patient, always had time, and was always helpful. But first, of course, you had to convince his secretary, Mrs. Jamieson, who stood guard, that your business was legitimate and merited the invasion of Dr. McNeill's privacy. Once over that hurdle you were permitted to enter the inner sanctum. No idle time was passed in chit-chat or persiflage, but in a short space of time my feet were set upon the right path. I had come with a problem in the name of Queen's University, and that was enough for Dr. McNeill.

He had little time to write or prepare speeches, for which he was in greater demand than he could satisfy. He wrote many a foreword for the *Tricolor*, the student yearbook. Each was a gem. These are among my favourites:

The mental garden should be constantly cultivated. Its beauties can be kept alive and its fragrance savoured only by using moments of leisure and solitude for the deepening processes of memory. The practice of learning and of repeating aloud treasured passages from the great writers enriches the whole intellectual life. Be one engineer or physician, school teacher or lawyer, homemaker or nation builder, one will joyfully find that great literature fully assimilated and lived with day by day can be the purest of pleasures and the great refreshment to the spirits of men.

Discussion, writing, active work of any kind 'trouble' the deep pools of the mind as the angel troubled the water of Bethesda and miracles happen. Then a man waxes wiser than himself, writes a book that is beyond him, does an impossible task.

To a young lady who came to him to autograph her copy of *Tricolor* he wrote:

Dear Miss Johnson: When good comes to you, as it surely will, remember the lines

So watch old armourers' eyes
Their young knights' emprise
Wistfully brighter.

In a tribute to Lois Saunders, the first full-time librarian at Queen's, Dr. McNeill was high in his praise. There were no empty phrases in anything he wrote; the sentiments came from the heart. Miss Saunders had a great gift for languages, she was an artist, and she loved books. On a limited budget she managed to build up a well-balanced library that was one of the best in Canada. Not the least of her attributes, in Dr. McNeill's eyes, was that she was able to accomplish so much with very little. He wrote:

No one could have done more with so little money. Her own salary was only $400 to start with and when four years later the Trustees thought she could have another $100, they voted to try to get it out of the School of Mining. In her first year she bought 791 books, in her last year 1294. For most of her time she had only about $2000 a year for all purposes except salaries. But she never overspent. Her youth as one of a clergyman's family of eleven children left ingrained lessons of economy. Nothing was wasted. Paper that wrapped incoming books was carefully saved to do up those mailed to extramural students. String must be untied, not cut. Even corks were carefully put away. She had no knowledge of bookkeeping and her unorthodox methods worried the auditor. At the end of the year vouchers and petty cash had to be sought in miscellaneous drawers and in various handbags, but they were always found, though once the expenditure had to be reported vaguely as 'about $1,000.' Those were small and simple days.

In a tribute to Lord Tweedsmuir at a memorial service in Grant Hall he said:

This hour, though shadowed with sadness, is lighted with gladness. A knightly spirit has gone by to the sound of triumphal exclamations:

Servant of God, well done, well hast thou fought
The better fight.

That the dust of the ground can take so valiant a shape is the urge of our striving. That the dust of the ground can flower so whitely into virtue is the end of our hoping.

Once more the idealism of a Scottish manse has enobled a life and enriched the world. Once more the English Bible has been a lamp to a way-farer's feet and a light to his path.

116

It is small wonder that he was almost an automatic choice of spokesman whenever tributes were in order. Prof. James Cappon – 'A quickening and liberating power'; Dr. John Watson – 'His voice is yet heard. ... and his power still goes out unbound like the sweet influences of the Pleiades'; J. M. Macdonnell – 'Queen's would have been a much lesser place without him'; Dean John Matheson – 'He spent his life for something that will outlast it. No man can do better than that'; Dr. R. Bruce Taylor – 'He was a master of kindling thought and vivid words that stirred the imagination and revealed truth like flashes of lightning'; Dr. R. C. Wallace – 'His sincerity is a radiating force as compelling as the late President Roosevelt's smile.'

His addresses were memorable. *The Story of Queen's,* which he delivered as part of the University's Centenary Celebration in 1941, is the most succinct history of the institution ever written.

I have told you the story of Queen's from its dim beginning in the thought of godly men to its present state of substantial being. For 40 years adversity dogged it, uncertainty racked it. But courage and sacrifice and vision always saved it. The wisdom of Euripides has been made manifest:

There be many shapes of mystery;
And many things God makes to be
Past hope or fear.
And the end men looked for cometh not;
And a path is there where no man sought.
So has it fallen here.

And then there was the unforgettable *Have You Anything To Declare?,* delivered at Convocation in the fall of 1947 after he had been given an honorary degree. Directed to the graduating students, it was a message for all people of intellect everywhere. In essence, he asked, 'What have you in heart and mind that will qualify you for admission to the more abundant life?' He gave as the answer an inventory of Character, Skills or Knowledge, and the Cultural Heritage.

The address was immediately hailed as a masterpiece. The *Ottawa Journal* said that 'for scholarship, for understanding, for grandeur of advice and beauty of form, this was one of the noble utterances of our time.' The president of the *British Weekly* wrote: 'If it were within my competence I should like to put a copy of the address into the hand of every undergraduate in the United Kingdom.'

The Board of Trustees published it for general distribution. The supply was quickly exhausted, as requests were received for extra copies for distribution in schools. It was found necessary to have a second printing, a third, and then still another. There was a reprinting in Scotland. Requests were still being received at the Alumni Office 25 years after the event.

It was always a reason for rejoicing when I was able to publish in the *Review* something from the pen of Dr. McNeill. One such, 'Queen's or Victoria: Which Was First?' came my way in 1943. It was a spin-off from *The Story of Queen's,* where Dr. McNeill had said that 'Centenaries are not what they seem,' pointing out that Victoria had had a centenary five years before, Toronto 14 years ago, McGill 20 years ago, yet Queen's had begun teaching before any of these. Some friends of Victoria had been aggrieved to hear that their university was a few months younger than Queen's. The article was written to give the evidence. In logical, relentless procession, the facts were paraded by Dr. McNeill and the issue was settled once and for all, at least to Queen's satisfaction.

His contributions to the good life were many and varied. He selected the inscriptions for the Memorial Room in the Students' Union and for the building itself. He wrote citations for honorary degrees. He coached the student debaters to such effect that they were able to hold their own and more against touring teams from Great Britain and the United States. He recorded the voices of friends, students, members of staff, and distinguished visitors to the campus. Included for posterity are such voices as those of the Rt. Hon. Vincent Massey, Sir William Hamilton Fyfe, Sir Edward Peacock, Dr. L. W. Brockington, Archibald McLeish, Dr. Alfred Lavell (who tells the story of the Queen's yell), a galaxy of overseas vice-chancellors, President Roosevelt (transferred from a recording of his Convocation address at Queen's), and Winston Churchill (transferred from a radio broadcast originating in Boston). The recordings are now a valued part of the University archives.

Dr. McNeill possessed a delightful sense of humour. Not for him the thigh-slapping, wisecracking school of humour, or the loud guffaw. His sense of timing was superb. People not familiar with this side of him were taken by surprise. They associated him with an aura of austerity. Harry K. Hutton, Head of the Department of Extension, 1946-52, and later associated with the College of Education at Penn State, recalls the opening of Dr. McNeill's lecture on

'The King's English' at a conference of the Queen's Theological College alumni: 'In one respect at least I shall excel a good half of those who have spoken from this platform. I shall be understood.' It was a typical touch. Short and emphatic, witty, but, as Mr. Hutton says, safely short of that brand of wit which burns or scars.

Over the years he had stored away letters that had struck him as notable and when the time was right he would bring them out. A sample from his mail-bag:

'I notice that you give the degrees of B.A., B.SC., M.A., D.SC., Ph.D., LL.D. I intend to take them all and would esteem it a great favour if you could advise me as the best order in which to take them.'

'Are there any boys who wear short pants in the University and about how many? I am getting a fall suit and would like to know if Queen's University has any special colours for a suit and any special style; if so, please give me details and samples, if possible.'

'For some reason that I cannot understand I failed in all my matriculation examinations except one. But I am not discouraged. I hope you will admit me. I have to offer an undaunted ambition and a pass mark in Physics.'

He found no humour in the attitude of students who came to University with less than dedication to study. He said:

The late President Eliot of Harvard constantly referred to the university as 'this society of scholars'. It is perhaps asking too much in these days of popular education that the majority of students should be scholars in the strict sense, but it is not unreasonable to expect that intellectual interests should prevail. The modern comfortable notion that the greatest good comes from friendships and games and social functions and a variety of extra-curricular activities should have no place in a university; certainly not at Queen's. Those who wish merely the pleasures and amenities of life should seek them elsewhere. Queen's needs to strengthen its old tradition of hard work, solid thinking, and useful living. They belong together. In the long run they are conditions of survival for individuals, institutions, and nations.

He had a gift for friendship. He attracted a wide cross-section of people, mostly colleagues. In the late Forties and the Fifties it became the custom for them to gather, usually at Dr. McNeill's home, to celebrate his birthday. Regulars included Dr. Frederick Etherington, Dr. W. A. Mackintosh, J. M. Farrell, Q.C., Francis King, Q.C., Dr. M. B. Baker, Dr. John Orr, Dr. R. C. Wallace, Dr. A. L Clark, Gordon J. Smith, Dr. J. A. Gray, Dr. P. G. C. Campbell, J. E. Wright, Dean D. S. Ellis, Dr. R. O. Earl, Prof. Arthur Jackson, Dr. P.

M. Macdonnell, M. C. Tillotson, Prof. H. G. Conn, Dr. G. H. Ettinger, Dr. H. A. Kent and Prof. R. G. H. Smails. A smaller group of the above, calling themselves 'The Ruffians', used to meet at the home of Dr. Etherington to watch the prize fights on television.

A great source of comfort and inspiration for Dr. McNeill was his wife. They were married at Bates College in 1906, and three years later came to Kingston. In 1911 Mrs. McNeill was appointed Adviser of Women, and in 1918 she became Queen's first Dean of Women, in which capacity she served until 1925. Subsequently she lectured in the Department of Spanish and gave special instruction in Italian. She was devoted to her husband and helped to make their home a focal point for students and staff. Dr. and Mrs. McNeill travelled extensively in Great Britain and Europe before her death in 1948.

Dr. McNeill did not lack for honours. He received honorary degrees from Acadia, Western Ontario, and Queen's, where his citation read: 'One who has rendered conspicuous service to Queen's University. An exponent of English prose, pure and undefiled, a financier of unusual sagacity, a careful husbander of university funds, a wise counsellor and a warm-hearted friend, [who] has made a mark on Queen's that will endure.'

He was elected a Fellow of the Royal Society of Canada (English and History). A painting of him by well-known Canadian artist Archibald Barnes is included among the portraits of those who have rendered distinguished service to Queen's. He served as honorary president of the English and History Section of the Ontario Educational Association. He was proud to have been an honorary president of the Alma Mater Society. He was awarded the Montreal Alumni Medal. When he retired in 1947, 350 attended a dinner in his honour in Grant Hall. He was presented with a playback recording machine, an oil painting by André Bieler, a copy of William Blake's *Illustrations of the Book of Job*, and honorary life membership in the Alumni Association. His friend and colleague, Dr. George Herbert Clarke, Head of the Department of English, composed a poem in his honour entitled *First Officer*.

For two months prior to his retirement he served as Acting Principal. Shortly after he relinquished the reins of office he was appointed to the Board of Trustees, where his experience was a great source of strength. In 1953 an annual scholarship was made available at Queen's for graduates of Prince of Wales College, Charlottetown, P.E.I., named in his honour. It included full tuition in any faculty for a person who maintained distinguished standing in the third and fourth years; subsequently the scholarship was converted into Summer School prizes in English.

Dr. McNeill died on May 8, 1959, in his 83rd year. Tributes were heaped on his memory.

Dr. H. A. Kent, Principal of Queen's Theological College, said: 'If I could find one word which would best describe him, I think it would be the word loyalty.'

Dr. W. A. Mackintosh: 'His work was marked by thorough preparation, systematic analysis, lucid exposition.'

M. C. Tillotson: 'An educator in the broad sense of that term.'

Gordon J. Smith: 'A man among men.'

Dr. A. Vibert Douglas: 'A man of character with a powerful will, yet withal a gentle spirit and a diffidence born of sensitive self-criticism.'

A brief committal service was held at Cataraqui Cemetery, where Dr. McNeill was laid to rest in the ground hallowed to Queen's. By him lie in adjacent graves five former Principals – George Monro Grant, Daniel Miner Gordon, Robert Charles Wallace, W. A. Mackintosh, and John J. Deutsch – plus many other Queen's folk.

Though I am not a Queen's man born, nor a Queen's man bred,
Yet when I die there's a Queen's man dead.
So works the magic of this place.

So spoke Dr. McNeill on the occasion of the Centennial Celebration in 1941. It is a most fitting epitaph.

Dr. McNeill's concern for Queen's did not end with his death. He left his entire estate to the University. In making out his will he had taken great pride in the fact that he was returning to Queen's more than he had ever received in salary. A condition of the bequest was that a chair in English Language and Literature should be named in memory of James Cappon.

A Gentleman of Colour

It is doubtful if any football team anywhere anytime made a more spectacular entrance onto a field for a game than did the Queen's Golden Gaels during the latter years of Alfie Pierce.

Alfie stood on the playing field to greet the players, headed by their captain, as they ran in single file from the dressing room under the stands. He was flamboyantly dressed in the University's colours – blue tunic with red cuffs, yellow waistcoat with red buttons, and red trousers – a tall, stooped, dusky man, with large feet, gnarled hands, and a certain nobleness of countenance and dignity of bearing. He threw a football to the captain, who then led his men into a pre-game warm-up. If this took place during the various times when the team boasted a bear mascot, the bear would be somewhere near the head of the procession.

Flanked by a couple of comely cheerleaders, Alfie then made his way in a plodding shuffle, as if his feet hurt him, and they did, to the bleachers on the student side of the field. The ritual that followed is engraved in the memories of thousands of alumni and Kingstonians.

'What's the matter with Alfie?' demanded the cheerleaders.

'He's all right!' The fans roared.

'Who's all right?'

'Alfie!'

'Who says so?'

'Everybody!'

'Who's everybody?' And the reply would come thundering back:

'Queen's! Queen's! Queen's!
Oil Thigh Na Banrighinn Gu Brath!
Cha Gheill! Cha Gheill! Cha Gheill!'

Alfie would stand there, while the Gaelic war cry reverberated around the stadium, brandishing his shako, student trophy of a football trip to Montreal, at arm's length, and as the noise died down he would turn around and hobble back to the grandstand side of the

Alfie flanked by cheerleaders Lois Buckley (left) and Tommy England
K. Carey & R. Bowley photo

field. His part had been played, tradition had been observed, and the game could now get under way. The entire performance had taken only a few minutes, but it was an impressive ceremony, carefully choreographed, uniquely Queen's. It was an integral part of the football season and added much to the enjoyment of the spectacle.

Who was Alfie Pierce?

He was the son of a runaway slave who operated a livery, serving coaches between Kingston and Toronto, and he had begun his association with Queen's at the age of 15, a few years after he had been orphaned. Several are credited with being his patron: Wicky Wilson, W. F. Nickle, Guy Curtis, all associated with football. The popular version is that he was playing in the yard of the old Gordon Street School – where Ban Righ Hall now stands – and caught the eye of Guy Curtis, the durable athlete who wore Queen's colours for an inordinately long time, whether actually in attendance or not. Guy is said to have invited him over to the Queen's playing field just across the street, and so began Alfie's career as mascot, handyman, masseur, and pensioner.

From then until his death he spent most of his time at Queen's, except for one interlude, when he drifted away during the years of World War One, in which time he worked for a Nicholson who had the contract for sprinkling the streets, and he slept in the stables on York St. It was J. S. McDonell, secretary of the Athletic Board of Control in the early Twenties, who invited him to return to the scene he loved so well. He took up residence at the Jock Harty Arena in the winters and in Richardson Stadium during the summers. His duties were never clearly defined, but one of the responsibilities he assumed was to keep youngsters out of the playing area, which he did by threats in his peculiarly husky voice – folk-lore has it that he strained his vocal cords cheering for Queen's – and by a brandished cane. The kids had no difficulty in evading him – his broken-down arches were a sufficient handicap – but it is doubtful if Alfie knew himself what action he would have taken if he had captured his quarry.

Although his life was devoted to teams at Queen's, he had an athletic career of his own. In his youth he was a first-class baseball player, a good football player, and a star performer in lacrosse. He competed against such Eastern Ontario teams as Prescott, Cornwall, Madoc and Tweed, and he was still playing in his early 40s.

As a rubber, Alfie was taken to the out-of-town games at the expense of the players themselves. Yet his duties were essentially those of mascot, or good-luck charm, for the he-men of the early days of football usually considered a rub-down as effête and, except when suffering from a strained muscle or other injury, men like Guy Curtis, Arthur Ross and Stuart Rayside would change immediately after a game and leave.

Long after he had been woven into the Queen's fabric, Alfie liked to recall the days of his idol, Guy Curtis. Each man provided his own uniform then, and consequently the team would present a somewhat haphazard and casual appearance. Each player also provided his own boots and, in lieu of cleats, nailed strips of leather across the soles. Curtis on one occasion played in running shoes, with one Queen's stocking and one green stocking, and once he played in his stocking feet.

One of the stories about Guy Curtis that eludes documentation is referred to in the line of the song *Queen's College Colours*: 'Remember Captain Curtis and the conquerors of Yale!', popularly believed to refer to a football game between the two institutions of learning. The game is said to have been played in Buffalo, about 1893, the first half under American rules and the second under Canadian. Captain Curtis is credited with having led his team to victory in both halves. In an interview with the *Queen's Journal* in 1932 Alfie is reported to have remembered the actual scores: 12-2, first half; 15-5 second half. Dr. Arthur Ross, a teammate of Curtis, once told the writer, however, that Queen's never did play Yale in football, but in hockey, which would have been highly laudable but less sensational.

After Curtis finally left the campus, he kept in touch with Alfie, paying him a visit whenever he came to Kingston. When Curtis died, W. F. Nickle, by then a King's Counsel and one-time Attorney-General for the Province of Ontario, took Alfie to the funeral.

Alfie was one of the most loyal of Queen's fans. The Gaels were his team, win or lose. When they fell on bad times his faith never wavered; they would return to the favour of the gods. He once distinguished himself during the course of a championship game by calling out: 'He was offside, Mr. Referee! I saw him! I saw him!'

Fanatically loyal as he was to Guy Curtis and the others of early vintage, it was the team of 1923 that Alfie selected as the best of all. The captain was Bill Campbell, and the lineup boasted such luminaries as Frank 'Pep' Leadlay, Harry Batstone, Johnny Evans, Red

McKelvey, Bud Thomas and Liz Walker. He never tired talking of these heroes of the Twenties.

As he grew into a legend, he became more and more enshrined in the memories of those with whom he came in contact, and a frequent question asked of Queen's folk was, 'How is old Alfie?' He became a focal point for graduates returning to the campus. His callers included athletes, scholars, executives and dignitaries. Sir Edward Peacock, Queen's Trustee, financier, banker and adviser to the Royal Family, always looked up his old friend.

Alfie's age was a popular matter of conjecture, and estimates varied by as much as 25 years. There was no doubt in Alfie's mind. 'I was born on the Queen's birthday in 1874,' he would tell anyone who took the trouble to go to the proper source of information. Although Alfie knew the date, he contributed to the confusion by celebrating the event whenever the spirit moved him – at times of Reunion, for example, when there was a concentration of alumni and well-wishers who might be expected to give him a present.

When he died the records bore him out. He had been born in Kingston on May 24, 1874. His parents were Albert and Margaret Pierce, and he was baptized in St. James Anglican Church by the Rector, Rev. F. W. Fitzgerald, on August 9, 1874. When he was 12 his father died, and three months later his mother passed away. Alfie was cared for by a half-brother, ten years older than himself, until the latter moved from Kingston.

Alfie always claimed he had been named after the Queen's Consort, Prince Albert, and that the name had been converted to Alfie. No matter that his own father's name was Albert; Alfie preferred the relationship with the Royal Family.

Generation after generation of students accepted Alfie for what he was, part and parcel of the Queen's tradition. In 1950 they named a trophy in his honour, to be awarded annually to the outstanding freshman athlete at Colour Night. Alfie flatly refused to sit through the dinner, but he did consent to make the presentation, and he waited outside Wallace Hall, attended by several students, until called upon. The chore completed, he left the gathering, to thunderous applause.

The next day, congratulated by a student, Alfie asked, in his peculiarly husky voice: 'Did I really do all right?'

The *Journal*, in commenting editorially on this episode, said: 'Yes, Alfie, you really did all right.'

Alfie died on February 15, 1951. The tributes poured in. Here is a sampling:

From Principal R. C. Wallace: 'Somehow, we feel that a very real part of Queen's has gone.'

S. H. McCuaig, K.C., Arts '13, Edmonton: 'Such a thing could only happen at an institution like our own.'

W. F. Nickle, K.C., Arts '91, Kingston: 'No one will fill his place.'

Frank Leadlay, Sc.'25, Kingston: 'Alfie was as much a part of Queen's to me as the buildings and the football teams.'

Charles B. Fox, Arts'95, St. Louis, Mo.: 'His loyalty to the team and to the college was always an inspiration to those who carried the colours of Queen's on the football field.'

It was a spontaneous expression of goodwill from colleagues, athletes past and present, graduates and students, a remarkable display of affection. The *Review* attempted to sum it all up: 'It just won't seem the same without old Alfie around.'

He was given a funeral that was impressive in its simplicity and dignity. For two hours his body lay in state on the ground floor of the Gymnasium. His long-time associates on the Athletic Board of Control stood guard as the lines of the many who came to pay their respects filed past. St. James Anglican Church, situated within a few hundred feet of the Jock Harty Arena, where he had lived and died, was well filled for the service. The pall-bearers were six student athletes: football captains Al Lenard, Ross McKelvey, Jim Charters and Sam Sheridan, and Alfie Pierce Trophy holders Tip Logan and Don Griffin.

He was buried in the Church of England Cemetery at Cataraqui, near his mother and father. The grave has been marked with a stone, the gift of the Class of Medicine '34:

Alfie Pierce

1874 – 1951

A faithful servant of Queen's University

Dead for many years, his legend still lives on. He is remembered by many as the personification of what has been called the Queen's spirit. Twenty and more years after his death a caricature still appears in student promotional publicity with the inscription 'Alfie Sez'. His ghost has been reported in the Students' Union by reputable witnesses. In his own humble fashion he has made a lasting impression on the University and the community. May his shadow never grow less.

Dollar Bill

Where he came from, no one knew. He just appeared on the campus one day in the early Twenties and in no time at all he was known to all within the sound of his voice as Dollar Bill, a nickname that he proudly proclaimed to the world. His given name was William Allen.

There were many rumours about his origin, racial and otherwise. He seemed to be American. It was said that he had served time in Kingston Penitentiary for having killed a man in a fit of anger, a credible surmise in view of his temperamental short fuse. Prof. James Roy, who had done considerable research both of a scholarly and practical nature, said he had been in prison for highway robbery. Some credited him with circus experience; with his colourful and amazing vocabulary he could have been a carnival spieler, and with his physical dexterity he could have been an acrobat.

He first showed up as a waiter in Marshall Reid's restaurant, a modest and temporary hall housed in a wooden building on the east side of the New Arts Building. It was patronized by workers and visitors to the hospital into which Grant Hall had been converted during World War One, and the members of the football team also ate there.

I first met Dollar Bill in the fall of 1927 when I was a freshman. Bill would drop into the Arts Club Room in the basement of the New Arts Building, where students congregated between classes; it was the only place in the building where smoking was permitted. He would start up a conversation with some promising prospect, or rather he would start declaiming, to capture attention, and proceed at some length until his audience had been sated and started to drift away.

In an interview I had with Bill for the *Journal*, I tried to capture some of the flavour of his speech: 'To use his own words, he doesn't desire the platitudes nor the applaudits of the mass aggregate.' Or, again: 'Chiropractically speaking, he could die, starve, or go to other extremes for smart people, but he has an abomination for titulation.'

Bill claimed that many of the great actors and actresses of the day used phrases that had been originated by him, but for which he received no credit. 'There is one phrase, however, that they cannot steal from him, and that is "the apex of the pinnacle." You may travel from coast to coast and north and south, but these few words will proclaim to the world that you know Dollar Bill,' I recorded for posterity. 'Bill says Napoleon, Kaiser Bill, and other celebrities rose to great heights and attained the apex, but they never reached the apex of the pinnacle.'

I had good fun interviewing Bill, but I hit one false note. I said, 'He may be a bum, but he's proud of it,' and the story came out with the headline 'Halleluiah! I'm a Bum!' and Bill was annoyed.

'I'm not a bum,' he protested.

Indeed he was not. I've been told that in the early days he would accept the occasional dime or quarter, but he was not a cadger, and he was to build a reputation as a good Samaritan who helped the downtrodden and the distressed. He was a free soul, a bit of a philosopher, a man who stood on his own two feet and took pride in his independence.

Along with his cafeteria duties, Bill served as refreshment vendor at the Jock Harty Arena. He ran a modest tuck shop in a cubby-hole under a section of the seats, to which hungry patrons made their way. It was not a particularly convenient location, and not content to have the customers search him out, Bill was wont to don skates and to encircle the ice surface with a trayful of chocolate bars, Cracker-Jack, chewing gum, and other delicacies. With the tray balanced on one hand, he would make his rounds with many a pirouette and a flourish, talking non-stop all the while.

Bill was a broad-shouldered, clean-shaven man of indeterminate age, with a healthy, glowing complexion. His ideas of hygiene were his own and Spartan in style. Gord McMahon tells of seeing Bill take a shower in the Gym, creating a thin lather with yellow laundry soap and scouring himself with a coarse scrubbing brush. This was not a sometime, but a daily ritual.

During the early years of his connection with Queen's, Bill volunteered for or was pre-empted as a mascot for the senior football team. For a time he even made the out-of-town trips. The players and their party enjoyed a coach car to themselves, and Bill would ride with them. As a point of honour he would not buy a ticket or even accept one free from the team manager. When the conductor appeared on his appointed rounds, Bill would quietly fade out the opposite end of the coach, clamber up on the roof, walk back along the swaying car and, after a suitable interval, climb down and rejoin the group. I can not personally vouch for this feat, but it has been authenticated by many who witnessed it, including Bill Campbell, Frank Leadlay and Jimmy Wright.

Trips with the team were lively affairs. Bill could not stand to be tickled, and when his Achilles heel was discovered his life was made miserable by the likes of Bozo Norrie and Hank Brown, who would pin him in a corner and tickle him mercilessly while he screamed in frenzy. In such innocent pastimes were the hours whiled away.

Perhaps because of such incidents, Bill stopped travelling with the team. However, he would show up with the crowd of students who made a ceremony out of meeting the team at the Inner Station on their return and gathering at the Gym to hear the captain and other heroes speak briefly in acknowledgment. As this was in the days when the senior team won 26 straight games, including three Dominion and four Intercollegiate championships, the opportunity for such displays came at regular intervals.

Ever the showman, Bill would appear on horseback for these functions. I seem to remember that he wore special clothes, a green tunic perhaps, and a hat such as a topper, or stovepipe, or bowler. He was never one to be overlooked, and he was never happier than when he was front stage, centre.

Among his many accomplishments was an ability to attend public events without buying a ticket. On one occasion he announced that he intended to crash into the Intercollegiate Assault-at-Arms in Grant Hall without paying. The management alerted the ticket sellers and appointed students as a special force to thwart this challenge to vested authority, but when the show was ready to begin there was Bill, his face flushed with success, as he arrogantly and triumphantly took his place among the paid customers. I was in my teens at the time, and I was much impressed to see Bill's victory over the Establishment. Those were the days of One-Eyed Connolly, a gate-crasher of international renown, and it seemed to put Queen's in the big-time to have such talent on the doorstep.

Bill also helped Trainer Billie Hughes to look after Boo-Hoo, the first of many bear mascots adopted by the football team over the years. He must have liked animals, as pictures in the 1929 and 1930

Dollar Bill, complete with fur cap, in
rare photo by Fran Welch

yearbooks show him with a large dog. In both pictures he is in char-
acteristic winter garb, sans overcoat, and wearing a peak cap, a
sweater under his jacket, a shirt and no tie, and gauntlets. Later he
was to adopt a fur cap with flaps that were never tied down. Hip
rubber boots were another part of his regular wardrobe after he
shifted his scene of operations to Barriefield.

What prompted him to leave the campus, Bill alone could say, but
didn't. Perhaps he had outworn his welcome at Queen's. The students who used to be amused at his antics perhaps became more
sophisticated, and certainly were more inclined to jeer rather than
applaud his oratorical performances. Or perhaps Bill merely became
more ambitious and decided to go into business for himself.

In any case he took dead aim at the laws of Prohibition, and went
into the bootlegging business. He moved into a cottage on the out-
skirts of Barriefield, where he began to cater to private parties at
which he was the purveyor of food and drinks. He served a deli-
cious dish in which chicken was the main ingredient, although there
were those who suspected it was really the flesh of rabbits. He used
wine or beer freely in the preparation of his culinary delights.

A year later he moved into a nearby abandoned airplane hangar
on the banks of the Cataraqui River, thereby acquiring quarters that
permitted more scope to his talents. The hangar was divided into

compartments by rugs and blankets strung on wires, and the walls were festooned with pictures of bathing beauties from the photogravure sections of the Sunday papers.

Guests were expected to respect the privacy of others, and anyone caught trying to find out who was next door ran the risk of ignominious and permanent banishment. Perhaps at a later date he did bar female customers, as some have claimed, but your scrivener and his spouse can vouch personally that such was not the case in the early years.

Bill ran the place with an iron hand and was arbitrary about who was admitted to his premises. If he did not like the looks or the manner of a prospective customer, or if the mood was not upon him to play host, admission was denied and there was no court of appeal. One importunate customer who insisted on entry at 2 a.m. one morning was routed by a blast of gunfire through the door.

The specialty of the house was a Collins made with three ounces of gin, which sold for a modest 50c per copy. A mickey cost $1, a 26er went for $2, and a 40-ouncer for $3. A quart of beer was 25c.

No liquor was kept on the immediate premises. This was forbidden by the law of the land, and Bill was a law-fearing man when it suited his purposes. But the law said nothing about water, and Bill kept his stock in the Cataraqui. When he felt so inclined he would put on a bathing suit and roller skates and make a spectacular production of sliding down a ramp, splashing into the water and emerging with a bottle in each hand.

His stock came mostly from the Province of Quebec, where there was none of this nonsense of denying a man a drop of the pure. On one occasion he is said to have brought in replenishments from Hull by ambulance and on another he is said to have outwitted the police by transporting a stock from Montreal by hearse.

He was raided periodically, paid a fine, but never went to jail. He regarded such incidents as an occupational hazard and, if the magistrate or judge happened to be one of his customers, neither party gave the slightest hint of acquaintanceship. For that matter, Bill was the soul of discretion with all his customers, and when their paths would cross in town never gave any indication that they were other than complete strangers.

He was a familiar sight on the streets of Kingston. He came into town daily for supplies. He rode a bicycle with a large cardboard box in front and another behind. Sometimes he wore hip rubber boots into the tops of which he had stuffed empty soft drink bottles, which made a disconcerting clanking sound when he moved.

Bill died under tragic circumstances, from coronary thrombosis. His body was not found for several days, and common gossip was that the rats had discovered him first. The *Whig-Standard* for Monday, November 5, 1945, published a brief note that 'William Allen, 65, known to everyone familiar with Kingston as "Dollar Bill", was found dead in Barriefield Sunday morning. ... Deceased was last seen alive at eight o'clock Thursday evening.' The following day the paper carried a notice about the death of 'William J. Allen, aged 68 years. Funeral took place from R. J. Reid's Funeral Parlors on Tuesday, November 6, for cremation at Toronto.'

There were all kinds of rumours about his quarters being ransacked by opportunists searching for a reputed fortune. Estimates ranged all the way up to $15,000, which in 1945 was about as big an unclaimed treasure as people could credit. A more reasonable story was that Bill left an estate of $6,000, that the executor was Bob Greenlees, a long-time friend and adviser, and that a wife and son, somewhere, someplace, were the beneficiaries. Bob Greenlees ran a garage at the corner of Queen and Wellington Sts., and Bill was in the custom of parking his bicycle there when it suited his purposes.

Death did not end the legend of Dollar Bill. Wallace Havelock Robb wrote a poem of 30 stanzas, published in 1947, entitled *The Bootlegger of Barriefield,* in which the refrain was:

Dollar Bill was on the level
And he had a lickker hoard,
He consorted with the devil,
In the service of the Lord.

In a prelude the poet wrote that 'William Allen was a character; he was, beneath his rough exterior, a learned, cultured gentleman and certainly, a distinguished personality in a sea of mediocrity.'

Robertson Davies wrote his play *Fortune, My Foe* with Dollar Bill readily recognizable in the person of Chilly Jim. The scene: 'James Steele's equivocal establishment near the city of Kingston, Ontario. It was built as a hangar for a small seaplane. ... The hangar had been floored, and is arranged as a simple cabaret; on the left the audience sees a counter which is almost a bar, but no bottles are visible, only soda water, pitchers of fruit juice, and a plate of oranges and lemons. ... The atmosphere of the place is clean and pleasant, but

133

untidy. ... Leaning upon the bar is the proprietor of the place, James Steele, who is always called Chilly Jim; he is of middle age, muscular, keenly intelligent, and of strong individuality.'

Says Chilly: 'Take me for example; by rights I should be a failure. I'm a self-educated philosopher and I'm a happy man. But you wouldn't believe the number of people that waste time worrying because I'm not in jail.'

Of his *modus operandi* Chilly Jim comments: 'This is an absolutely legal and unbeatable system. I sell nice, healthy fruit drinks and if, when a friend comes in, I choose to give him something to put in his glass, who can complain about that? What's more, I never keep liquor on the premises. The river is Crown property – navigable water – any liquor found on it is Crown property, too. A beautiful, beautiful system.'

James Roy, in *Kingston: The King's Town*, published in 1952, paid tribute to Bill:

He was usually found in Vinny Morrison's restaurant, sucking a big, black, ill-smelling cigar and holding forth to all and sundry on the most varied topics in the most amazing English. ... Bill regarded himself as a sort of crusader whose mission in life was to try to circumvent a tyrannical government, which not only deprived men of their liberty but took away from them their right to have a drink when they wanted one. ... He was a strange character, a man whom nobody knew, who gave shoes and candies and presents to children; a perverse man whose ideas of right and wrong were all twisted up inside him; a man who broke the law deliberately because he believed he was doing right, and gave away all his considerable earnings to charity.

Alvin Armstrong included a sketch on Dollar Bill in his newspaper series entitled 'Historic Kingston', printed in the *Whig-Standard* as part of Kingston's 300th birthday celebrations. The series was later published in book form and entitled *From Buckskin to Broadloom*. He described Bill as a kind of modern Robin Hood, who treated the poor at the expense of the rich.

And, in 1974, Floyd Patterson devoted one of his talk show programs on radio station CKWS to Dollar Bill. Many were the calls that came in praising this humble man for his many acts of generosity. It was an amazing tribute that showed his memory was still green and fresh almost 30 years after his death.

There have been many Kingstonians who fancied themselves as important figures who never achieved this sort of attention.

134

Leonard W. Brockington,
Rector Magnificus

Through Principal Wallace, Leonard Brockington had come to Queen's in 1947 to deliver the Alma Mater Society Lecture. He was an instant success. The capacity audience in Grant Hall took him to its heart, a spot he was never to relinquish. This delightful and entertaining personality, with the magnificent features, the mellifluous voice and the carriage crippled by arthritis, convulsed students and staff with his stories and anecdotes, his apt quotations drawn from a prodigious memory and from a wide variety of sources – the Bible, Shakespeare, Milton, the classical poets, A. P. Herbert and Bob Edwards of *Calgary Eye-Opener* fame; it came from him in a never-ending stream, a *tour de force*. And the message was an appeal for a greater awareness of his listeners' Canadian heritage.

Before the year was out Dr. Brockington was the unanimous choice for the post of Rector. He accepted, and thus began a mutually delightful relationship that was to continue until his death 19 years later. No one had ever served more than one term; he was to serve six and start a seventh. Every three years he accepted reappointment. It was a position in which he took great pride. He held or was to hold such positions as President of J. Arthur Rank's Odeon Theatre chain in Canada, Chairman of the CBC, adviser on Commonwealth affairs to the British Ministry of Information and Chairman of the United Nations Loyalty Panel. While a host of distinctions came his way, he gave priority to his position as Rector of Queen's in any listing of honours or titles.

At the first meeting of the Board he attended, he took a cigar out of his pocket, lit up, and started to smoke. It was an unwritten rule that no one smoked at Board meetings. Principal Wallace looked at Chancellor Dunning, who looked at Chairman J. M. Macdonnell. Brock puffed away. No one said a word. Then the Chancellor slowly and deliberately took a pipe from his pocket, filled it with tobacco, tamped it, struck a match, and started to smoke, too. Not a comment was ever made, but at the next meeting there were ash trays at every place.

His services on behalf of the student body and the University were never-ending. Not content with attendance at Board meetings, he was a frequent visitor to Convocations and other official functions. A request from the students for advice on such issues as the Student Health Plan, the Medical Faculty's fiat on the training of internes in teaching hospitals, or the projected AMS Theatre brought him posthaste from Toronto, even though his crippled condition made it impossible for him to travel in comfort. When arrangements could be made, he travelled by automobile, preferably ensconced in the front seat, where he sat, curled up, chain-smoking cigars and dropping ashes down the front of his suit as he gestured and talked and told stories from his vast repertoire and even sang music hall songs.

Through his auspices the university community was introduced to many of his friends, including such luminaries as Marian Anderson, Sir Alan Herbert, Nicholas Monsarrat, Lord and Lady Tweedsmuir, Healey Willan, Yousuf Karsh, Max Freedman and Grattan O'Leary. He arranged for films to be shown free of charge, classics from the J. Arthur Rank organization. The Douglas Library was the beneficiary of the John Buchan Library plus one of the most famous books ever printed in Britain, the Kelmscott Press edition of Chaucer. I once provided transport from Ottawa to Kingston for a chair that had belonged to Robert Burns. Many such gifts came to Queen's, purchases made as tributes to Dr. Brockington or arranged by him through wealthy patrons. Some were personal benefactions, such as a first edition of *Blackstone's Commentaries*, autographed presentation copies of books by prominent living writers, and manuscripts of John Masefield, E. J. Pratt, and others.

As a raconteur he was in a class by himself. He was quite capable of stringing together anecdotes, stories and reminiscences over a period of several hours. It was a memorable experience to be in his company. Some of his head-to-head story-telling duels with the likes of Donald Gordon and Sir Alan Herbert, in which they took impatient turns in topping each other's efforts, were classics of their kind. He was never in any hurry to go to bed, being 'an indifferent sleeper' in any case, and he styled himself 'The Squadron Leader of the Night Hawks'. Persons of more regular habits, such as Principal Mackintosh and Dr. W. E. McNeill, early learned in self-defence to leave themselves an escape hatch to avoid being trapped into sitting up with him until the small hours of the morning.

'Brock' swapping yarns with Yousuf Karsh. *Globe & Mail photo*

137

If you were in Brock's company a lot, you naturally heard some of his stories more than once, but his performance was so flawless that you were seduced to laughter even when you knew the punch line. It was a virtuoso performance. He never apologized for repeating a story. 'Whenever Sir Thomas Beecham,' he said, 'stands up in Albert Hall to conduct Tchaikowsky's Fifth Symphony, half the audience doesn't walk out saying "We have heard that one before." '

His memory was fabulous. He claimed it was a card file memory, but allowed that in later years he was having trouble with the index. If so, it wasn't apparent. He seemed able to come up with the perfect story for the occasion. As he aged he said he was between his dotage and his anecdotage.

No figure of his day was in greater demand as a speaker. The *Globe and Mail* described him as an orator of the Churchillian School. Dr. A. W. Trueman called him the greatest exponent of the art of rhetoric of his time. Another said he was a master of all the skills of the spoken word. He was described as an inspiring and courageous speaker who during World War Two thrilled the Allied world with his reassuring and eloquent broadcasts which encircled the world. Again, he was called the wartime voice of Canada.

Some of his most eloquent statements were made on behalf of Queen's:

This University to its imperishable honour has never excluded from the full and equal communion of its fellowship any of its students whether Gentile or Jew, Protestant or Catholic, White or Coloured, Believer or Agnostic.

*

Like all true universities, Queen's, which represents all Canada, city and country, east and west, men and women of many races, has sent out into the world teachers and pastors, doctors and engineers, who have carried with them from this place into the service of their native land wealth in poverty, comfort in sickness, society in solitude, strength in despair, and light into darkness.

*

No university has been more passionately and steadfastly concerned than we have been with the sacredness of the individual, the quest for truth, the service of humanity, the radiations of the healing strength and the warmth of the Canadian air which sweeps and sweetens the dusty and the musty places.

138

The history of this university is the story of a fire that would not be quenched.

*

This university is determined to survive as a free institution, uncontrolled by State or Church, making no distinction of race or colour or creed. It will continue quietly and not blatantly as a protest against the fallacy of bigness, as an advocate of the excellence of quality, as an example of the personal and national good that springs from intimate association between devoted teachers and eager learners, for it proposes to remain what it was established to be, a teaching university, not a factory of diplomas but a forge of character and an armoury of citizenship.

*

I can say with truth that no men and women have had, for their numbers, a greater influence on the life of Canada than the men and women who have learned the lessons of citizenship in the College on the banks of the St. Lawrence. To the government of Canada, to the healing of Canada, to the guidance of Canada, to the building of Canada, to the inspiration of Canada, the contribution of its men and women has been noble and enduring.

Pride in his adopted university shone through everything he wrote and everything he said about Queen's. His very eloquence was an educational and cultural plus for the students who had an opportunity to hear him. Coupled with his love for Queen's was his love for his adopted country:

Canada is indissoluble and perpetual. I have felt that Canada will find her national soul in the fulness of her splendor on that day when we take pride in each other and this nation realizes that her inheritances of two languages and two cultures is a strength, not a weakness.

*

I am proud to be a citizen of Canada, a land too wide for intolerances or narrow radicalism, a land where the prevailing wind is the wind of freedom. And for one like myself, the Commonwealth stands above all for human brotherhood. We are all citizens of one city – the World.

*

I hear the beat of the pioneer hammer, and the swing and stroke of the frontier axe, and I pay silent homage to that army of men with bent backs and gnarled hands who tamed the wilderness, cleared the forest, shaped the iron, and on the virgin soil of Canada set their signatures with the hopeful plow.

He once said of his speeches: 'I try to have a beginning and an end and see that the middle moves logically from one to the other.' That he achieved this objective seemed to border on the miraculous. He seldom was able to produce a coherent manuscript for the convenience of the press; more often he had only a few scribbled notes with cryptic jottings such as 'strawberry festival' or 'the Sphynx' to remind himself to tell a particular story.

His great friend on campus, Padre Laverty, said that the chaos of composition had to be seen to be believed, with papers and books strewn over the floor, on chairs, and all in imminent danger of being ignited by live ashes from his cigar.

He was scheduled to make a national broadcast in 1949 on 'Queen's and Canada' and he did not get around to his preparations until the day the address was to be delivered, to the concern and dismay of Dr. McNeill. He put his thoughts together in less than three hours, and half an hour before the broadcast he carried his disorderly collection of papers into the studio. The speech was one of his best, not only notable in style and content, but perfectly timed.

When he died the tributes were impressive. The obituary in the *London Times* ran to 600 words. He was cited as a great man who was 'a guidepost and a landmark in the state'. Lord Tweedsmuir said, 'He was Canada's greatest interpreter. It is doubtful if a spokesman of this calibre will ever be found again.'

A *Globe and Mail* editorial spoke for us all:

Aristocratic, he was not an aristocrat. He knew cabbies and bellhops and office boys as well as politicians, tycoons, and poets. He was no prude. He could sing bawdy songs, rattle off limericks and tell lusty tales. But some of his speeches were as close as we have ever come to having a Canadian national anthem. He died Thursday evening, at 78, and left us a legacy of wit, pride and compassion. Old-fashioned gifts. All of them.

Among those present ...

Some of the more interesting students have come from foreign lands. One that made his mark early was Robert Sutherland, a Jamaican of African and British ancestry, who enrolled in 1849. When he died in 1878 after a career as a small-town Ontario lawyer, he bequeathed to Queen's his entire life savings, plus some property. The gift amounted to $11,000, which is the equivalent of $70,000 plus today. He left the money to Queen's because, according to his will, 'I was always treated like a gentleman there.' This generous act was commemorated in 1975 when Kingston Mayor George Speal, Com.'54, on behalf of the City, presented Principal R. L. Watts and the University with a plaque honouring Sutherland. Jamaica's High Commissioner to Canada participated in the ceremony.

Another was Toshi Ikehara, a Japanese student in the Class of Arts 1896. He had been attracted to Queen's after meeting Principal George Monro Grant on shipboard while en route to Canada to attend school. He came to Queen's, and he became probably the most popular student on campus, elected to many offices, including the secretaryship of the Alma Mater Society. He was also noted as an extraordinarily fine penman, and the earliest pages of the Domesday Book, the University chronicle, are in his hand. He returned to Japan, where he became a prominent businessman and a noted collector of oriental antiques.

In my day there was a powerful personality by the name of George Ketiladze. George was a white Russian, from Tiflis, who left his native land after World War One and made his way across Europe, without benefit of passport. He stole his way past some border points and charmed his way past others by entertaining officials with his skill as a magician. In France he managed to get aboard a ship of Jewish refugees bound for Canada. He was discovered, and on arrival in the Maritimes was lodged in jail. He made friends with the warden and was allowed to play the warden's piano, and this led to periods of parole to provide music for the silent films in the local movie house.

He applied to Queen's for admission to Engineering. Dean A. L. Clark became interested in his case, and admitted him on probation despite the lack of any documentary evidence as to educational qualifications. His English was limited, but he overcame this handicap, as well as any other obstacles to his ambition.

As a student George was literally and figuratively a Big Man on Campus. He had a commanding presence. A strong man, physically, he was the perennial Intercollegiate heavyweight wrestling champion. An accomplished pianist and composer of considerable skill, he wrote the music for the annual revue, the Frolic, as well as making a few ventures into the commercial musical world. As a magician he was in demand at student gatherings.

George graduated in 1929 with a B.Sc. degree in Electrical Engineering, and his first job was installing sound equipment in movie houses. Later he taught in the Ottawa Technical School, and then moved to the United States to facilitate his courtship of an actress, whom he eventually married. They joined an artists' colony on Long Island, and George went into show business, taking the professional name of George Jason. During World War Two he travelled all over the world doing shows for the U.S. Armed Forces. Afterwards he appeared in seven Broadway plays and acted on television. He died in 1959 in Saginaw, Michigan, while on tour with his 'one-man' show.

Among the most generous benefactors of Queen's have been members of staff.

Dr. W. E. McNeill took great pride in the fact that he left the University more than he had ever received in salary. Through his estate a chair in English Language and Literature was established in memory of James Cappon. His home at 32 Queen's Cres. was also left to Queen's and now houses the Ban Righ Foundation for Continuing University Education for women and the Student Counselling Service.

Dr. John Orr, who lived in the McNeill home after Dr. McNeill's death, climaxed a lifetime devoted to the service of Queen's by also leaving more than he had received – $280,000. His sister Lillian, one-time secretary to Dr. W. A. Mackintosh, left $40,000. Dr. Orr was a member of the teaching staff from 1925 until his retirement in 1963, at which time he was head of the Department of Bacteriology. He was then appointed Director of Residence Planning, but, even more important, he continued to plan and supervise such events as installations of Principals, special Convocations and other special ceremonies with a graciousness and dignity that were models of their kind and which reflected his own attributes.

The biggest windfall from a member of staff came from Dr. Frederick Etherington, Dean of the Faculty of Medicine for 18 years and an outstanding surgeon. He left an estate of $1,276,586, of which $51,000 was bequeathed to relatives; 70 per cent of the balance was left to Queen's and 30 per cent to Kingston General Hospital. His wife, formerly Agnes Richardson, made a contribution to the cultural life of the University community that is without parallel. A patron of the arts, she was influential in the appointment of a resident artist and a resident musician, and she furnished a music room in the Douglas Library. A fitting memorial is the Agnes Etherington Art Centre, which occupies and overflows the Etherington home she willed to Queen's.

Other staff benefactors stand out in the records. William Nicol, first occupant of the Chair of Mineralogy, provided most of the funds for Nicol Hall, long-time home of mining and metallurgy. It was erected at a cost of $70,000 in 1912. It is interesting to note that an addition built in 1961 cost $284,781.

For a man who hated the money-raising aspect of his position, (though he was extremely good at it), Principal George Monro Grant was a generous benefactor. In the endowment campaign of 1878 he subscribed $2,500. His annual salary was $2,750. Little wonder that members of his staff were inspired to contribute $3,500 out of their own even more modest stipends.

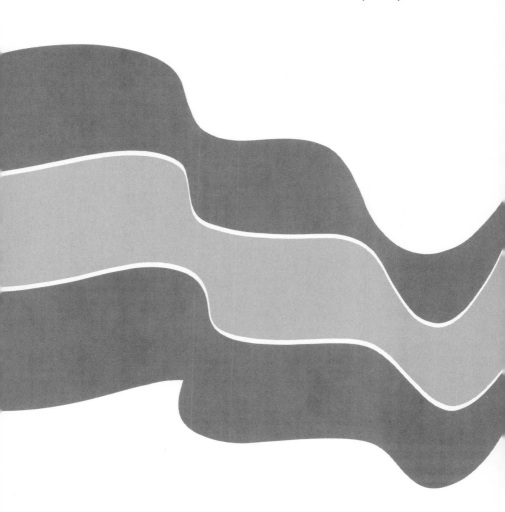

IV
And now,
sports fans...

Part of a 'pulchritudinous procession' – the cheerleaders of 1956, with drum major-ette Joan Murphy

Gridiron histrionics

What was the most dramatic moment in the history of team sports at Queen's? Not which team was the greatest – I don't want to start any riots – but which team provided the most drama?

Well, in my time, it had to be one of the football teams. Of the five major sports – football, hockey, basketball, boxing and wrestling, track and field – football was almost a way of life, at least for the majority. All sports had their moments of glory, but football, in good years and bad, involved more people than all the rest combined, and generated an enthusiasm and spirit peculiarly its own. The raucous fans, the cheers, the bands, the cheerleaders, such talismans as Alfie Pierce and Boo-Hoo the bear mascot, the colour and the excitement were an integral part of the hysteria that swept the campus every fall. Those sunny afternoons in George Richardson Stadium, those junkets to Toronto and Montreal, those highly dramatic gladiatorial displays in a grassy arena were for many a source of memories to carry with them for all time.

So, okay, which team? Was it one of those which won four straight Intercollegiate championships and three Grey Cups, the teams that went almost four years without a loss? Was it the team that won the college title in 1955 after a drought of 18 years? Was it the team that won the Vanier Cup? A strong case could be made for each, and there are fans who are willing to back up their arguments with a physical show of strength, but surely the nod must go to yet another: the Intercollegiate champions of 1934, a team that captured the imagination of the entire sports world and inspired even more hyperbole than usual in a milieu where superlatives are the norm. A poll of sportswriters across the land put the Good Housekeeping seal of approval on the feat by proclaiming it the most thrilling sports event of the year.

The team of destiny did not show all that much potential at the start of the 1934 season. The Gaels were not impressive in eking out a 2-1 victory over Western and a last-minute 5-4 win over McGill.

They had a good team, on paper at least, but they were not 'clicking', wrote Sam Lundy, sports editor of the *Review*.

The unlikely source of inspiration for this team was the loss of five players on the eve of a crucial game with Varsity, fresh from a 34-1 win over Western. The five, including one already lost to the team through injuries, were banned from participation in athletics for the remainder of the year by an AMS Court ruling as members of a group of 24 who belonged to a fraternity in contravention of a student government ban. Coach Ted Reeve decided to carry on with the remnants of his squad, 14 in all, inevitably to become known as the 'Fearless Fourteen', bolstered only by a reactivated senior and an intermediate who had never played at the senior level.

Queen's won a titanic struggle 4-3, before a bumper Reunion crowd of students and graduates and citizens who could scarcely believe their eyes. The rest of the season went like that, Queen's losing 7-6 in the return game in Toronto, winning 8-4 over McGill in Kingston, and losing 5-4 to Western.

The stage was now set for the play-off with Varsity, in Toronto. The Tricolour fought back from a 7-1 deficit to win 8-7, Johnny Munro kicking the winning point late in the fourth quarter. In fact, Johnny scored all the points – a touchdown and three singles. It was a cliff-hanger all the way, replete with strategy and counter-strategy – fake placements, intercepted forward passes, fumbles, even an end run in the time-honoured tradition of the Twenties. In the words of Robert Southey, waxing poetic about the Battle of Blenheim, 'Twas a glorious victory!'

'It was a victory in the face of adversity, misfortune, and injury,' said one writer, carried away by the frenzy of the moment. These sentiments were echoed from coast to coast. It is doubtful whether the Queen's spirit ever received a bigger boost.

The players who shared the glory with Munro were Harry Sonshine, Bob Elliott, Ed Barnabe, Johnny Edwards, Curly Krug, Reg Barker, John Kostuik, Doug Waugh, Abe Zvonkin, Archie Kirkland, Marty Jones, Johnny Wing, Bob Weir, Jack Lewis, Mal Bews, Mel Thompson, Joe McManus, Jim Scott, Ted Young, and Gord McMahon. If that adds up to considerably more than Fourteen, Fearless or not, remember that injuries forced Coach Reeve to improvise as he went along. The talisman and good-luck charm of this team of destiny was the trainer, Senator Jake Powell, 'a tremendous source of inspiration and a fine, proud man,' Johnny Munro once told me.

Although the saga of the great football teams of the 1920s is really outside my orbit, it must be included because the dramatic highlights of Queen's in football are incomplete without it. Actually, I saw all the home games and I came to know many of the players well in later years and to number some of them among my friends. I heard many of the wonderful stories of that era at first hand.

Those were great teams. The birth of a new era started in 1921 when Queen's played in the George Richardson Stadium, a new home and an impressive one after the uneven turf of the Old Athletic Grounds on Earl St. Queen's defeated Varsity 9-5, a feat that had not been accomplished since 1908. They lost by one point to Toronto on the latter's home grounds, or they would have won the title. They did win the Yates Cup in 1922, and also the Eastern Canada and the national title as well, an accomplishment they were to repeat in 1923 and 1924. In 1925 they won the Intercollegiate championship, but lost in the Eastern finals to Ottawa in a stunning upset. Up to that point they had won 26 games in a row.

There was lots of colour on those teams. They played wide-open, heads-up, flamboyant football. It was a heady experience when they captured their first Intercollegiate championship since 1904, but when they continued on to a 12-11 victory over Toronto Argonauts on a snowy field in Toronto it was almost more than the supporters could absorb. The 13-1 win over Edmonton Eskimos in the Grey Cup final in Richardson Stadium was anti-climactical. It was only to be expected of supermen.

The spark plugs were Frank Leadlay and Harry Batstone, both of whom are now enshrined in the Canadian Football Hall of Fame. The field general was Johnny Evans. It was a hard-tackling crew, led by Bill Campbell, Bud Thomas, Curly Lewis and Liz Walker. The end run as executed by the backfield was a spectacular manoeuvre. The onside kick was a valued part of the repertoire.

Also on the 1922 team were Pres McLeod, Dave Harding, Unk Muirhead, Orrin Carson, Red McKelvey, Roy Reynolds, Chicks Mundell, Fred Veale, Jack Delahaye, Eddie Dolan, Coley Johnston, Don Nickle, Babe Grondin, Ken McNeil, Jack Bond, Jim Saylor, Bert Abernethy and Norm Burley. These men were campus heroes, household names. At this distance it is difficult to describe just how these men were idolized. They were larger than life size.

As the players graduated, other great athletes were available to take their place, including such as Tiny Adams, Bert Airth, Jimmy Wright, Pee-Wee Chantler, Hank Brown, Gib McKelvey, Bozo Norrie, Snag Skelton and Carl Voss. They helped to carry on the dynasty. Although it was not apparent at the time, the end of an era when college teams could compete successfully with club teams was approaching.

And now for the team that won the Yates Cup in 1955, bringing Queen's a championship for the first time in 18 years. The Gaels had frequently been strong contenders, but hadn't been able to make it all the way. There had been good players during the intervening years, such as Bob Stevens, Stu Kennedy, Harry Lampman, Tip Logan, Jack Roberts, Dick Harrison, Jim Charters, Al Lenard, Pete Salari and Ross McKelvey, but there weren't enough of them.

On the team that finally turned the tide were Ron Stewart, Gary Schreider, Lou Bruce, Jocko Thompson, Gus Braccia, Jim Hughes, Paul Fedor, Russ Thoman, Jay McMahan, Al Kocman, Bill Surphlis, Pete Redfern, Chuck Safrance, Paul Beck, Dave Wilson, Dave Harshaw, Brian Wherrett, Gary Lewis, Floyd Bajally, Clair Sellens, Don Roy, Jack Milliken, Jim Cruickshank, Karl Quinn, Scott Latimer, Jim Telford, Russ Radchuck, Jack Abraham, Vic Uzbalis, Bob Bevan, Bob Cranston, Claude Root, Frank Geard and Ron Lane.

On the way to the title, Queen's nosed out Varsity 11-10 with Jocko Thompson kicking a field goal with 23 seconds remaining on the clock. That one play saved the Gaels from being a bridesmaid once again. In the play-off with Toronto in Kingston it was Queen's all the way, 18-0. Bill Surphlis provided one of the highlights when he ran 77 yards from scrimmage for a touchdown.

The strength of this team was indicated in the number who went on to play professional ball: Stewart, Schreider, Bruce, Hughes, Thoman and Fedor. When Stewart graduated his number was retired; he went on to play and star for the Ottawa Rough Riders for ten years. One of the best professional prospects was Gary Lewis, who instead followed his father's footsteps as a doctor in Seattle, father being the same Curly Lewis who had played snapback (centre, to you, Mrs. O'Flaherty) on the 1922 Grey Cup squad and was rated among the best of his day. Gary had the distinction of captaining the Queen's team for three years.

A lot of credit belongs to the quarterback, Gus Braccia, a transfer from Temple University in Philadelphia. His contribution was appropriately commemorated by the popular campus singing group, the

Queentones, who came up with new lyrics for the stirring Scottish bagpipe number, *My Bonnie Lassie.* One verse of *My Bonnie Braccia* went like this:

We'll meet him at the shore
Playing the pipes for him
Dressed in a kilt and a tam-o-shanter too.
That's why the drums are drumming
That's why the pipes are humming
Our Bonnie Braccia's coming
Coming to Queen's.

Alas, Gus received his military call-up and was gone after one season. Johnny Moschelle stepped into the breach at quarterback, and the Gaels repeated for another championship in 1956.

Again Queen's and Varsity met in the play-off, and again it was in Kingston, thanks to Orrin Carson's lucky quarter used to decide choice of home field. Varsity led 2-1 with less than a minute to go when Jocko Thompson split the uprights with a placement, and Queen's were the winners, 4-2.

The team that won the Vanier Cup and the first truly Canadian Intercollegiate championship was one of the best-balanced squads ever developed under Frank Tindall. The team went through the regular season with only one loss, defeating the defending champions, Toronto, in both their encounters.

After winning the Yates Cup, the next step was a trip to Winnipeg to meet the University of Manitoba Bisons in the East-West Bowl, a game which the Gaels won 29-6. Several hundred fans, including many members of the bands and several cheerleaders, made their way West for the game, some hitchhiking all the way. In many cases accommodation was provided by alumni.

A crowd of 20,000 was on hand for the tussle between Queen's and Waterloo-Lutheran for the Vanier Cup in Varsity Stadium. Queen's won this handily, 42-14, and the national championship was theirs.

On this squad was Don Bayne, a unanimous choice for quarterback on the all-star Canadian Press team. Others picked for stardom were Keith Eaman, Rick Van Buskirk, Heino Lilles, Bob Climie, Brian Parnega, Doug Walker and Jim Turnbull. Also in the line-up were Joel Anderson, Chris Brennan, Ron Brooks, Tom Chown, Ron Clark, Doug Cozac, Theron Craig, Doug Cunningham, Steve Davis, Brian Donnelly, Ron Faulkner, John Gordon, Paul Gordon, Terry Haggerty, Cam Innes, Jamie Johnston, Kees Kort, Paul Landros, Dan McCarthy, Lorne McConnery, Don McIntyre, Jim McKean, George McKenzie, Bill McNeill, Mike Nihmey, Derek Orr, Glen Penwarden, Jim Sherritt, John Stirling, Al Strader, Jim Tait, George Wade, Dave Whiteside and Peter MacPhail.

There were other outstanding teams, and not all of them won championships. Some of the best players played in a losing cause, but win or lose the thrills arising from football seemed never ending. In my freshman year Harry Batstone finished his career and, despite injuries, had a remarkable season, aided by the likes of Bubs Britton, Cliff Howard, Ike Sutton, Fred Warren. ... Red Gilmore, a deadly placement kicker, gave Queen's a win over Varsity and a tie with McGill in the dying seconds of two 1931 games. ... And who will ever forget Johnny Munro returning two of Jack Sinclair's kicks on the run in the final seconds to save a Queen's win over Varsity? ... Or that day in 1935 when Ed Barnabe, filling in for Munro, scored all the points in a 6-4 victory over the Toronto Blues? ... And that day in 1937 when Bernie Thornton kicked a placement on the last play of the game to give Queen's a win over McGill? That kept the Tricolour pennant chances alive, and they did indeed win the championship over Varsity in the second of two overtime periods. ... Or that day in 1949 when Al Lenard threw a 55-yard forward to Tip Logan from his own goalline and the latter ran the remainder of the way for a touchdown? Queen's lost this one 22-21, but it had to be one of the most thrilling games ever played between these arch rivals.

The Sixties were great years for the Gaels. They won the Yates Cup five times and were runners-up in the other five seasons. There were some great players, including such men as those who went on to professional careers – Jim Young, Skip Eaman, John and Peter Quinn, Andy Shaw, Pete Thompson, Bayne Norrie, Mike Law, Tom Beynon, Larry Plancke and Tom Chown – and others of outstanding skills, such as Cal Connor, Bill Edwards, Terry Porter, Gary Strickler, Frank Tindall Jr., Dave Skene, Guy Potvin, Heino Lilles, Doug Walker, Doug Cowan, Robin Ritchie and Doug Cozac. The last big year for the Golden Gaels was 1970, when they won the Yates Cup and lost 24-20 to the University of Manitoba in overtime.

One of the most spectacular displays put on by any Queen's team came in 1973, when the Gaels went into the final quarter of a game with York behind by a score of 22-0 and in 15 minutes ran up 30 points to win 30-22. Behind back-up quarterback Doug Latham, the Gaels exploded for touchdowns by Stu Lang, Greg Anderson and Alex Melvin. With less than two minutes to go, John Wintermeyer kicked a 38-yard placement to put the Gaels ahead 23-22. An interception provided one final opportunity and Lang scored a touchdown with nine seconds left on the clock. All this was accomplished in virtual secrecy; the game was played in the C.N.E. Stadium and there were only a few fans on hand.

Although the championships have tailed off, there have been some outstanding players, such as Mike Lambros, Bob Howes, Stu Lang, Dave Campbell, Bob Climie, Dave Hadden, Doug Cozac, Joe Pal, Brian Warrender, Gord McLellan, Tom Shultz and Darrell Penner, to name a few.

Richardson Stadium was moved to the West Campus in 1971, and a lot of the fans, particularly the Old Guard, failed to move with it. In the interests of declaring a national champion, the schedule now starts before all the students are on campus, and sometimes when they return their team is practically out of contention. Queen's no longer plays against her traditional rivals, Toronto and Western. Football is still the major sport, but it does not hold the same pre-eminence.

AND ON THE SIDELINES ...

Co-incident with the emergence of Queen's as a football power in the land was the one and only Alfie Pierce, whose career is chronicled more fully elsewhere. Alfie made a contribution that was unique.

Bear mascots showed up from time to time, all named 'Boo-Hoo', starting as far back as 1922. There was even a march composed for the piano by Oscar Telgmann, entitled 'The Mascot' and dedicated to one of the early Boo-Hoos.

When the bands blossomed forth in kilty uniforms after the war, another dimension was added to the football panache. And those beautiful drum majorettes: Marj MacGregor, a happy choice for the first of a comely and pulchritudinous procession (the *Journal* once heralded the start of a new season with a banner headline *MARJ IS BACK!*), the beautiful Tance Alcock, the sexy Dyer girls, Peggy and Sandy, Joan Murphy, and happily on and on and on.

The Queen's teams have had few coaches. Bill Hughes, a McGill graduate, coached those championship teams of the Twenties, Ted

Reeve was in charge for most of the Thirties, and Frank Tindall became the Dean of all Canadian college coaches, with a span of 29 years, outlasting even the durable Johnny Metras at Western.

Reeve and Tindall had a lot in common. They both had a creative sense of humour, both were low-key, both were capable of inspiring their players to play beyond their capacities, and both made friends of their players on and off the field and for life. They both believed in football for all the right reasons, including the not always universally accepted thesis that it should be fun as well as competition.

Ted Reeve came to Queen's in 1933 and stayed until 1938, when he left to try his luck as a coach in the Big Four. He had been an outstanding football and lacrosse player, a sports columnist for the Toronto *Telegram*, and Queen's was his first crack at coaching.

Defence was the name of the Reeves' strategy, with the final outcome being decided surprisingly often by one or two points. He was quite content for the team to get within kicking range for a single point. An opportunity for a field goal was like a run on the bank. His teams didn't score many touchdowns, but the opposition usually scored even fewer. One or two touchdowns were a season's output. His teams won three championships.

One year the ball struck the goalposts an inordinate number of times. Wrote Tedder after one such occasion: 'Queen's used the goalpost play again on Saturday and it worked. Against McGill we arranged to have an upright block a McGill placement. Against Varsity we had Wing play a punt-carom off the cross-bar which enabled him to follow up and recover the ball. The Goalpost Play – the Flower of the McGuffey Genius.' McGuffey was Ted himself; other aliases were the Moaner, Alice Whippersnapper, Nutsy Fagan, and Bozo the Airedale.

Ted Reeve never had a contract at Queen's. A verbal agreement was all that was needed. When he decided to try his hand as coach in professional ranks, the news came as a shock, but he carried with him nothing but good wishes. In his column he wrote:

We don't know how a fellow feels when he leaves a college he has attended as a student. It must be quite a wrench. For our six years as an employee down at Queen's have given us hundreds of happy days and a store of pleasant memories. After all, when you coach a team for six years without once having anyone butting in on you or criticize; when, even on the worst days, the members of the Athletic Board and the supporters and students merely say: 'Never mind that one, you are doing fine, we'll win the next

154

1950: King Boo-Hoo V with cheerleader Peggy Chisholm. *Toronto Star photo*

three,' you have something to remember. Always. That is the way they are at Queen's. From the freshmen in their tams right through to professors and doctors, men famous in their fields of learning, who are still impressed in how things are going with the Tricolour on the 40-yard line.

And another thing. You learn a lot at college even if you are not a student. We don't know whether it is the same everywhere, but at Queen's there is certainly a tremendous college spirit. And a tie between students and graduates that is a very strong one. You learn, too, how hard most lads work to get through. You learn to admire these youngsters (many of the kind we used to call white collar guys) for the way they muck in the mines, slug it out in the steel works, or do summer work in the bush on the rocky road to an education. They do it the hard way. And like it.

Yes, there were a lot of happy days down there. When the trees were turning gold and red against a background of the old gray, stone college buildings, the smell of burning leaves hung on the autumn air, and the Galloping Gaels were whooping through practice at Richardson Stadium. Coaching was all right, like that. And the man who gets that job is a fortunate fellow. We hope he enjoys it as much as we did.

*

A feature of the 1952 Colour Night was the presentation of a plaque and a wallet to Jack Jarvis, coach of the boxing team for 25 years. (He was to continue for another ten). In his own quiet way he had made a remarkable contribution, producing many champions, but even more significant than the number of champions he produced was the sportsmanlike manner in which he did it. None of the lads he trained was ever seriously injured. He knew the capabilities of his charges well. One man would be allowed to continue although he was taking heavy punishment; another might go on until tagged with a solid hit, when Jack would jump through the ropes and wrap his arms around him. The fight was over. There would be no more that night.

Jack was quite emotional when the presentation was made, but he managed to make a speech in acknowledgement. True, he dropped his notes, and when he retrieved them from the floor they were not in the proper order. He faithfully followed the script as it came to hand, however, and the result was hilarious. It mattered not. The audience was with him all the way.

The next day, Fred Bartlett, head of the School of Physical and Health Education and one of the prime organizers of the presentation, asked Jack how he liked the wallet. Tears welled up in Jack's eyes. He assured Fred it was the nicest wallet he had ever seen.

'How did you like what it contained?'

Jack looked blank. He drew the wallet from his hip pocket. 'I didn't know there was anything in it,' he said. He looked. There were five crisp $100 bills.

Queen's Football Hall of Fame

Who was the greatest player ever to represent Queen's on the football field? Was it Guy Curtis, immortalized in *Queen's College Colours?* Was it Frank Leadlay or Harry Batstone, who scintillated in the Twenties and who are in Canada's Football Hall of Fame? Was it Ron Stewart, who starred in professional football for a decade after his record-setting days at Queen's? Or was it Jim Young, who at time of writing is still a stellar performer with the Vancouver Lions, after making the grade in the National Football League?

It is a question that will never be answered to the satisfaction of all Queen's football *afiçionados,* of course. Each of the above mentioned has his own following, fans who are eloquent on the subject of their particular choice and who, without any encouragement whatsoever, are prepared to delve into their memories for deeds of derring-do performed by their hero.

In 1970 the Queen's Football Club, headed by Heino Lilles, decided to enshrine in a Hall of Fame the outstanding performers on the gridiron for Queen's over the years. A committee was struck consisting of Dr. Jim Melvin as chairman, Mike Rodden, Ted Reeve, Frank Tindall, Dr. Bill Campbell, Dr. Hal Dunlop, Dr. Jack Kerr, and your humble servant. Ted Reeve, Frank Tindall and Mike Rodden did not attend meetings, but they made a most valuable contribution to the deliberations by mail or by telephone.

Ted Reeve, after picking the best he had played against or coached, advised Dr. Melvin: 'This is quite a task you have been pegged for. I know, as I got nailed on the committee for the Canadian Sports Hall of Fame. The main point is to remain anonymous, incognito, unknown, and just vote by mail, as everyone thinks his choice is tops.'

The members of the Melvin committee held several meetings and developed guidelines to help in their final selections:

1 Only players who had performed since the Intercollegiate was formed in 1898 were to be considered.

157

2   Players were to be judged on their performance at Queen's and not upon a subsequent career in football.
3   A player must have played senior football for three years; under exceptionable circumstances two years' experience was considered.
4   Members were not eligible for selection until ten years after their student playing days.
5   For the first year, 24 players were to be elected to the Hall of Fame, and thereafter the number selected was to be greatly reduced.
6   For the first year six players were to be selected from each of the following groups: (1) Pre-First World War, (2) the Twenties, (3) the Thirties, (4) the late Forties and the Fifties.

The members did their homework. Lists such as Captains and Most Valuable Players were studied, former players and coaches were consulted, all-star team selections read. Finally the following nominations were approved:

GROUP I – Tout Leckie, Hugh Macdonnell, George Taylor Richardson, Mike Rodden, Ernie Sliter and Jack Williams.

GROUP II – Harry Batstone, Bill Campbell, Johnny Evans, Frank Leadlay, Art Lewis and Red McKelvey.

GROUP III – Reg Barker, Howie Carter, Bob Elliott, Howie Hamlin, Johnny Munro and Harry Sonshine.

GROUP IV – Lou Bruce, Jim Charters, Al Lenard, Gary Lewis, Ron Stewart and Jocko Thompson.

A Fifth Group was recommended, to consist of those who had contributed much to the cause of football at Queen's: Orrin Carson, W. P. Hughes, Senator Powell and Ted Reeve.

These were the recommendations that were forwarded to the Football Club. In the meantime the Club had, in effect, disbanded. The chairman was temporarily in England, other members had moved out of town, no meetings were being held, there was no one around to take any action. The result was that no final decision was ever made.

Some day the project will, no doubt, be revived. For what it is worth, then, this may be regarded as a report on the spadework that has been done, which may save some research. And it may be helpful, particularly in the case of the players of the early days, to include a further list of those who were considered but not selected on the first round, and who in many instances may be at least

Ottawa Football Night, 1964: eating, Lou Bruce and Kaye Vaughn; looking on, from left, Hap Shouldice, Dr. J.A. Beggs, Gary Schreider and Ron Stewart

equally deserving. It is quite possible, of course, that if and when a Hall of Fame is established, the original list of selections may be revised.

GROUP I – Art Turner, Ed Elliott, Jack Hazlett, Ken Williams, Bill Dobson, Teddy Etherington, Arthur Ross and Tupper McDonald.

GROUP II – Bud Thomas, Dave Harding, Hank Brown, Liz Walker, Cliff Howard, Bubs Britton, Ike Sutton and Tiny Adams.

GROUP III – John Kostuik, Bernie Thornton, Ed Barnabe, Curly Krug, George Sprague, John Wing, Archie Kirkland, Frank Earle, Nick Paithouski, Johnny Edwards, Art Stollery, George Carson, Red Gilmore and George Caldwell.

GROUP IV – Gary Schreider, Tip Logan, Harry Lampman, Ross McKelvey, Hal McCarney, Jack Roberts, Bill Surphlis, Don Robb, Gary Strickler, Dave Skene, Terry Porter, Bob Stevens, Pete Salari, Jack Cook, Stu Kennedy, Dick Harrison and Robin Ritchie.

The lapse of time now permits the formation of a Group VI, with such strong contenders as Don Bayne, Bayne Norrie, Heino Lilles, Skip Eaman, Pete Thompson, Larry Ferguson, Jim Tait, Doug Cozac, Bill Edwards, Doug Cowan and others.

And, in the wings, awaiting the qualification of the time clause, are Brian Warrender, Dave Hadden, Mike Lambros, Darrell Penner, Stu Lang and other latter luminaries.

For the contributors' group, how about some of those soccer players who helped to introduce football at Queen's and played on the first team in 1882? People such as R. A. Gordon, C. Jackson Booth, T. G. Marquis ('How Rugby Began at Queen's' by W. I. Garvock, *Queen's Review,* August 1937); the Pirie Brothers, Guy Curtis, Charlie Fox, Stuart Rayside, Jim Smellie, Arthur Ross, Charlie Webster, who played before the Intercollegiate league was formed; Coach E. O. Sliter, Principal of K.C.I., and J.S. McDonell? And, of course, the Dean of them all, Coach Frank Tindall?

Somewhere in the offing, and not too far offing, is Alfie Pierce, who made his own unique contribution, as did Boo-Hoo, the bear mascot, who appears on the scene from time to time.

PICK A LEWIS, ANY LEWIS

A notable feature of the suggested list of nominees for charter membership is that of a father-and-son combination: Art Lewis of the

The Lewises – Dr. Gary of the Fifties and Dr. Art 'Curly' of the Twenties

Twenties and his son Gary of the Fifties. In an article on his selection of an All-Star Intercollegiate Football Team, 1919-1926, Bill Hughes, who coached the famous Queen's football machine 1922-23-24-25-26, wrote of his pick for centre:

Art Lewis, of Queen's, possessed everything that an all-star centre should have – magnificent physique, perfect control of the ball in snapping, a tower of strength on the defence and a keen sense of play that enabled him to anticipate many a move on the part of opponents before it got under way.

This might very well be a description of Gary, who was elected Captain of the Gaels for a record three times. Bob Masterton, coach of the Varsity Blues, had a play which he saved for those infrequent occasions when Gary was hurt or resting. Coach Frank Tindall says, flatly: 'Gary was the best centre I've ever seen.' At least one sports writer picked him as the best professional football prospect of that brilliant team which included the likes of Ron Stewart, Gary Schreider and Lou Bruce. But Gary, like his father, embarked on a medical career instead, and, again like his father, is a successful proctologist in Seattle, Washington.

I always heard Art Lewis referred to as Big Curly Lewis. It was something of a surprise to meet him years later and find that the son towered over the father.

TOUCH OF GOLD

Ted Reeve, who picked Curly Lewis as probably the best man, position for position, he had played against, along with Bud Thomas, once said of Jack Kostuik that 'if he had kept playing after graduation he was, I am positive, among the Canadians who could have made it big with the Bears, Giants, or any other professional team in the land. He was that strong and fast. Too bad he had to go and waste his time with Denison Mines, etc.'

Frank Tindall –
Rarity among coaches

When Queen's gave Frank Tindall tenure as a football and basketball coach, Ted Reeve thought it was a move that made a lot of sense:

Come to think of it, those Tricolour types in Kingston have always operated in this rather forthright Scottish manner, as far as we know. In our six years there we never signed any papers or contracts and the association with Chas. Hicks and the Athletic Board made for half a dozen of the happiest autumns of this sports beat, which has generally been on the sunny side of the street, we are grateful to remark. Of course we had Senator Jake Powell and his Loons going for us on the field. Kostuik, the bull of the woods; Kitty, Sonsh, Stolberg, Peeroy and the Frog, Pooper, Curly, Popadapolous, Gee Whiz Johnny and his 60-foot spirals when you needed them, Tuffy, Kidney Foot and the rest of a weird and wonderful squad.

So, we know, now that they are a tuggly part of the Alumni Association, that they know what sort of a gent they have in Frank Tindall. With his integrity, ability and patience mixed with that easy-goin' turn of real fun. ... amid all the hooting and turmoil on the sports pages of late, that was a nice quiet and solid statement that came from the sturdy old Limestone City to brighten up this week.

Frank had first come to Queen's in 1939. The war put a temporary end to Intercollegiate sports. He returned in 1948 and stayed until 1975, a rarity among football coaches, a permanent fixture.

A graduate of Syracuse University where he had been a star athlete, he first came to Canada to play football for the Toronto Argonauts and was a member of the Grey Cup championship team of 1933. He also helped his good friend Warren Stevens coach the University of Toronto Blues.

Under Frank the Gaels won eight Intercollegiate championships. Queen's were national champions in 1968, and were the unofficial champions on other occasions. Over the Tindall years the Gaels won 111 games, against 84 losses and two ties, and outscored their opponents 3,572 to 2,972. Out of 851 who have played football for Queen's since the Year One, Frank has coached 443, better than 50 per cent.

1968 was a vintage year. The Mentor with quarterback Don Bayne, the Yates Cup, the Western College Bowl Trophy and the Vanier Cup. *Wallace R. Berry photo*

163

But statistics do not come close to telling the full story of the Tindall era. His teams did well, for the most part. That is self-evident, and it is interesting that he managed to survive and prosper in a highly vulnerable profession, but the real success of his career is the manner in which he performed, the personality of the man himself, the impact he had on his players, and the honour and respect that he brought to Queen's in the performance of his duties.

Part of Frank's success was that he was so much more than a coach. He was a naturalist, and a conservationist, and an outdoorsman. He liked to fish. He had a natural curiosity about animals, insects, flowers, and the woods. He was a bit of an artist – he did a little drawing, and a little sketching, and a little sculpturing and wood carving. He attracted people as if he were a human magnet. When he lived in an apartment in town, the walls bulged with people dropping in; some were friends, some were casual acquaintances, and others just heard the noise and decided to join the party. He moved to the country, and the stream never dried up. He built a cottage on a well-hidden island in the St. Lawrence and people still got there. If they didn't have a boat, Frank would pick them up in his.

It doesn't matter whether he's home or not– there are always some of the neighborhood children shooting baskets at the hoop attached to the garage. He goes into the garden to do a little work and in a few minutes he is surrounded by all the youngsters for blocks around, including toddlers in diapers. Every stray dog adopts him; he feeds the birds; he grows African violets and exotic cacti. He is a combination of Pied Piper, Peter Pan, Herb Shriner, Albert Schweitzer and Francis d'Assissi.

Called upon to say a few words at any gathering he invariably steals the show. His sense of humour is contagious, his timing professional. A local sportsman once said, 'Frank can break me up just telling me what he had for breakfast.' Over the years he developed a talk about small towns and the life to be found therein, and if he seemed slow to get around to this topic there would be shouts from impatient admirers. It got so that his friends acted as bird dogs and sent in any reference to a small town that they came across.

He'd tell about going downtown on a Saturday night to watch a couple of haircuts. ... 'With luck we might get to see a crew cut.' Or the town that was so small a man's third best friend was his worst enemy. Or the town where the biggest industry was returning bottles to the store. Or where a favorite pastime was to walk out to the highway and count American licence plates. Or where the lights on the Main Street dim when you plug in your electric razor. Or where, when you see a girl out to dinner with a man old enough to be her father, it *is* her father. Or where the head of the Mafia is a Polack. Or where everyone knows what everyone else is doing and buys the weekly newspaper just to see how much the editor has dared to print. Or about the good football prospects: the lad who picked up a plow in one hand to point out a direction, or the lad who could fit square pegs into round holes.

Not the least of his assets has been his wife Mary. Ted Reeve once paid tribute to her as a 'helpmate with the open house and the ever-ready skillet for those ever-hungry linemen.' They make a great pair.

Frank never had sufficient help in his coaching duties. There was rarely enough in the budget to cover much in the way of assistants. He was fortunate early on to have the help of Hal 'Moose' McCarney, who had played for him 1948-50 and who commuted from Gananoque for 21 years to help out as an assistant coach. Hal went to all this trouble through a sense of loyalty to Frank and a love of the game. He never made much money out of it – only a little more than what it cost him for gasoline.

For several years an old football buddy from Argonaut days, Andy Mullen, used to show up in the fall for a spot of coaching. Andy, who was working for the state civil service in New Jersey, would take a couple of weeks' holidays and then cadge another week by reporting sick. For his reward, whenever the team lost, Frank would publicly acknowledge Andy as the head coach. Others, Jim Jerome for one, would drift in and out of camp to make what contribution they could, in the name of friendship. Everybody had some fun, a lot of laughs, and that in itself was considered an adequate rate of pay.

Probably the most succinct appraisal of Frank Tindall was made by Dr. R. C. Wallace when Frank was being considered for the post of coach. 'I don't know anything about football,' said Dr. Wallace, who was nothing if not forthright, 'but I know a man when I see one.'

The Ballad of Casey Waugh

The ponderous right-hand punch travelled backwards towards the floor, reversed its field in a tremendous loop, and caught the target on the side of the jaw. Down went the gladiator, all six-foot-plus, draped diagonally across the ring. The referee started to count, but the fight was over. Several minutes elapsed before the man revived.

In this dramatic fashion Queen's won her first Boxing, Wrestling and Fencing championship in 20 years. The occasion was February 27, 1932, and the site was the new Gymnasium, opened only the year before. The winner and new heavyweight Intercollegiate champion was Freeman 'Casey' Waugh and the loser was George Maughan, who was to get up off the canvas and live to fight another day on his way to being Intercollegiate and Canadian champion and Canada's representative in the Olympics.

For Casey it was his first and last fight. He hung up his gloves and retired undefeated. He had achieved what he had set out to do: he had given Queen's representation in what would have been otherwise an uncontested class. While he was totally lacking in experience, he had plenty of courage and determination. Otherwise, his only credentials were that he had played on the senior football team and was a soloist in St. Andrew's Church choir.

The setting was dramatic. Queen's, Varsity and McGill had gone into the second night of the annual competition with 13, 11, and eight entries qualified, respectively – enough for any team to win the championship. McGill had a point to its credit, having won the fencing honours. This advantage was soon wiped out, and the Saturday night finals developed into a struggle between Queen's and Varsity. The lead changed hands several times, with Queen's dominating the boxing events and the Blues the wrestling. Bobby Seright, one of the best ever to represent Queen's, made history when he won two classes, an accomplishment never attempted before or since. Grant Baker and Merve Peever won their bouts, and two wrestlers, Ash Hutchison and Henry Hosking, were the victors in their weights.

Came the final bout of the evening, and Queen's and Varsity were tied with six points each. Casey Waugh was opposed to Maughan of McGill. If Casey won, Queen's would be champions; if he lost, Varsity would gain the title by virtue of a better showing in the fencing.

Whatever optimism may have lingered in the breasts of the most avid Queen's fans in the capacity crowd of 2,000 evaporated when the tall and well-proportioned Maughan threaded his way down the aisle, ducked through the ropes and stepped into the ring. When Referee Jack Day talked to the two fighters, the disparity in size was marked. Maughan towered a good foot over Casey and seemed to have at least that much advantage in reach. But what Casey lacked in height he made up in the width of his shoulders and in determination. No reluctant dragon he – at the bell he came out of his corner with a rush and let fly with a haymaker that would have torn off Maughan's head if it had connected, but it was well wide of the mark. The momentum of his attack spun Casey off his feet, and he wound up on the seat of his ample pants. He was up again promptly. He loosed another roundhouse punch and still another while Maughan expertly and coolly jabbed him off balance. One of Casey's wild swings, plus a clout from Maughan, resulted in our hero sliding along the floor, under the ropes, and out onto the apron of the ring.

Casey was a frustrated warrior at this point – but a study in determination. He thought it might be a good idea to go into a clinch, so he crawled back into the ring, proceeded on all fours to where Maughan was standing, and grabbed him around the knees. The McGillian made a move as if to hit him, shook his head, pulled his punch, half smiled at the crowd, and stepped back while Casey regained his feet.

It was at this moment that our hero unleashed his thunderbolt. Everyone in the hall saw the blow abuilding as Casey drew back his right arm as if he were going to hurl a javelin and put his balance on his right leg, his left lifted a few inches off the floor. Inexperienced fighters are guilty of telegraphing their blows, but this was ridiculous. Of the whole assembly Maughan was in the best position to see what was developing, but he stood mesmerized and the lethal wallop caught him on the side of the jaw. Down he went as if pole-axed and lay on the canvas, with nary a twitch. Referee Jack Day started to count and went through the required 10-second routine, although it was apparent that he could have continued indefinitely.

The highly partisan crowd was too stunned to react immediately.

They had been watching what seemed to be the inevitable destruction of their man, bemused by his awkward lunges. It took a moment or two for the situation to sink in. Then pandemonium broke loose. The fans swarmed into the ring. Casey seemed a little dazed himself. It must have taken him fifteen minutes to make his way out of the ring and down to the dressing room. The *Whig-Standard* estimated that he had shaken hands with at least 1,500.

Before the fight the *Journal* described Casey as 'Queen's heavyweight boxing representative of whom much is expected.' It said, optimistically, 'Waugh will handle the heavy class. With a hard punch and exceptional speed he stands a good chance to win a title.' Afterwards the same paper commented, 'Waugh, previously conceded little chance. ...'

At a party in Ottawa some years later some fans were reliving Casey's hour of glory in the presence of Casey and his wife, with Casey's wry comments not the least of the entertainment. As the group dissolved in laughter, Mrs. Waugh turned to her husband and said, 'And I thought all these years you really could fight.'

Where are they now? George Maughan, after serving in the Navy as Surgeon/Lt.-Commander, become a professor at McGill and one of Montreal's most distinguished obstetricians and gynaecologists. He is still in private practice. Casey Waugh had an international military career with the Army from 1940 till 1959 – including a stint in New Brunswick when Camp Gagetown became known as 'Casey's Empire'. In 1959 he was seconded by the Department of Justice to be special assistant to the Commissioner of Penitentiaries. Now back in his native Kingston, Casey came out of retirement recently to become involved with security for the Sailing Olympics.

A few years ago the Alumni Office acquired the gloves that Casey wore on that historic occasion.

'You will note,' said Casey, in that dry manner of his, 'that the left glove is unmarked. As a matter of fact it was never used. I could have gone into the ring without it.'

This was undoubtedly the greatest single dramatic episode in the long and glorious history of Queen's athletics. It was never recorded in song, but it deserves a place in the folk-lore of the country, to be passed along from father to son.

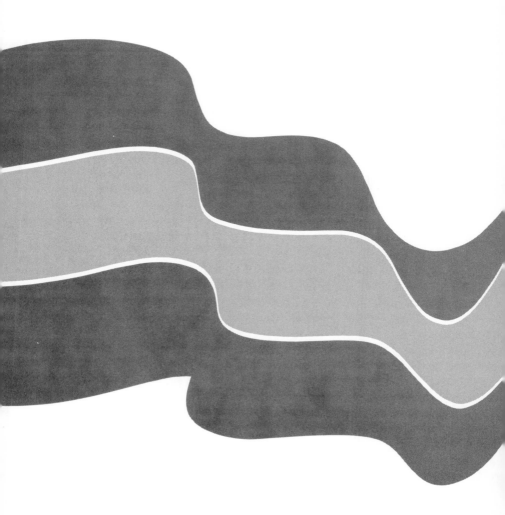

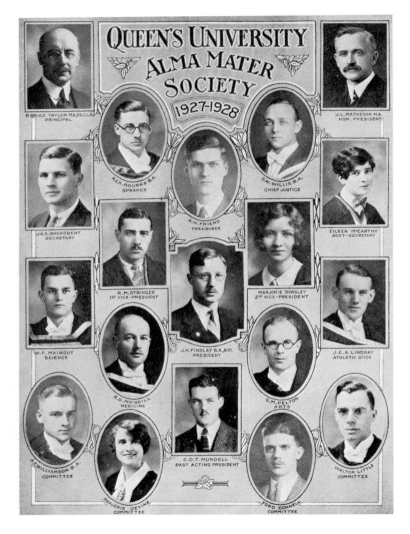

170

In view of the fact that the Queen's campus was relatively quiet during the turbulent and troubled times of the late Sixties, with little of the disturbances and confrontations prevailing elsewhere, it comes as something of a shock to look back on the strike of 1928 when the students locked horns with the administration.

The situation attracted widespread attention in the press. Such demonstrations were not only unheard of, they were not to be countenanced. *The Kingston Whig-Standard* reported that it was the most serious protest ever made by students in Canada, although not the first: 'A few years ago students of McGill went out on strike, but it was over in three hours.' The *Whig* said that 20 years previously a strike was threatened at Queen's, but it never materialized. More serious than any of these was a strike in 1895 at the University of Toronto that lasted for several days, in which William Lyon Mackenzie King was one of the ringleaders.

I can speak with some authority of the Queen's strike that did come off, for I took part in it. I was only a freshman, but I could recognize injustice when I saw it. I was prepared to storm the ramparts, fight to a finish for what I thought was right, jeopardize my chances for a degree. Well, actually, I was not quite sure what it was all about, but when the others got to their feet and hurled their defiance at authority, I yelled along with them. When it was decided that the only effective course of action was to go on strike, I went out on strike, too. But not without first checking with my mother. She was horrified, but reluctantly gave me permission to go along with the majority. I don't know if Che Guevera or Emiliano Zapata or Jean Marat or all those other firebrands obtained parental blessing before setting forth as revolutionaries, but I was new at this sort of thing.

The issues that precipitated the strike were three, and took place over a period of ten days, late February and early March, 1928. First, a student was assaulted and seriously injured by another student. Second, a drinking contest between two students resulted in their hospitalization. Third, an open dance was held after the annual Frolic, a dance which the Senate regarded as a breach of an agreement reached only a short time previously.

The point at issue was really student self-government. Under the terms of the Alma Mater Society constitution, the AMS Court 'shall be responsible for the punishment of offences by students of the University, except those involving academic standing.'

In the case of the student charged with assault, the Athletic Board of Control and the AMS Court had found the assailant guilty and had agreed on a sentence. The University Senate expressed concern that the punishment did not fit the crime, but otherwise supported the verdict.

In the drinking-bout case, the Senate moved quickly, and found the students guilty. They were suspended, but allowed to write their supplemental examinations in the fall, provided they cleared out of town immediately. The Alma Mater Society held no brief for the culprits, but thought that what they had done was their own affair and no concern of the Court or the Senate.

Right on the heels of this *contretemps* followed the episode of the Frolic dance. The Frolic was an annual stage production consisting of skits, songs and comedy acts, some of which were funny, most of which were painfully amateurish, and practically all of which were mildly risqué and ribald, to the indignation of the Senate, which had long taken a dim view of the venture. Also in disrepute was the traditional dance, held in City Hall after the Frolic and open to the entire student body. Because of the circumstances, the dance started at midnight, carried on into the small hours of the morning and was, in the view of all those not privileged to attend, a veritable orgy. The Senate had wanted to outlaw the Frolic and the dance, but a compromise had been reached: the show was to be laundered and the dance was to be a private affair for the members of the cast and the production staff. This was a considerable concession in view of the fact that the students had been trying for years without success to have the hours for their weekly dances in Grant Hall extended from 7 – 11 p.m. to 8 p.m. – 2 a.m.

With typical ingenuity three students who belonged to a boarding-house club known as *Pi R²* proposed to circumvent the agreement by arranging a dance in the name of the club in a downtown hall, the Venetian Gardens. The Senate turned thumbs down on this ploy.

Then the organizers turned the affair over to the proprietor of the boarding-house and the dance was held in his name. The three original organizers were at the dance.

The Senate decreed 'the three students had not given the most elementary evidence of good faith, and that so serious a challenge to the will of the Senate could not be overlooked.' On these grounds they were suspended for two weeks, which would mean the loss of their year because of attendance regulations.

The AMS executive was concerned because they did not think there had been a violation of the Senate – AMS agreement. The Aesculapian Society was upset because of what they considered to be unfair treatment.

Meetings formal and informal were held all over the campus, and communiqués passed back and forth among the various groups. Some members of staff, particularly in the Faculty of Medicine, openly sympathized with the students, and they and others worked diligently towards a *détente*. Students met with students, students met with staff, staff and students met with university officials, everybody got into the act, but there was no progress toward a settlement. Some hotheads among the students called for the resignation of the Principal, of Prof. R. O. Jolliffe, whom they regarded as one of their main opponents on the Senate, and of Dr. W. E. McNeill, Registrar and Secretary of the Board of Trustees. There was some loose talk of making a bonfire out of the classroom benches in Kingston Hall and the chairs in Grant Hall. No acts of anarchy actually took place.

The Senate met again, and after due deliberation reduced the sentence from two weeks of suspension to one. Not satisfied, the Aesculapian Society decided to call a strike. Arts and Applied Science agreed to go along with this plan, but Levana refused. At a mass meeting held in Grant Hall, which was filled to capacity for the historic occasion, the students voted overwhelmingly to go out on strike. The controversy had now taken an ugly turn.

In a public statement Principal Taylor gave the party line: The Senate is the body responsible to the University for the control and regulation of university life. Whatever recognition it may have given to student government has not involved any delegation of authority or abrogation if its duty. Anything therefore in the conduct of the students which tends to bring dishonour or reproach upon the Univer-

173

sity is a matter which comes within the purview of the Senate.

John Findlay, president of the Alma Mater Society, spoke for the students:

The Senate... took the matter out of student hands, thereby breaking the constitution of the Alma Mater Society, which they had ratified, and abrogating the principle of student self-government which they endorse and advertise in the University calendars. ... The students having failed to get what they considered justice or a sympathetic hearing felt that the matter had become of sufficient importance to be brought urgently to the attention of the friends of the University. A strike seemed the only available procedure.

The momentous decision to strike was taken at 11 a.m. on Thursday, March 22. The student leaders sent a telegram to R. O. Sweezey, a member of the Board of Trustees living in Montreal and also President of the Alumni Association, who had offered his services as a mediator. A mass meeting was called for the morning of Friday, March 23, and Mr. Sweezey, who had spent most of the night conferring with students and members of staff, addressed the gathering. He said he would endeavour to the best of his ability to try to settle the points at issue if the students would return to classes immediately. A vote was taken, the result was approval of this proposal, we cheered Mr. Sweezey lustily, and went back to classes with a collective sigh of relief. The strike lasted just 23 hours, from noon one day till 11 o'clock the next morning, but it seemed we had lived a lifetime in that period.

The Principal did not react favorably to Mr. Sweezey's intervention, and it took a great deal of persuasion to bring him around to agreeing that there would be no punishment for classes missed. Mr. Sweezey got on the train for Montreal. The Principal had second thoughts and decided not to back down from his original position, which had called for unconditional surrender. The student leaders wired Mr. Sweezey, and he got off the train at Brockville and returned to Kingston for some more desk-thumping. His point of view prevailed, and the strike was over.

While all this was taking place the newspapers were writing reams of editorials. Here are a few comments:

Kingston Whig-Standard: We believe, however, that for the honor of the university, this decision must be respected and obeyed by the students, and we are inclined to think that on careful consideration the students will agree with us.

Stratford Beacon-Herald: If there were no discipline there would be no Queen's University.

Toronto Star: Youth should not demand freedom to run amok.

Ottawa Citizen: The evidence as reported is not exactly in favor of the view of the affair taken by the students who have gone on strike.

Border Cities Star: Many of the students appear to be under the impression that they are doing the university a great favor by attending its classes. The sooner they are disabused of this idea the better.

Guelph Mercury: The chief work of any university is discipline, and with that destroyed there can bé no university.

Toronto Telegram: The strike at Queen's University was happily disassociated from sabotage. No bridges were burned by the students, which might have prevented their adoption of the excellent strategy immortalized in the lines:

The Duke of York, he had ten thousand men
He marched them up the hill
And marched 'em down again

. ... Folly, for a strike on such a trivial pretext indicates a lack of the wisdom necessary for self-government of the student body.

St. Thomas Times-Journal: Many of the students must be familiar with the words of Hamilcar – 'I know my son Hannibal will be a great general, because of all my soldiers, he best knows how to obey.'

Hamilton Spectator: The first and most important lesson to be learnt is discipline. It may be a disagreeable lesson, but it is the most essential of all.

Peterboro Examiner: The Senate of Queen's is to be commended for refusing to be intimidated; its firmness and a wiser second thought on the part of the students have averted a nasty situation.

Implied or explicit throughout all the editorial comment was the theme that the students had acted irresponsibly, that their spokesmen had showed few qualities of leadership, and if these were the best that universities could produce the country would be in a bad way for captains of industry, doctors, engineers, teachers and statesmen.

The Principal's Report for the year was more reticent than the press on the subject. In fact, the only reference was over the signature of Dr. R. Bruce Taylor:

Several times in the last ten years the Principal has drawn the attention of the Trustees to the fact that Student Government was failing in its objects.

The situation this year has been no worse than at any time since the war, but a series of instances within a few days of one another made it clear that Student Government would have to be reminded it had its duties as well as its privileges.

A special meeting of the Executive of the Trustees was called and the whole situation was considered, assurance being sent forward to the Senate that the Executive was behind it in its efforts to maintain standards of conduct. Action was taken by a unanimous Senate in two cases which the Alma Mater Society themselves declined to handle. The students felt that the action of the Senate had been precipitate and went on strike. After 24 hours the students returned to their classes, their conduct in the meantime being orderly. Apparently the normal course of life was at once resumed and it is confidently hoped that next session will find both administration and student life united in the effort to uphold the dignity of the University as well as the liberties of the students.

None of the Faculty Deans made any reference to the strike in their reports. Even more remarkable, neither did the AMS president.

How many of the irresponsible leaders wound up on skid row?

John H. Findlay added an M.Sc. degree to the B.A. and B.Sc. he already held and later got a Ph.D. from Princeton. He became director of electronics development, Sandia Corporation, Albuquerque, New Mexico.

Jason A. Hannah, Chief Justice of the Aesculapian Court, added M.D., C.M. degrees to the B.A. he already held, and became a pioneer in prepaid medical care. He was granted an LL.D. by a grateful alma mater in 1974. His citation read: 'Distinguished graduate, generous benefactor, faithful friend, and Trustee of this University' etc., etc., etc.

R.D. MacNeill, President of the Aesculapian Society, graduated in Medicine. He was a veteran of World War One, served in World War Two, and was a medical examiner for the Canadian Pension Committee.

There were no repercussions from the strike. Both sides were satisfied, or at least reconciled, with the outcome. Student self-government became stronger and more responsible and the AMS executive and the Senate conducted themselves with more respect and understanding for the other's position in the years that followed.

There is one feature of the whole affair that baffles me at time of writing. I had been a member of the cast of the Frolic that year (optimistically if inaccurately entitled 'Not a Breath of Scandal'), and as such was privileged to attend the dance that followed. I have absolutely no recollection of the affair. Even if it had not been an orgy surely it should have left some impression on my unsophisticated mind. If it were an orgy I could not have been so worldly wise at the age of 19 to have accepted wild and wanton behaviour as a natural way of life. Nor am I alone in my failure to remember. Jim Wright was the stage manager for the production and as such should have been up to his armpits in the shenanigans, but he has no recollection whatever of even being there, either. Is it possible that the proceedings were so shocking that the mind, in self protection, has shut them out?

At the heart of 'The Strike': Medical Concursus et Iniquitatus, or the Aesculapian Court. Left to right, standing: W.H. English, C.H. Berry, H.A. Brown and D. Allen. Seated: C.W. Kelley, G.C. Ferguson (Senior Judge), J.A. Hannah (Chief Justice), R.M. Stringer (Junior Judge) and K.B. Waller

Beware of the Greeks

> *By resolution of Senate no student registered at Queen's University may form or become a member of any chapter of any externally affiliated fraternity or sorority at or near Kingston.*

This fiat was promulgated in 1934 and was intended to provide muscle for an Alma Mater Society regulation forbidding students to form or become members of any externally affiliated fraternity. It first appeared in the University calendars in 1935 and has been there ever since.

In announcing the Senate action, Principal W. Hamilton Fyfe said:

> Whatever the advantages of fraternities in other universities, our constituency seems to be unanimous in the opinion that they would not suit the spirit and atmosphere of Queen's. The Board of Trustees and the General Alumni Association have expressed their satisfaction with the stand taken by the Alma Mater Society in vindication of the rights of student government. The Senate of the University evidently shares this feeling since in support of the student body it has now resolved to forbid students registered at Queen's to form or to become members of any externally affiliated fraternity in Kingston.

What had brought the matter to a head was the fact that a medical group had affiliated with a national fraternal organization in defiance of an AMS edict. The members were found guilty by the AMS Court and lost their political, social, and athletic privileges for a year. The Senate moved swiftly to implement the decision, as cited above.

The controversy over fraternities had been simmering over a period of years. A fraternal-type club known as Delta Omega Kappa had been formed in the early 1920s, and a medical group became established later. *The Queen's Review* took notice of the potentially explosive situation by presenting the facts pro and con. An article by J. Alex Edmison, Arts '26, who had belonged to a fraternity at McGill, stated his belief, in the December 1929 issue, that fraterni-

178

ties 'would contribute little to, and possibly detract from, that traditional spirit so long associated with student affairs at Queen's.' In the January 1930 issue, J. C. Macgillivray, Arts '23, proclaimed that 'Fraternities are an accepted and recognized part of the life at all the more important universities in Canada and the United States, and they would have a decidedly beneficial effect on student life.'

In January 1931, the Alma Mater Society wrote into its constitution a clause forbidding the formation within the University of fraternities and sororities, composed of members of the AMS. This appeared to settle the matter for all time, but two years later, at a sparsely attended AMS annual meeting, the regulation was rescinded.

When the AMS elections came up in the fall, the Arts-Levana-Theology party campaigned on an anti-fraternity platform and swept the polls in convincing fashion, winning five of six executive positions. It marked one of the rare occasions that the Meds-Science party did not dominate the elections.

The executive set up a fact-finding committee of three students to make a thorough investigation. It reported that there were two bodies on campus fulfilling the functions of fraternities and calling themselves by that name. Their main functions were defined as social and professional. Socially the fraternities provided the facilities of a men's residence, for which the University had a need. Professionally the outlook and interest lay beyond life on the campus. The report was fair-minded and unbiased and contributed a note of sanity to the controversy. The facts were allowed to speak for themselves.

The AMS executive shortly afterwards produced a proposed constitutional amendment of two sections, the first banning all Greek-letter organizations and the second bringing under reasonable control any clubs of students living together for social purposes and governed by a constitution.

At an open meeting held in Grant Hall and attended by 1,000 students, the ban on Greek fraternities was once more imposed, after a barrage of speeches for and against the motion. The matter of control of social clubs was also discussed at this and a subsequent meeting, but failed to obtain the necessary two-thirds majority.

Lorne MacDougall, Arts '31, a former editor of the *Journal* writing for the *Review* an unemotional resumé in the March 1934 issue, said that the fraternities refused to back down, the AMS was prepared to prosecute, and the administration was worried. Private conversations followed between both factions and members of staff, and ultimately a compromise was hammered out. It was conceded that since the amendment of the Constitution, the 'social and social-and-professional organizations' had taken such action that they no longer came within the definition of a fraternity as written into the constitution. A committee was set up to supervise the activities of the existing social bodies and any others that might be formed.

The Arts-Science group fell into line, changing their name from Delta Omega Kappa to D.O.K. Club. The Medical organization persisted in the use of Psi Delta Phi, but it was felt this defiance could be overlooked. Peace was restored to the campus. The students left for the summer.

That is, most of them left. As usual, the Medical undergraduates were around for a few weeks longer. On May 25, two days after Medical Convocation, Psi Delta Phi became Beta Sigma Chapter of Nu Sigma Nu, a prominent international medical fraternity. Nine members of staff in the Faculty of Medicine were also pledged as members.

This was the situation that faced the AMS executive on its return in the fall. This executive was, in effect, a rump parliament, with only two remaining of the 1933-34 elected members of the executive. There were, of course, a number of ex-officio members. The truncated executive would not achieve full membership until after the elections on October 25. The acting president, Vice-President Nora McGinnis, was in charge until that time. She could have chosen the easy way out and put off deliberations until the new executive was in office, but she decided otherwise. Under her leadership the executive ordered the prosecution of all the undergraduate members of Beta Sigma Chapter for contravention of the AMS constitution.

Upwards of 800 were on hand in the Gymnasium on October 16 when the 24 student members were brought to trial before the AMS Court. The Judges and the Prosecuting Attorney were gowned, the atmosphere was hushed and subdued. Morris Leishman of Science was the Chief Justice, and on the bench with him were Anton Forsberg of Medicine and Donald Lapp of Arts. R.W. Young of Theology was the Prosecuting Attorney; Russell Thoman, Sheriff; Arthur S. Bayne, Chief of Police; Paul B. Young, Clerk of Court; and Malcolm Young, Crier. Medsman J.C. Finley, one of the defendants, appeared as defence counsel.

A plea for adjournment was made on behalf of the accused, on the grounds that the summonses had been served only the day before and therefore there had not been sufficient time to prepare the defence. The plea was denied, whereupon Mr. Finley declared that his group had no recourse but to withdraw. The 24 men filed out of the courtroom.

Mr. Justice Leishman immediately found each of the accused guilty of contempt of court and instructed the Prosecuting Attorney to proceed with the presentation of evidence. After a brief resumé of the facts, the Judges conferred and soon after brought in a verdict of Guilty against each defendant. The decision meant a ban on participation in student political, athletic, and social activities for not less than one academic year.

The announcement was received in stunned silence. Included among the accused were four active members and one incapacitated member of the senior football team, a team which had won its first two games and was considered to have a good shot at the championship. A large percentage of the student body just couldn't believe that the Court could make its decision hold up. The campus became a hive of unrest.

In this emotionally charged atmosphere, the football team consolidated the Court's position by winning a crucial game against the University of Toronto a few days later. Coach Ted Reeve had not replaced the men who had been disqualified, and the Fearless Fourteen, as the wracked team came to be known, nosed out Varsity 4-3 in a thrill-packed game. Gaels lost two games and finished tied with Toronto, they won the title in a playoff, 8-7, thereby making headlines all over the country. In a poll conducted by the Canadian Press, the success of the riddled Queen's team was cited as the most thrilling moment in sports of the 1934 season. The Court decision received wide support. The Athletic Board of Control approved. The alumni body at large was predominantly in favour, judging from the flood of letters. The cause seemed to capture the imagination of the graduates, of whatever vintage and wherever located.

One Medical graduate found prose inadequate for his purpose. In a poem that appeared in the November 1934 *Review,* he recorded his feelings in verse, the last stanza of which read:

And so the story travels
Wherever Queen's men be:
It's Queen's for all and all for Queen's,
That's true Fraternity.

Additional endorsement was forthcoming at the annual meeting of the Alumni Association, at the semi-annual meeting of the Alumni Directors, and at a meeting of the Board of Trustees. Vice-Principal McNeill summed it up when he commented: 'We have had from coast to coast the most favourable publicity that we have had in my day at Queen's – and that goes back 25 years.'

J.M. Macdonnell, Arts '05, chairman of the Trustees, said:

The thing which has so favorably impressed both our own graduates and the public is this – that the students of today have stuck to a principle laid down by themselves, even at the risk of wrecking that dearest of all their possessions – a football team with a bright hope of championship. ... We old-timers feel that this recent action of the Alma Mater Society is in the very best tradition of Queen's University, whose 'peculiar race and grace and testimonial' (to use the words of John McNaughton) is that vehement, almost fanatical loyalty with which she has always been able to imbue those who have come under her influence.

The rout of the fraternity men and their supporters was complete. Within a few weeks after the close of the football season the Queen's Chapter sought and obtained withdrawal of its charter; the AMS lifted the ban on the 24 members and reinstated them with all rights and privileges.

For the fraternity men it had been a traumatic experience. These were not irresponsible malcontents, but men of substance and reputation on the campus. What had led them to flout constitutional authority in such a flagrant manner?

One of the group, a distinguished doctor, told me years later they had been led to believe – or thought they had reason to believe, or perhaps they had jumped to conclusions – that they had the assurance of the Principal's support in the matter of affiliation. And presumably they had the support of the nine members of staff who joined along with them.

So it was a sad denouement, when the matter came to a showdown, that the students were out in left field, alone. There was nothing but silence from those from whom they might have expected support. The names of the student members were proclaimed from the housetops, but no identification was made of the members of staff who presumably had been friends and advisers, as well as fraternal brothers. The students felt deserted and betrayed and disillusioned, and the bitterness still lingers on in the breasts of many.

The Principal's Report of 1934-35 gives no hint of sympathy:

Fraternities are obviously of value in very many universities. We do not want them at Queen's, because the whole University is itself a fraternity, and our brotherly spirit would inevitably suffer from rival loyalties and from the exclusive spirit which fraternities tend to foster. By the action of the Senate and of the Trustees, fraternities are now forbidden and all students entering Queen's will be required to sign an undertaking not to become members of any externally affiliated fraternity or sorority in or near Kingston. So, thanks to the good sense of the students and their elected representatives, a stormy chapter found a happy ending to the satisfaction of Queen's Alumni far and near.

The D.O.K. Club faded from the scene shortly afterward, but the Medical group carried on what became known as Medical House at 49 King St. E., where it still flourishes. The membership never again challenged the edict of student government; their subsequent history has been quiet and uneventful, and their contribution to student life has been substantial and commendable.

It is interesting to note that while sororities were banished along with fraternities, there has never been a sorority. The closest was the co-operative known as Boucher House at 144 Lower Albert St., and that was not really close at all.

The fraternities of the Twenties and Thirties were believed by many to be the only ones to surface at Queen's, but such was not the case. Dr. E. H. Wood, Arts '10, Medicine '14, told me that a chapter of Phi Sigma Kappa was quite active in the late 1890s and early 1900s. He had been a member himself and he remembered many of the names of the others, including that of Prof. P. G. C. Campbell. This information made sense of a fraternal pin that had been donated to the Alumni Association archives by the daughters of a Queen's graduate.

The fraternity must have kept a very low profile, because the *Journal* evidently did not know of its existence when this editorial was written in the issue of February 6, 1903:

Queen's is to be congratulated upon having so far escaped the affiliation of Greek-letter societies and other disorders of a similar kind. Up to the present the University has been distinctively democratic in ideas and ideals; and it is in the democratic spirit that much of our strength lies. ... Those who are familiar with the working of the cliques do not hesitate to attribute nerveless-ness and inefficiency to the cheap and tawdry exclusiveness imported by the Alpha, Beta, Gamma follies.

Then in May 22 the same year, the editor, apprised of the existence of a fraternity, said:

And now comes word of a Greek-letter society established in connection with Queen's, or at least a chapter or paragraph or something of the kind. The installing officers hailed from New York and Canton. The attitude of the *Journal* towards the innovation in question is already known, and space forbids restating it here. We cannot but feel that the Greek-letter departure looks a little like running to seed, yet indications are not wanting that the sapless branches and dry leaves will make an inconspicuous showing amidst the vigorous over-topping growth of our democratic institutions.

Selah!

In spite of such criticism the fraternity carried on for several years and then apparently fell victim to an edict of the University authorities, who banned Greek-letter societies from the campus. Dr. J. Arnot MacGregor, a member of the Class of Arts '15 and later Medicine '21, told me that he and some of his fellow-students started up an organization known as the 'Eat-A-Pie Club', which violated no law and still approximated the sound of a Greek-letter society.

The membership consisted of student leaders in athletics, music, dramatics, and scholarship. The club had its quarters in a house on Alfred St., near the University, owned by two gracious ladies who acted as hostess and waitress. It was really a co-operative, with the boys buying their food wholesale, and proved to be highly popular. There was a long waiting list, and vacancies occurred only when the members graduated. No wonder; the food was excellent, the menus were varied, and the cost worked out to $3.50 per week.

A picture of the members dated 1914 shows 27 contented customers and one landlady gathered in what appears to be the dining-room, which is festooned with paper streamers and Christmas bells. The venture lasted several years and came to an end shortly after illness struck down the ladies who provided the motive power.

Although fraternities have never been a live issue since that historic night of the AMS Court decision in 1934, the question has arisen from time to time as to the reason for what seems to be a strange and unreasonable ban. When the questionners learn the background, they still raise their eyebrows, but to date no one has made a serious tilt at the windmill.

From time to time the *Journal* lifts the veil of mystery surrounding fraternities at Queen's in response, no doubt, to public interest. In 1964, some enterprising reporter had the initiative to interview some of the men who had belonged to the Medical chapter and present their side. He reported that Dr. Fyfe had attended a tea at the frat house after the affiliation and had presented the members with a painting. This gift was destroyed in anger after the court decision. 'Even to this day,' he wrote, 'many of these doctors feel hurt, and for them Queen's does not call up the same memories, quite, as for the other alumni.'

In 1975 it seemed that new evidence was being introduced when it was stated that fraternities had been phased out at Queen's '30 years ago when a young frosh was stripped and tied to Macdonald's statue and left there over night; he later died of pneumonia.' Where this startling bit of information originated has evaded documentation. One is led to the conclusion that it was an inaccurate recollection of what may well have been only a rumour in the first place.

As for the great majority of the students, they have no opinion one way or the other; no opinion, that is, until the question becomes a matter of public controversy again. Then, I feel – with no evidence I can produce, just a feeling – that most of the students would again unite in their opposition to the whole idea of fraternities on the Queen's campus.

Rector L. W. Brockington once put the case succinctly in an address delivered in reply to a toast to Queen's by the Rt. Hon. Louis St. Laurent, then Prime Minister of Canada:

This University has no fraternities and no sororities. I will correct myself. It has one fraternity. And that is a brotherhood that without the key of wealth and any distinguishing mark or race or creed is open to all who seek and find within the walls of this place true patriotism, a sacred thirst for learning, the love of truth, and the hatred of intolerance and cruelty. It has one sorority, and that is the sisterhood of true women dedicated to the building of homes, the teaching of children, the nursing and healing of the sick, and all those compassions which have been throughout the ages the benediction of womankind.

These bold words were spoken, of course, long before Women's Lib had expanded the horizons of women far beyond homemaking and nursing, but the sentiments are still the same.

The Chair of Social Science

As the major auditorium on campus for more than 70 years, even after the new Jock Harty Arena syphoned off some of the events, Grant Hall has provided a happy setting for a large variety of attractions. The range has been from such solemn functions as Convocations and church services to gay affairs such as *conversaziones* and formal and informal dances, hairy rock groups and big name bands, string ensembles and symphony orchestras of international renown, and such disparate affairs as plays, operettas, banquets, receptions, reunions, mass meetings, conventions, student courts, and boxing, wrestling, and fencing competitions. It also served for a time as a military hospital.

The strangest event that the clock in the tower ever looked down upon, however, happened on the night of November 28, 1933, when Senator Lawrence A. Wilson was host to a standing-room-only crowd of students, staff, and citizens. He brought along his own entertainers, musical artists from radio station CNRM in Montreal. At the door the 1,700 guests were presented with noisemakers and buttons featuring a picture of the Senator. In return he was made Queen's first and only Professor of Social Science.

Involved in this three-ring circus somewhat more than they might have wished were Principal W. Hamilton Fyfe and Dr. W. E. McNeill, University Treasurer. The story current at the time was that the University was expected to grant an honorary degree in return for a gift of $25,000 – a windfall in those depression years, but a transaction out of character with Queen's and tradition. Whatever, the Senator did come to town and he was so pleased with his reception that he voluntarily raised the ante to $30,000.

Not only were Principal Fyfe and Dr. McNeill uneasy about their role in the proceedings, but they were apprehensive about the behaviour of the students, whose reactions were not to be predicted with any certainty. As it developed, there was no cause for concern. From the time a large delegation of students, accompanied by the

Queen's band, met the Senator and his entourage at the Outer Station with a highly enthusiastic welcome, until departure many hours later, their behaviour left nothing to be desired. They wholeheartedly accepted the Senator in the spirit of goodwill and *bonhomie* in which he came, and, indeed, their own good nature was so spontaneous and infectious that it contributed in no small measure to the undoubted success of the venture.

Who was Senator Wilson? He was a native of Montreal, of Scots and French parentage. He had been engaged in the wholesale wine-importing business and had made a great deal of money. He had been elected three times as a Liberal M.P. for Rigaud. He was well known in Quebec for his philanthropy, but his visit to Queen's was a rare venture outside his native province, aside from his senatorial pursuits in Ottawa.

He travelled to Kingston by special train, and he brought with him some close personal friends, an orchestra, and a troupe of outstanding musical talent, comedians and jugglers. He was met at the station by five bus-loads of students. He and his party were greeted by the band with *Queen's College Colours* and by a hearty Queen's yell from the students. The band also contributed a spirited rendition of *For He's a Jolly Good Fellow*. The *Queen's Review* described it as 'one of the most enthusiastic and vociferous welcomes ever accorded a public man in this city.'

His party in Grant Hall was scheduled for the evening, and he put in the afternoon by visiting Victoria School, Kingston Collegiate Institute, Regiopolis College, St. Mary's School, the House of Providence and the Home for the Aged, as well as touching bases with Archbishop O'Brien and Bishop Lyons. He was accompanied on this tour by Dr. Fyfe, Dr. McNeill, and Mayor Bruce Hopkins. In the schools he spoke briefly and distributed the noisemakers and buttons with his likeness. He was received with enthusiasm wherever he went.

In Grant Hall that night the 71-year-old Senator and his party filled the platform. In the front row were members of his family, including his son, Capt. L. M. Wilson; his daughter, Baroness S. W. Eysenhardt, and the Baron; friends and colleagues – Senator Pierre Casgrain, Milton L. Hersey, LL.D. '08, and Dr. W. H. Atherton, of the University of Montreal, each of whom spoke briefly in praise of the Senator; M. and Mme. Emile Grothe, M.L. Bissonette, and Dr. E. Deguire, Mayor of Côteau de Lac, where the Senator made his home.

Introduced by Senator H. H. Horsey, Arts '95, the main speaker was Senator Wilson himself. He said he accepted the ovation as a tribute to the humanitarian work he was doing rather than to himself alone. 'I made my money from the public,' he stated, 'and now I am trying to return it where it belongs. As a youth, I was very poor. Fortune saw fit to favour me and I became wealthy; but I was left with a duty to perform to the poor and the sick with whom I come in contact. That is exactly what I have tried to do in my life.'

Moneyed men were not the greatest philanthropists, continued the Senator; the emancipators of history – clergymen of all denominations, nuns, country doctors, and mothers – all ranked higher than the mere possessors of money bags. He decried those millionaires who hoarded securities and evaded income taxes. Part of Senator Wilson's own political life had been spent in fighting tax evasion, and recently he had been praised by the Rt. Hon. R. B. Bennett for his accomplishments in that field.

In thanking the veteran philanthropist, Dr. Fyfe spoke warmly in appreciation of his contribution to the University's endowment, and presented him with an illustrated address signed by Dr. McNeill and himself.

Dr. Fyfe paid tribute to the Senator as a practitioner of social science –

the science of making people sociable, the art of getting people to forget their worries and differences and grumbling grievances and to enjoy themselves with the whole-hearted simplicity of children. That is a science and an art which we highly appreciate at Queen's, and as I am sure we shall never find anyone else so learned and so skilful in that art and science, we hereby appoint you our first and only Professor of Social Science.

Other honours were offered to the friendly philanthropist. A. R. Winnett, President of the Alma Mater Society, announced that the executive had given the Senator honorary membership. Little Miss Helen McArthur, daughter of Prof. Duncan McArthur, presented Senator Wilson with a beautiful 'Q' made of chrysanthemums and tied with Queen's ribbons. A little Indian girl, Muriel Maracle, descendant of the illustrious Chief Joseph Brant, handed him a tomahawk as a tribute to the fact that the Senator's grandmother was a full-blooded Iroquois.

Whoever and whatever the spotlight was on, the Senator was very much in evidence. His interjections, asides, soliloquies and observations on the passing scene never stopped. His good humour pervaded the entire proceedings, and he had the audience with him all the way.

Now the professional entertainers took over. Led by the prestigious Agostini, the orchestra rendered several classical numbers. Among the outstanding artists who also performed were Mme. Jeanne Maubourg, formerly of the Théatre Royale de la Monnai, Brussels, Covent Garden, London, and the Metropolitan Opera, New York; Mlle. Jeanne Miguolet, coloratura soprano, formerly of Roxy's Gang, in Radio City; and M. Jacques Gerard, Canadian tenor of the Opera Comique, Paris. M. Louis Chartier acted as *maitre de ceremonie* and M. Henri Letondal as *radio annonceur.* Senator Wilson's happy remarks and part of the musical programme were broadcast for an hour over a Dominion-wide hook-up by the Canadian Radio Broadcasting Commission.

After the party broke up, I was introduced, as a reporter for the *Whig-Standard,* to the distinguished visitor by the publisher of the paper, Rupert Davies. The Senator's interest in me was enhanced by the fact that I would be filing a story for the Canadian Press. When we shook hands I felt a lump of something pressed upon me. As soon as I could I investigated and discovered a ten-dollar bill and a five-dollar bill. In the meantime I had assured the Senator, yes sir, indeed sir, that I would see that he received adequate coverage in the newspapers of the nation.

The Senator passed me over to his secretary, a serious, intense young man, who wanted to know what letters the Senator would now be able to place after his name. He indignantly rejected the information that a chair in social science carried with it no such privilege, and stomped off in obvious displeasure. Months later it was rumoured that the Senator felt he had been deceived by the University and was threatening to make a fuss about it. True or not, nothing came of it, because he died in March of 1934.

Certainly the Principal's Report for 1933-34 gave no support to the rumour. Dr. Fyfe wrote:

. ... We therefore welcome with peculiar gratitude the late Senator Lawrence A. Wilson's generous gift of $30,000, which was entirely 'without strings' and has been added to the general endowment, with the exception of a sum of $5,000 set aside to form a student loan fund, an arrangement to which he gave his very glad approval before his death. In Senator Wilson we found a friend only to lose him, and his sudden death in March brought to Queen's a sense of personal loss. His visit in November was a remarkable event. The seal of our welcome may gave given enemies cause to blaspheme – and some friends, too. But the proceedings were redeemed from reproach by the simple kindliness of our visitor, who became for the evening also our host, and by the enthusiasm with which the students responded to his friendly gestures. Queen's is indebted both for his gift and for his joy in giving.

But this is getting ahead of our story. The festivities in Grant Hall over, there was still more to come, this time with the University as host at a supper in the Gymnasium. Exhibitions of swimming and diving, boxing, wrestling and fencing rounded out the program. At a late hour the party broke up, and the visitors returned to their special train.

The *Whig-Standard,* besides reporting on the visit in detail, commented editorially:

Senator Lawrence A. Wilson made many warm friends in Kingston last night, not alone by his generous gift of $30,000 to Queen's University, but by his warm hospitality and his ever-present air of friendliness and good nature. Senator Wilson is a self-made man. He came from the humble home of Scotch parents, and has made his way to the top of the ladder by dint of hard work. He has made a lot of money. As he says, he made it out of the people, and he believes it to be his duty to give a large portion of it back to them. In the giving of it he likes to spread joy and happiness, and judging from the vociferous reception given to him last night by the students of Queen's University he succeeds admirably in doing so.

Senator Wilson does not hide his light under a bushel. He professes no hypocritical self-modesty. He is a big-hearted, generous, kindly man who has made a lot of money. He is the Pollyanna of the Canadian Senate and we believe he is doing a tremendous lot of good. May he be spared for many years to continue the good work!

This pious hope was not to be realized, but the Senator did leave his mark on Queen's. The phrase *sui generis* fits him like a skin-diver's suit.

VI
The Rectorship

Fall Convocation 1957: Rector Leonard Brockington (second left) with honorary graduate Sir Alan Herbert (left), Principal Mackintosh and AMS President Rich Milne
D.G. Dewar photo

The Rectorship –
A distinguished peculiarity

The position of Rector is peculiar to Queen's in Canada, and is one of the many traditions that the University inherited from its Scottish prototypes. There are other rectors, or *recteurs,* but not in the same meaning of the word. According to one encyclopedia: 'A head of a university or college may be known as rector, but in Scottish universities a rector is an official elected triennially by the students.'

The Act of 1912 had provided for the election of a Rector at Queen's, by 'the registered matriculated students. ... to hold office for three years, or until his successor is elected.' Commented the *Journal:* 'Queen's has always given her students great liberty and almost complete self-government, and in establishing the new office of Rector the University is but taking one step further in this direction.'

The Rev. Dr. S. W. Dyde was the first to fill the position. He was one of the grand old men of Queen's, in the same league with George Monro Grant, John Watson, James Cappon, Nathan Dupuis, W. G. Jordan, John McNaughton, Adam Shortt, and the other giants. He was an alumnus (B.A. '83, M.A. '84, D.Sc. '87) and had taught Mental Philosophy for 16 years in association with his mentor, Dr. Watson. He left Queen's in 1911 to head Alberta's new Robertson Presbyterian College in Edmonton, and he was Principal there when chosen Queen's first Rector in 1913. He returned to Kingston in 1917 as Principal of Queen's Theological College, held that post till 1926, but went on teaching until 1934, when he was 73 years of age.

In 1916 Dr. Dyde was succeeded by Dr. James L. Robertson. This outstanding Canadian agriculturalist had been elected over another candidate, Sir John M. Gibson, K.C., lawyer, industrialist, soldier, and one-time Lieutenant-Governor of Ontario. This was the only occasion where there had been more than one nomination for the post until students began contesting the position in recent years. All other appointments were by acclamation.

The Rectors of Queen's, with their years of election, have been:

1913   The Rev. Dr. S. W. Dyde
1916   James L. Robertson
1920   Brigadier General A. E. Ross
1925   W. H. Coverdale
1929   Oscar D. Skelton
1935   The Rt. Hon. R. B. Bennett
1937   The Hon. Norman McLeod Rogers
1940   The Earl of Athlone
1944   B. K. Sandwell
1947   Leonard W. Brockington
1968   Senator M. Grattan O'Leary
1969   R. Alan Broadbent
1972   Gary Gannage
1974   Bruce Trotter
1976   Morris Chochla

The Rector was designated as the students' representative on the Board of Trustees, but there is little evidence that the earlier appointees considered the position more than an honour. Most of them did, however, deliver a rectorial address at some time during their term of office.

Dr. B. K. Sandwell, editor of *Saturday Night* and one-time head of the Department of English at Queen's, described his position as follows:

The office of Rector dates from the earliest days of university institutions, away back in the Middle Ages, a period which in my youth was regarded as somewhat unenlightened because it was excessively addicted to wars. The simplest considerations of etymology make it clear that a Rector is a much more important person than a Principal or a President, for the Rector derives his title from the Latin *regere,* to rule, govern, direct, or guide, while the Principal is merely one who goes first and the President merely one who sits further forward. There are, I find also, several kinds, grades or degrees of Rector. I myself belong to the lowest kind, the common or garden Rector, *Rector Vulgaris* or *Canadensis.* But in Germany there is the *Rector Magnificus,* which sounds like a very good grade indeed, and even the *Rector Magnificentissimus,* a title bestowed when the officer in question is also the ruling head of the state, so that I suppose we may assume that the Herr Doctor Aldolf Hitler, if still alive, is Rector Magnificentissimus of several once great and flourishing but now *gleichegeschaltet* universities. In Scotland there is of course the Lord Rector, but Canada, having abolished lords along with

Rector B.K. Sandwell

knights and baronets, must obviously get along with a more democratic sub-species.

One thing is certain. The matter of installation of a Rector at Queen's is an infinitely more dignified affair than it is at Scottish universities. In 1950 Queen's had two representatives at the installation of Rector MacCormick during the University of Glasgow's Fifth Centenary Celebrations: E. Michael Howarth, Arts '49, who was at Oxford on a Rhodes Scholarship, and Miss Joan Torgeson, Arts '51, now Mrs. H. G. R. Knapp, who was on an exchange scholarship at St. Andrew's. Both gave a report to the Alma Mater Society, reprinted in the *Review,* and both spoke of the high-spirited participation of the students in the various ceremonies.

Wrote Miss Torgeson:

A Rectorial is the noisiest occasion of all because the Rector is nominated, elected, and installed by the students themselves. During the week preceding his election, classes are practically abandoned, days are devoted to publicity stunts, nights to paint jobs and raids.

... Fortunately Rector MacCormick expected the worst, but we, as 'honoured guests', were totally unprepared. ... Before the entrance of the university and city dignitaries, we found ourselves the main target for the rolls of paper, fireworks, bags of flour, ripe fruit, rotten eggs, and other sundry articles with which the students massed below and above us had had the forethought to arm themselves.

... The barrage thickened when the City Fathers and University officials entered in their velvet and ermine gowns, and when the Lord Rector himself appeared on the platform he was submerged beneath a welter of streamers and heavy artillery and almost deafened by an unanimous roar. ... However, the Rector plunged into his speech.

... There was not the slightest let-up in the noise or the target-practice as MacCormick began to speak, and ... his progress was hindered not only by the incessant clamour but by such interruptions as a mock-athlete running in to present him with a lighted candle, a live duck being thrust on to the platform, two amateur trapeze artists crossing the auditorium on a rope suspended between the galleries, and an egg which, glancing off the Rector's sleeve, landed on the mortarboard of Chancellor Lord Boyd Orr.

... The 'ceremony' was cut short by (student president) Donald Macmillan, who apologized to the guests for 'the unprecedented exhibition of hooliganism.' However, in the opinion of most students, their conduct was little worse than at preceding rectorials, and the only unprecedented event was the president's apology. Nevertheless, they hoisted him good-humouredly on their shoulders and bore him from the littered paper-strewn hall.

We can be thankful that the tradition of the office and not the undisciplined behaviour has been adopted at Queen's. In fact the rectorship caused scarcely a ripple in student life, and occasionally the three-year term was extended through oversight.

The appointment of Norman McLeod Rogers gave the students a relationship with the office that had been lacking. Mr. Rogers had been a popular Professor of Political Science before he went into politics and eventually became Minister of Labour and then Minister of Defence in Ottawa. When the rectorship became vacant in 1937, he was the students' unanimous choice. He was proud of the appointment, and the students felt they had a friend on the Board.

B. K. Sandwell was another who cherished his appointment. He wrote:

The editor of *Saturday Night* was last week invited by the Alma Mater Society of Queen's University to assume for a time the functions of Rector of that University. This is a purely honorary post corresponding to the office of the same name in Edinburgh, Glasgow, Aberdeen, and other Scottish universities from which Queen's derives its traditions; and it imports, we believe, no duties other than that of delivering the rectorial address at some time during incumbency.

It is, we feel, among the highest honours ever paid to this journal, because it proceeds from a body of students, that is of serious young men and women from all over Canada, who have the dignity and prestige of their university very much at heart. The confidence of such Canadians is something which we have worked hard and long to attain, and which we profoundly appreciate.

Dr. Sandwell delivered two rectorial addresses during his term and also made several visits to the campus to meet with the students. It was a happy relationship.

As I have chronicled separately, the rectorship took on a new dimension with the appointment of Leonard W. Brockington in 1947. He was faithful in his attendance at meetings of the Board of Trustees. Not only was he a strong supporter of any causes in which the students were interested, but he also became a most eloquent spokesman on all matters pertaining to the University. He was very proud of his association with Queen's.

Dr. Brockington was succeeded as Rector by his good friend, Senator M. Grattan O'Leary, journalist, orator and national figure. He lasted only one year. His appointment had been marked by controversy as to whether a student could not fill the post to better advantage. This was at the time when students had been admitted to the Senate and were campaigning for direct representation on the Board of Trustees. The dissidents finally succeeded in ousting Senator O'Leary from office, as was their prerogative, but it was not the students' finest hour.

The Constitution was studied again, and the way was now clear to elect a student to the rectorship: A number of good candidates contested the election, and the winner was Alan Broadbent, a postgraduate student in History, and the son of Alan Broadbent, Permanent President of the Class of Arts '29. The choice was a good one. Alan took his duties seriously, represented the students ably on the Board of Trustees, performed with dignity on ceremonial occasions, and interpreted his role effectively as a sort of campus ombudsman.

His successors, Gary Gannage and Bruce Trotter, were also carefully chosen and represented the student body creditably. These first three student Rectors adopted a reasonable approach in representing the student viewpoint, and the University was well served.
[When graduate studies at Oxford forced Bruce's early retirement in the summer of 1976, he was succeeded by another student Rector, Morris A. 'Mo' Chochla, Sc.'74, Law'78.]

*

Most of the buildings on campus bear the names of persons who have been prominent in the history of Queen's or who have made a significant contribution in one way or another. A roll call of the names thus commemorated merits an accompaniment of drums and cymbals.

One name that has earned preservation and which has not yet been assigned is that of Elizabeth H. D. de St. Remy, the first woman student to register at the University.

Miss de St. Remy was the headmistress of a girls' school in Kingston, and she asked the Senate to allow girls, upon her recommendation, to attend classes at Queen's. Chemistry and Logic, curiously enough, were the subjects deisred. On October 13, 1876, the Senate granted her request. The fees were set at $7 and $3 respectively.

Miss de St. Remy was the first to take advantage of this opportunity, and in fact beat the gun by registering in Logic on February 1, 1876. A native of Brantford, she had been educated privately by her father, a teacher. She was the 936th student and the first woman to enrol at Queen's. She was also an early dropout; at least she did not attend a second year, according to my research.

Mac de St. Remy of the Class of Arts '44, a prominent Kingston businessman, is a relative.

VII

My seven Principals –
Every man in the right place
at the right time

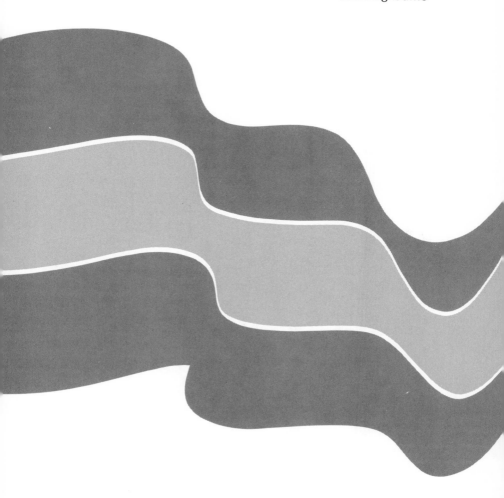

Boyes photo

200

R. Bruce Taylor

R. Bruce Taylor, M.A., D.D., LL.D., was the eighth Principal of Queen's and the last to be a member of the Presbyterian ministry. He was within two years of retirement when I entered Queen's as a freshman in the fall of 1927.

Dr. Taylor had come to Queen's in 1917 from Montreal, where he had been minister of St. Paul's Church, whence the University had also acquired Dr. William Snodgrass, who served as fifth Principal 1864-1877. A native of Scotland, Dr. Taylor had been educated first in the humanities, law and economics, later in theology and Semitic languages, studying at Glasgow and Aberdeen; then for 21 years he was a Presbyterian minister in Ayrshire, Aberdeen, London, and Montreal. For one year he was chaplain of the 42nd Battalion, Royal Highlanders of Canada, serving in France and Belgium.

At Queen's he faced a formidable task. As usual, the University was hard pressed for money. World War One had not yet ended, the student body and the staff were depleted, and the annual deficits were being picked up by the Chancellor, Dr. James Douglas. As an incentive the Chancellor issued a challenge that he would give Queen's half a million dollars if an equal amount could be raised from other sources. He died shortly afterwards, and the trustees of his estate allowed Queen's less than a year to meet the objective. Dr. Taylor succeeded, with the help of the Carnegie Corporation which contributed $250,000, and the grateful Trustees increased his salary by $2,000.

A second campaign in 1926 brought the endowment up to $2,800,000. Dr. Taylor also improved the financial position by persuading the provincial government to increase its annual grant; it climbed from $99,000 in 1917 to $350,000 in 1930. In addition he got a capital grant of $275,000 for buildings and $560,000 for improvement of medical teaching.

During his incumbency there was what D.D. Calvin described as 'unprecedented expansion'. Ban Righ Hall was erected as the first women's residence on campus; the Douglas Library gave the University a more adequate home for library facilities and administrative offices; the George Richardson Memorial Stadium and the Jock Harty Arena added new dimensions to Queen's participation in Intercollegiate athletics; a new Central Heating Plant on the waterfront superseded a Mickey Mouse effort attached to Fleming Hall; the Old Medical Building, gutted by fire, was rebuilt; the Department of Pathology obtained new quarters in Richardson Laboratory, and the Students' Memorial Union was finally opened – all of which contributed to a new campus life style.

Along with the physical plant, the education program was strengthened and enlarged. Degree courses were added in Commerce and Administration, extramural instruction was provided for the Institute of Chartered Accountants of Ontario and other provinces, the Arts program was completely overhauled and revised, and the Medical School was upgraded to the A standards of the American Medical Association.

Dr. Taylor had two recurrent problems, other than financial, that gave him concern over the years: student government and staff salaries.

He deplored what he considered to be the deterioration of student government, particularly in the area of the courts. He felt they were ineffective despite their great potential as a disciplinary force. His criticism was valid, but his hard-nosed, intransigent attitude brought him into conflict with some of the students. In one of his annual reports he wrote:

As the University has grown larger Student Government has become less and less effective. Every now and then it is whipped into activity and justifies itself. When a student generation with poorer standards or a group of men with less personality, comes along, the Student Government, forgetful of its duties, remembers only to insist upon its rights.

In a more benign mood he tempered this view with the observation that 'We can, however, make this broad statement that it is never difficult to appeal to the good sense of the student body and rarely a disappointing thing to trust in it.'

In the matter of staff salaries, Queen's was vulnerable, and with salaries lower than those paid at other universities, notably Toronto and McGill, was at a distinct disadvantage in attracting the better-qualified teachers. The giants of the staff, who had served Queen's loyally for many years, men of the stature of James Cappon, John Watson, W. L. Goodwin, John Matheson, A. L. Clark, Dr. J. C. Connell, G. Y. Chown, and Dr. W. E. McNeill, apparently accepted the *status quo* as one of the facts of life or felt that the atmosphere at Queen's compensated for other shortcomings, but O. D. Skelton, a jewel in the collection, was enticed to Ottawa, and the contribution he made there has long been a source of great satisfaction to the University.

A full professor was paid from $3,000 to $5,000, an associate professor $2,500 to $2,900, and an assistant professor $2,000 to $2,400. In comparison, an engineer on road construction got $350 a month, plus overtime, and a hospital dietitian with no experience could earn $100 a month, plus keep. Dr. Taylor laboured hard and long to improve the academic lot, with considerable success.

While he could scarcely claim much credit for the resurgence of the football team as a power in the land – indeed, he commented wryly at times on the emphasis placed on a mere game with more important matters close at hand – the fact remains that he took a great deal of pride in the accomplishments of the team, including a record three Grey Cups and a victory skein of 26 straight. In his final annual report he wrote:

In the excitement that attended the early victories it may well be that more attention than was fitting was given to this sport. The influence, however, upon the whole Queen's constituency was distinctly good. Now, in these changed times, it has come to be taken almost for granted that the Queen's team reach the place of honour.

With his hearty endorsement, and as a by-product of the University's endowment campaign of 1926, the Alumni Association was formed. The women graduates had had an organization of their own since the turn of the century and a solid history of achievement, with Ban Righ Hall as a monument to their imagination, tenacity and foresight. The new Alumni Association was needed to exploit the potential of the alumni body as a whole.

As a scholar, Dr. Taylor was the author of a four-volume work, *Ancient Hebrew Literature.* He also wrote extensively for periodicals on economic and public matters, as well as on scientific languages. He was Canadian editor of *The Book of Knowledge.*

It was as a public speaker, however, that his reputation largely rested. He was in great demand for a wide variety of functions in

Canada and the United States, and he interpreted this role as the most useful he could perform for Queen's. He held his audiences with bright humour, 'with vivid kindling words never dimmed by any commonplace, and with brilliant unexpected turns of thought,' wrote Dr. W. E. McNeill. 'He could make any Bible text, or indeed any theme, lastingly memorable.' *The Queen's Review* apotheosized him as 'a public speaker second to none'. Said the *Alumnae News:* 'If we can single out one gift that more than any other contributed to his success by bringing the needs and value of Queen's to the Canadian people, it is his rare gift as a public speaker.'

In his rich Scottish accent he referred to Queen's as a gr-r-reat gr-r-reat university, with rolling cadences, and this phrase became his trademark, words to be anticipated, enjoyed. I heard it for the first time when I was a high school student serving as a waiter at a faculty dinner in Grant Hall, a vogue of the Twenties. I was paid $2 for the evening, and I provided my own white coat. This worked out to about 25c an hour, because we had to wait around until after the program, mostly speeches, was over, in order to clear away the dishes. The hiatus provided by the evening's agenda provided a great opportunity for cultural advancement, of which I am afraid the Philistines among us did not always avail ourselves.

When he retired in 1929 Dr. Taylor referred to his time at Queen's as an absorbing 13 years. He wrote:

The presidency of a University is ranked in the United States as one of the dangerous trades, and the average tenure of office there is about six years. The labour is infinite and the labourer is on a pinnacle exposed to the criticism both of the witting and the unwitting. It is expected of him that he be a scholar, an educationist, a financier, an administrator, a man of deep silences, and an orator able to maintain his place on any platform. To be lacking in any one of these aspects is to be met with the charge that the old days were better – as indeed to sentimentalists they always are.

My own contacts with Dr. Taylor were rare. He was a remote figure representing authority. One just didn't question the 'Prink', as the Principal was then known to the student body, though not to his face. I was shocked by the temerity of those who challenged his fiats during the student strike in the spring of 1928. But I did meet him, and in his own house. As a member of the Drama Guild I had played the part of Finch McComas in Shaw's *You Never Can Tell;* subsequently the cast was invited to tea at the Principal's Residence, Summerhill. After his retirement I had occasion to visit him at his summer home on Wolfe Island, probably for the *Journal,* and was surprised and pleased and impressed to find that he remembered me. It was my first experience that a Principal was not so weighed down by affairs of state or so dedicated to serious thought that he had no awareness of his constituents.

For part of his retirement Dr. Taylor was minister of the Church of Scotland in Rome. Later he bought a house near Cannes, France, and settled down with his wife and books. In 1940 he got out of the country just ahead of the Germans, and moved to British Columbia. After the war he and his wife returned to France, where he died in 1955, in his 85th year.

In an appreciation written for the Board of Trustees, Dr. McNeill said: 'R. Bruce Taylor was a great personality, with an infectious zest for life and for books, for people and for things, a man of warm humanity, a scholar and a gentleman. His name belongs in the roll of those who have served Queen's well and gladly.'

William Hamilton Fyfe

For her ninth Principal, Queen's came up with William Hamilton Fyfe, M.A., LL.D., an outstanding classical scholar and a man Principal Grant had tried to attract to his staff 30 years previously. He was the first layman, and the first member of the Church of England, or indeed of any communion other than the Presbyterian, to hold the office.

Principal Fyfe was born in Chelsea, England, the son of James Hamilton Fyfe, barrister-at-law. He attended Fettes College in Edinburgh, matriculated with a foundation scholarship to Merton, at Oxford, and graduated with the honour of a double first in 'Mods' and 'Greats'. It was at this period that Principal Grant tried to get him for Queen's.

After graduation he was assistant master at Radley College, 1901-03, and then returned to Merton, where he became Fellow, Tutor, and Dean. During his 15 years at Merton he gained a high reputation as scholar and administrator, and in 1919 he was appointed Headmaster of Christ's Hospital, 'the Bluecoat School'.

It was from Christ's Hospital that Dr. Fyfe came to Queen's in 1930. He had a reputation as a scholar of fine quality and a man of real intellectual distinction, qualifications which were welcomed enthusiastically by the Queen's community.

When he arrived on the Queen's campus he was serenaded by a few hundred students led by Gib McKelvey and Oot Gourlay of the football team.

At Convocation that fall he was given an honorary LL.D. degree with the citation: '... derived from a fine race, inheriting a great name, scholar, teacher, writer, orator, administrator.'

In his inaugural address, Dr. Fyfe outlined his philosophy of education, introducing a note that he was to repeat many times during his tenure, a clarion call for intellectual integrity: 'Mere attendance at lectures, the patient inscription of notes, and their punctual regurgitation at examinations – all such routine is utterly valueless in

206

Boyes photo

itself.' His ideals encompassed all faculties, but he made it clear that he expected Arts to be pre-eminent in the life of the University. In addition to the regular production of school teachers, professors and teachers of religion, he said, 'we must produce in greater numbers than before the statesmen, poets, artists, and thinkers of the future; we must find the man power and the woman power for the era of Canadian art, philosophy, literature, and music which is just dawning – or, if it isn't, then Queen's must up and make it dawn.'

This theme is developed and expanded in the annual reports he made each year to the Trustees. Some of his suggestions were implemented. The honours course was revised. A resident artist, Goodridge Roberts, and a resident musician, F. L. Harrison, were appointed. The National Entrance Scholarships were established, one for each province.

But there were not many changes. The Depression took care of that. There was a steady decline in the income of the University. There was an annual decrease both in the grant from the provincial government and in the income from the slender endowment. This led to stringent economies which in turn served to hamstring efficiency. It was a struggle for mere survival.

The University surmounted the financial crisis largely because of the Draconian measures of Dr. W. E. McNeill, who, as Treasurer, served as hatchet man in introducing economies. The students, shivering in their eight o'clock classes because the heat was not turned on until later in the morning, blamed Dr. McNeill, not Dr. Fyfe. The same held true when the tuition fees were raised. Dr. McNeill once described himself as a lightning rod, designed to draw the wrath of the students from the Principal.

Annually, the Principal gave full credit where credit was due: 'He remains Treasurer, so we are not bankrupt,' he said in his first Report. Later, he cited 'the unsleeping care with which as Treasurer he conserves our dwindling funds.' And, in his final Report: 'Not only does he jealously watch our dwindling resources and devise those ingenious, small economies by which alone the University is kept out of bankruptcy, but in the decision of every question that arises his experience and wisdom are factors of dominant weight.'

The Canadian student as Dr. Fyfe saw him at Queen's was a matter for grave concern. 'The horizon of the typical undergraduate student is said to be bounded by the lectures, examinations, dances, films and gladiatorial games at which he is a frenzied spectator.

'I am not without hope that this familiar portrait may become before long a caricature.'

Dr. Fyfe, who himself played an English version of the game at Merton, thought too much attention was paid to football at Queen's. He deplored the annual football fever in the autumn, although he blamed the newspapers more than the students for this state of affairs. As for alumni interest, he saw it as 'the infantile enthusiasm of middle-age'. He viewed intramural sports in a different light: 'This association of athletic exercises with the proper functions of an educational establishment is in the best British tradition, and, so long as it does not interfere with intellectual or moral development, it should in my opinion be encouraged and preserved.'

He regarded the number of dances available on campus as an even greater threat. Once in a *Review* article entitled 'What I Have Found at Queen's', he reported 'student activities multifarious and innumerable; and unreasonable wealth of dances.' On another occasion he wrote that 'dancing is much more detrimental to university studies than rugby.' He was pleased when the student government restricted the number of dances to one a week.

My contacts with Dr. Fyfe were frequent, mostly after I had graduated and become a reporter with the *Whig-Standard*. Queen's was on my beat, and every morning I paid a call at the office of the Principal. If I could impress on his efficient secretary, Miss Mamie Anglin, the importance of my call, I would be permitted to ask my questions in person. I well remember seeking him out on one occasion for a comment on a *Toronto Star* news story that six Americans had turned up at Queen's for the football training camp. I knew that Dr. Fyfe was at his desk, because I had seen him through the door, which was always open. But when I entered his office he was not in view. He had overheard the purpose of my mission and had ducked out of sight. Then slowly his head emerged from behind his desk, where he had been crouching.

'You wanted to see me?' he asked, all innocence.

I asked for his comments about the American contingent in football camp. He gave this some thought, and then said: 'Let me get this straight. By football do you mean the round one or the pointed one?'

I did not get a story, but he made even a losing encounter pleasurable.

Whenever he had occasion to introduce me to visitors to the campus, he always presented me as 'one of the carrion vultures of the press, seeking whom he may devour.'

I remember, when I was a student on the staff of the *Journal,* that he issued a statement in which he thanked the students for their help in connection with a fire in Kingston Hall, but deplored the *defenestration* . This sent us scurrying for a dictionary. The one in the printing office was no help, and it took a hurried trip to the nearby public library to determine that the Principal was referring to the ejection of objects out of windows. It was a typical example of his ability to come up with the right word at the right time. Another time the phrase 'inspissated gloom' sent us scrambling.

As long as I have been associated with alumni business, there has been a controversy over the pronunciation of *alumni* and *alumnae.* The Alumni Directors once tried to resolve the problem by incorporating into the Constitution the fiat that the 'i' in alumni was to rhyme with 'eye' and the 'ae' in alumnae was to rhyme with 'knee'. This was passed with apparent unanimity, but, alas, when the Constitution was printed there was a howl of protest. The upshot was that the matter was dropped for all time, at least as far as the board was then concerned.

Dr. Fyfe, who was said to translate the morning newspaper into Greek and Latin as a mental exercise, once made a suggestion that in the interests of harmony it might be advisable to use *alumnuses* as the plural for *alumnus.* Other than this observation he did not enter into the argument.

Queen's University and the community took great pride in the erudition and scholarship of the Principal and the manner in which he graced his office. Mrs. Fyfe was also popular, particularly in the work of organizations devoted to the aid of the needy and to the advancement of the social welfare of citizens. A daughter Margaret (now Mrs. C. J. Mabey) graduated from Queen's in 1933. It came, therefore, as a shock when the announcement was made in 1936 that Dr. Fyfe had been appointed Principal of the University of Aberdeen. He had not been able to give even a hint that the move was pending, as this appointment was a prerogative of His Majesty the King.

In less than six years he had established himself as a champion of educational ideals of the highest order. People in all walks of life – at the University, in Kingston, and throughout the country – voiced their regret. Their feelings were made manifest in many ways, culminating in a family party in Grant Hall attended by 500. The atmosphere was charged with good will and emotion. Dr. Fyfe brought down the house when he said that one of the many memories he would have of Kingston is that the weather is always unusual for this time of year.

D. D. Calvin claimed in his *Queen's University at Kingston* that Dr. Fyfe was modestly dissatisfied with the results of his time at Queen's, and indeed it cannot be said that he succeeded in putting all his ideals into practice. But his influence was greater than he thought, both as an interpreter of the ancient tradition of British education and as an offset, perhaps, to the constant pressure of American ways. Certain it was that he brought a fresh and keen outlook to Canadian university life. He was to be missed above all for his humour and his light touch; however serious the discussion, it could never be over-solemn when he was present.

Of the many tributes paid to Dr. Fyfe, Dr. McNeill characteristically produced the most memorable:

Principal Fyfe girds his thinking with words of magic power. He is matchless in piercing logic and vivid speech, in conquering wit and disarming humour. Lord of language, he could not be dull or commonplace. Everything he says has distinction. 'His words wing on – as live words will.'

Dr. Fyfe was the second member of staff to become Principal of Aberdeen. The trail blazer was Rev. Peter Colin Campbell, Professor of Classics and the first appointment to the staff of Queen's, in 1841. In 1845 he returned to Scotland, and in 1860 when King's College and Marischal were united to form the University of Aberdeen, Campbell was made Principal and served in that capacity until his death in 1876.

At Aberdeen Dr. Fyfe capped his long career in education and added further lustre with contributions to the war effort in many capacities. His distinguished services were recognized by the honour of knighthood, conferred on him in 1942. He retired in 1948.

He came back to Queen's just once, on the occasion of the Commonwealth Inter-University Conference in the fall of 1954. By this time he was nearly blind, but the flashing wit, the friendly persuasion, and the presence were still much in evidence. Accompanied by Dr. W. E. McNeill and Dr. W. A. Mackintosh, he paid a visit to all those on staff whom he had known. He died in London in 1965, at

Principals past and present: Sir William Hamilton Fyfe (centre) on a visit to Queen's in 1954, with his successors, Dr. Wallace (right) and Dr. Mackintosh.
D.G. Dewar photo

the age of 86, survived by his wife, Dorothea, a daughter Margaret (who is a Queen's graduate) and two sons. Lady Fyfe died in January 1977.

Queen's University owes much to Sir William Hamilton Fyfe. As J. M. Macdonnell, Chairman of the Board of Trustees, said, 'It is no exaggeration to say that he has raised the name of Queen's throughout Canada. ... Again and again those who have come in contact with him, personally or through his speeches, have said to me, "That is the kind of man who *should* be at the head of a university." '

Dr. W. A. Mackintosh said: 'His ready wit, his apt phrase, his scorn of the pompous and hollow, his enthusiasm for the inquiring student, are not only pleasant memories, but contributed much to the spirit of the University.'

212

Robert Charles Wallace

Robert Charles Wallace was appointed Principal of Queen's in 1936, the first scientist to hold the post. He held or was to hold the right to list after his name: M.A., B.SC., Ph.D., LL.D., D.C.L, C.M.G., F.G.S., F.R.S.C. He had been President of the University of Alberta since 1928.

His selection met with enthusiasm. At the installation dinner, J. W. Dafoe, editor of the Winnipeg *Free Press,* said, 'Wallace was made for Queen's and Queen's was made for Wallace.' Later, the prediction was confirmed by Dr. McNeill: 'He has found his true home, intellectual and spiritual.'

His credentials, academic and professional, were of the highest. A native of the Orkney Islands, as was Mrs. Wallace, he was educated in Deerness Public School, Kirkwall Burgh School and Edinburgh University, where he obtained the degrees of M.A., B.SC., and D.SC. His several awards included the Royal Exhibition of 1851 Scholarship. He obtained his Ph.D. degree at Göttingen University, and held a Carnegie Fellowship at St. Andrew's University.

It was as an expert in Geology and Geography that he came to Canada in 1910, with an appointment as lecturer in the Department of Geology and Mineralogy at the University of Manitoba. From 1912 to 1928 he was professor and head of this department. He was Commissioner for Northern Manitoba, 1926-28.

No sheltered academic he. He knew Canada as few do. In his early period as a geologist, he went into the field each summer with the Dominion Geological Survey. As Commissioner of Northern Manitoba his headquarters were at The Pas, 500 miles north of Winnipeg. He travelled by canoe in summer and by dog team in winter, winning respect everywhere he went.

No matter whether he was in university or in the wilds, he towered as a leader. At Queen's his genius reached full flower. He fitted into the combined post of Principal and Vice-Chancellor as if it had been tailor-made for him. Dr. McNeill was to comment: 'Queen's

K. Carey & R. Bowley photo

214

University claimed Dr. Wallace, who seemed a man made in its own image.'

A man of deeply religious nature, he needed all his spiritual resources shortly within weeks of his arrival at Queen's when his son, a postgraduate student at McGill, died suddenly. He and Mrs. Wallace bore their sorrow privately and bravely.

At Queen's Dr. Wallace faced many problems. The Depression was just lifting, and there were many financial constraints. Very soon he found himself in charge of a war-time university, with a shortage of staff and an insecure student body. Queen's rose to its responsibilities nobly and the Principal saw that it did – then, and during the difficult post-war period.

Under his guidance there was steady progress. He added a School of Nursing (something he had also done for the University of Alberta), a School of Physical and Health Education, the Department of Industrial Relations, the Institute of Local Government, a Board of Graduate Studies, a Biological Research Station at Lake Opinicon, a School of Fine Arts, (which he had also set up at Alberta), and an English School for Quebec students and others whose native speech was not English.

The physical plant was enlarged. Chemistry and Chemical Engineering each got a new building, and the Mining and Metallurgical Laboratory an extension; Clark Hall gave the campus extended facilities for Technical Supplies and a bookstore; a new and enlarged Students' Union provided clubrooms, offices and common rooms for male students, with limited privileges for women students. The latter also got a new dining hall in Ban Righ and a new residence.

One of Dr. Wallace's most loyal admirers was Col. R. S. McLaughlin, President of General Motors of Canada. Colonel Sam became interested in Queen's and Wallace through Chancellor C. A. Dunning, and developed into the most generous Queen's benefactor of all time, starting with McLaughlin Hall for Mechanical Engineering. Ultimately his benefactions amounted to approximately $4.5 million.

One of his gifts was a substantial contribution towards the cost of rebuilding the Students' Union after the fire of 1947, and at his request the Great Hall was renamed Wallace Hall. A party was held to express publicly the University's gratitude for Colonel Sam's munificence. It was a great evening, the first of many for which Wallace Hall became a gracious focal point. Mrs. McLaughlin, called upon for a few words, stole the show from all the other luminaries.

Colonel Sam 'phoned the next day to thank the Principal for the party. Then Mrs. McLaughlin joined the conversation, and the upshot was a contribution from her for a quarter million dollars to complete the construction of a new women's residence, subsequently named Adelaide Hall in her honour.

With University co-operation, and to the great gain of the Faculty of Medicine, Kingston General Hospital expanded its patient, clinical, and research facilities. An Ontario Cancer Clinic was given space. A synchrotron was added to the equipment in Physics in the interest of atomic studies.

Dr. Wallace's goals included better teachers and better salaries. At a Reunion reception he once remarked that it was possible to estimate the age of a graduate by the names of great teachers he or she remembered, names such as Cappon, Dupuis, Watson, Jordan, Shortt. Great names all, but Dr. Wallace felt strongly that there were just as great teachers on *his* staff, and there were more of them. He took great pride in his appointments, and he pressed unceasingly for adequate salaries. Four times during his tenure the members of staff received raises, as well as other benefits.

At heart Dr. Wallace was first and foremost a teacher. He believed strongly in education and in the teaching process, and he spoke and wrote profusely of his thoughts on the subject. But he spoke on a wide range of other topics, as well. He was known outside his immediate field of scholarship as a profound and stimulating speaker on philosophical subjects. In the first address he gave at Queen's, in Convocation Hall, he provided the press with a copy of his remarks, but warned that in future he would speak without notes. On the rare occasions when he did have a manuscript, he did not refer to it, but he would repeat the text word for word, a remarkable example of clear thinking and concentration.

Although he did much to advance the interests of the professional schools, he felt strongly that the humane studies were of paramount importance. They must not only be kept strong, he said, but they must be integrated into the courses that were designated as practical. 'The Faculty of Arts will always remain the mainspring which supplies the dynamic for the professional subjects,' he said in one of his annual reports.

He also felt that the University should not be allowed to become large, that it should concentrate on those things which it could do well.

It would be inadvisable to permit the student body to increase – when the veteran needs are over – beyond a figure of 2,000 intramural students, if Queen's is to keep the closely knit student life which has been a great factor in her strength.

The policy should not be that of expansiveness, but rather of high quality in the fields which are available for cultivation. In this way, and in this way alone, can Queen's do its best service to herself and to Canada.

He was a tireless traveller, a familiar figure on the station platform at Kingston, either coming or going. He was the first Principal to be able to make use of the airplane, and use it he did. Some of his junkets made news. In connection with one of Dr. Wallace's visits to the West Coast, D. A. McGregor, Arts '05, in his column in the Vancouver *Daily Province,* wrote that 'it took Dr. Grant about 80 days to cover half the distance Dr. Wallace covered in three days. It took Dr. Gordon 144 days to cover a quarter of the distance.' On this particular safari he visited Vancouver, Victoria and Calgary, speaking and meeting alumni and professional groups, and was back in Kingston within three days to keep an appointment. Subsequent Principals did as much or more, but Dr. Wallace was a pioneer in this mode of travel.

Always on the go, he never seemed to be in a hurry. In appearance he had some resemblances to Abraham Lincoln; tousled hair, rumpled clothes, youthful, warm, friendly, oozing humanity, with a ready smile on his countenance. One Lincolnesque quality was his use of homely stories to illustrate a point.

Two come to mind. A traveller making a transcontinental train trip was at a loss as to the amount he should tip the porter. After some indecision he went right to the source, the porter himself. 'George, what do you usually receive as a tip?'

'I get an average of $5,' was the reply. The grateful traveller then produced a five-dollar bill.

'Thank you very much,' said the porter. 'I'd like you to know that you are the very first to come up to the average.'

A man dropped in at a Presbyterian church service in Winnipeg. At what seemed to him suitable intervals he uttered a loud, 'Praise the Lord!' The members of the congregation shifted uneasily in their seats. A few looked around to see where the interruptions were coming from. After several of these interjections, an elder tapped him on the shoulder and whispered in his ear, 'We don't "Praise the Lord" in this church.'

He was keenly interested in young people, and the students recognized the fact. He believed in student government. He always had time for consultation and advice. He kept in touch with those who ran student affairs. Every year he and Mrs. Wallace entertained the executive of the Alma Mater Society at dinner in Summerhill, followed by an evening of parlor games.

An elder of Chalmers Church, he was in his pew every Sunday he could attend. But before he went to church he visited any sick students or members of staff who might be in hospital, a practice firmly established by Principals in earlier days. 'When a Principal of a University takes time out every week to visit sick students, I know something about the quality of that man's character,' wrote 'R.D.C.' in *Medicine Chest.*

Once a 50-year graduate sent in a generous contribution accompanied by a warm letter. 'I like to think of Queen's as one of the modern universities where sound scholarship and serious thinking still prevail,' he said. 'New and beguiling deities are born to each new generation, but I have always put my trust in the rugged prophets on the Old Ontario Strand to denounce the interlopers. In these days we have a great prophet in Principal Wallace.'

He was considered by many the country's senior university principal. The Prime Minister selected him as one of three people – the only university head – to represent Canada at the London conference which created the United Nations Educational, Scientific, and Cultural Organization, known as UNESCO. He was one of its most active founders. He was widely regarded as the spokesman for Canadian education, and his advice was freely sought and freely given. His pronouncements were faithfully recorded. He was considered to be good copy by the daily newspapers.

The honours that came his way were impressive in importance and in number. The King made him Companion of St. Michael and St. George. He was the first Canadian Trustee of the Carnegie Foundation for the Advancement of Teaching. He was offered the headship of McGill and received feelers from several other universities. He was a member or fellow of ten learned societies, a member of ten government or educational committees, and president or chairman of most of them; he was a Fellow of the Geological Society of London and of America and of the Society of Economic Geologists; honorary member of the Royal Canadian Institute and of the Engineering Institute of Canada; member of the Committee on Reconstruction; chairman of the Sub-Committee on the Development of Natural Resources and of the National Advisory Committee for Children from Overseas; president of the Association of Canadian Clubs, of the Ontario Research Council, of the National Conference of Canadian Universities, and of the Royal Society of Canada. This list was respectfully compiled by Dr. McNeill for a tribute published by the *Proceedings of the Royal Society of Canada.* He was also president of the Canadian Association for Adult Education. It is doubtful if Dr. Wallace himself knew of the extent of his involvement in so many organizations; he just did what he was asked to do.

Each of 20 universities gave him an honorary doctorate. Vancouver columnist D. A. McGregor commented that 'if each carried a medal, there would not be room on his jacket for all his decorations, and, as each degree carried a hood and some a cap and gown, there is no possibility of wearing more than a small fraction of his distinctions at any one time.'

Dr. Wallace retired in 1951, at the age of 70. The major alumni branches held dinners in honour of both Wallaces, and Montreal

Principal and Mrs. Wallace dancing a Scottish reel with Queen's Bands members Connie Hope, Arts '54, and Eric Cheadle, Arts '53.   *Photo by Hepburn*

presented its prestigious Medal. At a formal reception in Wallace Hall, J. M. Macdonnell, Chairman of the Board of Trustees, said that the best thing Dr. Wallace had brought to Queen's was Mrs. Wallace. She replied, with characteristically quiet humour and mellifluous Scottish accent, 'I don't think I hindered my husband much. I wish I could have hindered him more.'

His retirement brought no slackening of pace. He became Executive Director of the Arctic Institute of North America, consultant to the Department of Education of Ontario, member of the Defence Research Board and its Selection Committee, and Advisory Editor of the *Encyclopedia Americana.* These were not honorary posts. They involved travelling, conferences, meetings, speaking, and writing.

He kept up a formidable pace until his death in 1955, because he knew no other way to operate. He once wrote, 'There is no way to knowledge and ultimate wisdom but by hard work and pleasure in doing it.' Surviving were his wife, who had been a pupil of his in the Orkneys and in Scotland, and three daughters, Sheila, Brenda, and Elspeth. The latter is now Mrs. C. W. Baugh, a member of the University Council and the Board of Trustees.

The funeral service was held in Grant Hall, and the staff, students, and graduates, with representatives of other universities and of learned societies, of church and state and the armed forces, and others important and humble, came to honour him. The hall was filled. Rev. A. M. Laverty, who had been Dr. Wallace's own selection for the post of University Chaplain, said, in his prayer: 'We thank Thee, O Lord our God, for this man of granite and grace, Thy servant so highly revered and so greatly beloved among us.'

The Kingston *Whig-Standard,* in an editorial, said: 'He will be sorely missed in Canada, but nowhere more than in Kingston whose city and university he served so well.'

The Ottawa *Citizen:* 'Dr. Wallace displayed throughout his life many of the characteristics attributed to the Scot – gravity, relieved by a dry sense of humor; granite-like principles; devotion to the ideal of an education both solid and rich. As Principal of Queen's, he found himself very much at home.'

The Rector, Dr. L. W. Brockington: 'Our world is bereft of a wise and gentle counsellor who never lost faith in the inevitability of human progress and the massive peace of humane goodwill. As our solace for the sorrow of a death so bravely faced, let us always remember our gratitude for a life so nobly lived.'

William Archibald Mackintosh

Dr. William Archibald Mackintosh, c.c., c.m.g., m.a., ph.d., d.c.l., ll.d., f.r.s.c., was the first Queen's graduate to become Principal and Vice-Chancellor of the University. He was appointed in 1951 and retired as Principal in 1961, but he carried on as Vice-Chancellor for another four years. His association with Queen's spanned more than half a century.

When Dr. Wallace stepped down, it was generally agreed that his would be a hard act to follow. He had been a Principal in the tradition of George Monro Grant, of beloved memory, and, indeed, had made all but the most stubborn of the Old Guard concede that he belonged in the same league. Yet it was relatively simple for the search committee to come up with his successor. William Archibald Mackintosh was highly visible. For four years of post-war pressures and adjustments he had fulfilled the responsibilities of the combined posts of the Sir John A. Macdonald Professorship, Head of the Department of Political and Economic Sciences, Director of the School of Commerce and Administration, Dean of Arts, and Vice-Principal of the University.

'Only an extraordinary productivity and capacity to compress tasks into their rightful priorities and time spans could have coped with the demands,' commented Vice-Principal L. G. Macpherson in the minutes of the Senate in 1971. 'After that *tour de force* it was inevitable that he should be chosen as Principal.'

For his installation at Fall Convocation on October 19, 1951, Dr. Mackintosh let it be known that he wouldn't mind a little informality in the best traditions of some of the proceedings of a similar nature in the past. He was taken at his word. The students in the gallery let go a barrage of confetti and paper streamers and raised a mighty Queen's yell. A flock of pigeons was loosed, which stirred up the air more than somewhat. The affair was of only a few minutes' duration, but it was chaotic while it lasted. It may be just a coincidence, but a demonstration from the students was never again solicited at an affair of this nature.

Wallace R. Berry photo

Dr. Mackintosh was born in 1895 at Madoc, Ont., within 70 miles of Kingston and 125 miles of Ottawa, the two cities where he was to spend most of his life and to wield a tremendous influence. He received his preliminary education in the schools of Madoc and at St. Andrew's College, Toronto. He graduated from Queen's in 1916 with an M.A. and the Medals in both History and Political Science. He was an all-round student: he was president of his year, played rugby and soccer, and won his 'Q' as the college fencing champion. In the summer holidays he taught school in Saskatchewan.

After graduation he went to Harvard for a year, left for Brandon College in Manitoba to lecture in Economics for two years, and then returned to Harvard to continue his doctoral studies. In 1920 he came to Queen's to work as Assistant Professor of Economics with the illustrious O. D. Skelton and W. C. Clark. And at Queen's he remained for the rest of his life, except for periods spent in Ottawa in the service of his country. He had a highly developed sense of citizenship, and he was always receptive to any government call on his services.

His career in public service was parallel in distinction to his career in education. It started back in the Twenties as a member of the Staff Advisory Board on Tariff and Taxation. From 1929 to 1934 he was director of research for the Canadian Pioneer Problems Committee. He was prominent in the work of the National Employment Commission and took a leading role in the work of the Rowell-Sirois Commission.

From 1939 to 1946, Dr. Mackintosh was on leave of absence from Queen's to work full time in Ottawa. At the beginning he was special assistant to the Deputy Minister of Finance, and during the later years he was in the Department of Reconstruction and Supply. In both jobs he dealt with issues that could not be assigned definitely to any one department, some of them international economic problems which took him to London, England, once a year for four or five weeks, and also involved frequent visits to Washington.

On one of his junkets to England he found himself held up at the airport at Gander, along with a planeload of others on important wartime missions. For security reasons the frustrated travellers were told nothing about when they might be expected to become airborne again or any other details that might have eased their anxieties. Then an airman sidled up to Dr. Mackintosh and whispered out of the side of his mouth: 'You will be departing at 1600 hours, you will be flying at a height of 5,000 feet for one hour, and then at 20,-000 feet for five hours, and the weather outlook is most favorable. *Cha Gheill!*' And with that he disappeared as quickly as he had materialized out of nowhere. Dr. Mackintosh often used this story to illustrate the ubiquity of Queen's folk and their friendliness and camaraderie to a fellow member of the clan.

In the hurly-burly of the early war years in Ottawa there was a need for a place where the senior civil servants who ran the establishment could meet and relax in private. Dr. Mackintosh, Donald Gordon and W. C. Clark acquired a property in the Gatineau Hills about an hour's drive north of Ottawa, labelled it the Five Lakes Fishing Club, and limited the membership to 40. The fishing never amounted to much, which did not bother anyone unduly, but the lodge, which would sleep 25, afforded a sanctuary where members could unwind, have a swim, and talk. It was from this Club that Dr. Mackintosh was summoned to act as mediator in the railway strike that loomed in 1950. In his book *The Canadian Establishment,* Peter Newman described the Club as a 'private and important forum for the exchange of mandarin views,' adding that it 'continues to be a status-laden sanctuary where members can meet on a summer evening and weekends to swim and talk.'

Dr. Mackintosh had much to do with the development of policies dealing with the mobilization of labour. He was influential throughout the war in framing wheat policy. He was a leading figure in the negotiations which resulted in the Bretton Woods agreements, being one of the Canadian delegates to, and chairman of, the most important committee of the conference. *The Financial Post* commented: 'Dr. Mackintosh comes as near to being a so-called "brain-truster" as anything we have in Canada.'

The negotiations which resulted in Canada's wartime loans and in the financing of the Allies, generally, were largely in his hands. He was a member of the Wartime Prices and Trade Board and played a key part therein with regard to policy. He was chairman of the Canadian section of the joint United States-Canada overall economic committee. During 1945 he was acting Deputy Minister of Finance.

He resisted all offers to remain in Ottawa, and returned to Queen's as soon as he could wind up his affairs. Grant Dexter, in the *Winnipeg Free Press,* said: 'There was, in fact, no aspect of our wartime economic policies in which he was not actively consulted and in which his judgment as a rule was not decisive.'

'The greatest gift he brought to Ottawa,' said the columnist, 'was plain common sense and an inborn belief in democracy as a way of life.'

His tenure as Principal coincided with a rapid expansion of the University in response to a great social need. In the decade 1951-61 there was a 40 per cent increase in building space. In one of his annual reports he described how this came about.

This arises primarily from three circumstances: First, the advance of knowledge, teaching methods and equipment coupled with necessarily meagre building programs from 1930-50 makes it necessary that in a number of fields we must provide additional and thoroughly up-to-date space for various departments if we are to maintain and improve our standing as a University. Secondly, the increasing number of students and the much greater prospective increase requires that in doing this, we would provide also for these increased numbers. Thirdly, we have reached the stage in Kingston when an increasing proportion of students must be provided with residence accommodation, for the traditional lodging house, if not disappearing, is certainly declining.

Buildings erected or renovated during the 10-year period included Clark Hall, for the students' bookstore and the Engineering Society clubrooms; Richardson Hall, named after the former Chancellor, designed for administration offices, and which, in the Collins Room, 'provides a meeting-place of beauty and dignity for the Board of Trustees, the Council, the Senate, and the Faculty Boards'; three men's residences – McNeill House, Morris Hall, and Leonard Hall, on Leonard Field; Chown Hall, a women's residence on Stuart St.; the Physiology Building, now Abramsky Hall, on Arch St., which not only provided the University with a modernly equipped building for teaching and research in a basic medical science, but released space elsewhere for badly needed expansion; Etherington Hall, the Queen's-KGH building on Stuart St., with classrooms, research laboratories, and offices for clinical medicine; Ellis Hall, on University Ave., for Civil Engineering; Dunning Hall, at Union and University, for the Departments of Political and Economic Science, Industrial Relations, the School of Business, the Institute of Local Government, and classrooms. In 1960-61 the Law Faculty's new building, Sir John A. Macdonald Hall, was opened. The Agnes Etherington Art Centre was also unveiled to the public during this period. In addition there

225

Principal Mackintosh with his 'Cabinet': left to right, J.A. Corry, Vice-Principal; H.G. Conn, Dean of Applied Science; R.O. Earl, Dean of Arts; and Dr. G.H. Ettinger, Dean of Medicine.   *Wallace R. Berry photo*

were extensive renovations to the Gymnasium, Carruthers Hall, the Douglas Library and Ban Righ Hall.

Dr. Mackintosh had misgivings that he might become known as a 'building Principal'. He did indeed, but not for the reason he feared. As Prof. Glen Shortliffe said at a party held in Dr. Mackintosh's honour on retirement,

Although we shall certainly remember him as a building Principal, we shall not be thinking of bricks and mortar when we use that expression. ... His real building has been in the strengthening and expansion of the best intellectual traditions of our University, a task to which he brought not only a vital soundness of judgment at a critical time, but also an imaginative vision of the future tempered only by that sensible caution we have all learned to respect.

He was a quiet, thoughtful, contemplative man, astutely perceptive, an intellectual, deliberate in his judgments, reserved in manner, logical in his decisions. 'He had a richly furnished mind of unusual quality which sought out the relevant facts in any issue, and respected them when found, but pondered long on their meaning,' wrote Dr. J. A. Corry.

Dr. Wallace said, 'Dr. Mackintosh has won his place, not by assertiveness – for he is a modest man – but by sheer ability and by qualities of personality. There is a saneness and a wisdom on which one can rely, no matter how difficult may be the issue of the moment.'

226

As Dr. McNeill put it, 'Dr. Mackintosh is a great economist because he is so much more. He has humour in his heart and poetry in his soul.'

These were some of his views on education:

A person may be impressively knowledgeable and yet be an uneducated person. He may be ignorant of many things and yet be an educated person.

*

I believe in persons, not methods. Nothing in education can take the place of the occasional glimpsing of the workings of a fine mind. Nothing can take the place of the evident pleasure of a master in some bit of excellence in a beginner's work.

*

One cannot master knowledge in general. One must master it in particular but with an awareness of the unfolding general pattern. It is well to know something about many things, but only in mastery is higher education attained.

*

If a person is to be considered even moderately educated he or she must be able to use at least one language with clarity, without ambiguity, and with economy. If, in addition, it can be used with taste and distinction, so much the better.

At a Convocation at the Royal Military College he said:

We shall not by our reason or in our time reduce this expanding universe nor the intractable humans who occupy so tiny a corner of it to tidy rational patterns. Behind the momentary certainties lie the shifting uncertainties of tomorrow. The test of maturity is the ability to live with uncertainty and reckon with risk. If we pass this test, it is because of an evolving faith which each will formulate in his own way.

One of his most endearing qualities was a quiet sense of humour. Yet, when writer Leslie Roberts was researching a story about Queen's, he complained that everyone he met spoke of Dr. Mackintosh's humour, but no one could give him an example. The truth of the matter was that Dr. Mackintosh had a gentle appreciation and expression of the little ironies of life. He was not a stand-up comedian firing off one-line side-splitters or knee-slappers. Wry comments on the passing scene were more in character.

Once he remarked to me he felt he was as conditioned as one of

Pavlov's dogs. He had been piped in to the head table at so many functions that 'when I hear pipes, I actually begin to salivate.'

He described the prerogatives of his position as Vice-Principal as 'taking the Principal's place in his absence and the privilege of being buried in the University lot in Cataraqui cemetery.'

In his inaugural address he said: 'The beauties of Frontenac County are a joy forever, but not to a university treasurer.'

Again: 'A university isn't a reform school in which all the mistakes of the parents and school teachers can be corrected.'

This saving grace of humour was not his only form of intellectual relaxation. This epitome of intellectualism, this man who numbered some of the finest minds on the continent among his intimates, this man who did not suffer fools gladly (although he made a valiant effort to disguise his innermost feelings), this man enjoyed as his favorite TV show the unlikely one about a talking horse. He contrived to schedule or manoeuvre meetings or conferences so that he could get to a television set in time to watch the latest episode of *Mister Ed,* the horse whose talents included an ability to converse. This appealed to his risibilities, and somehow this predilection for a program that can only most charitably be described as low-brow served to emphasize by contrast the rarefied atmosphere which was his more familiar milieu.

He was most approachable. I had many occasions to seek his advice, and no matter how full his 'In' basket might be, he always found the time to give me the benefit of his counsel. He would stare out the window as he pondered the pros and cons, while his right hand groped for a package of cigarettes from a side pocket. He would light up, inhale, exhale, still gazing into space. All his movements were slow and deliberate. The silence would grow almost unbearable. One had to resist a strong desire to fill in the void with some comment, but to do so would only have confirmed what you felt might be his secret conviction that you were a complete idiot. One learned not to disrupt his meditations, while he smoked, stared, pondered, scratched the back of his neck, reached for another cigarette. Finally he would swivel around, his eyes would come into focus, and he would then deliver his opinion. Invariably what he suggested as a solution seemed so logical that one felt foolish for having overlooked the obvious, the only perfect answer. It was indeed an impressive gift.

Life magazine once sent a team of photographers to the campus to do a picture story on a Medical Centenary Weekend. Hundreds of pictures were taken; ultimately half-a-dozen were published, all about the football game and its accompanying events. There were shots of the cheerleaders, the parade, the students, the victory procession. One alumnus wrote from Texas that he was delighted to have this pictorial reminder about 'the greatest little school in the country'. A graduate in New York commented that the publicity was worth thousands of dollars. Dr. Mackintosh's reaction was more restrained: 'Wouldn't you think they might have included one small picture of a student with a book?'

Many honours came his way. Eleven universities gave him honorary degrees, including his alma mater. His citation read:

Distinguished graduate and illustrious servant of this University who absorbed its essence as a student and nourished its inner spirit as teacher and Principal, balanced and discerning economist who has moved as a peer among the foremost of his kind in the world, weighty and much sought adviser of governments in war and peace, acclaimed in all his many roles for comprehensive grasp, masterly synthesis, and calm lucidity of mind.

At Brown University the citation read: 'To a unique degree you have demonstrated the trustworthiness of sound theory as a guide to action, and public responsibility as a factor in keeping theory in effective touch with reality.'

He was a Companion of the Order of St. Michael and St. George, and of the Order of Canada. He was awarded a Canada Council Medal. He was a Fellow of the Royal Society of Canada, and served as president. He also served as president of the Canadian Political Science Association, president of the National Conference of Canadian Universities, and chairman of the Association of the Universities of the British Commonwealth. He was an honorary member of the American Geographical Society, a member of the American Economic Association and the Royal Economic Society, and a director of the Bank of Canada.

He was the author of many publications. *Canadian Frontiers of Settlement,* a monumental study in eight volumes and a Canadian classic of its kind, was organized and edited by Dr. Mackintosh, who was also one of the contributors. He wrote the government White Paper on Employment and Income that had so decisive an influence upon national policy in the immediate postwar years.

When Dr. Mackintosh retired as Principal in 1961, there were many tributes from colleagues. He was called an outstanding Canadian personality, the ideal Queen's man, chief scholar in a community of scholars, an economist, a peer of the best abroad as well as at home.

He died in 1970. Among the survivors were his wife and one-time pupil, formerly Jean Easton; a daughter, Mrs. I. G. Morgan (Alison), and a sister Helen (who died in 1972). He had been predeceased by another sister, Agnes, who had herself been a brilliant scholar and a generous benefactor. All were graduates of Queen's.

Dr. J. A. Corry wrote:

Canada has lost an illustrious son, whom she trusted much and often honoured for his worth. Queen's University has lost the member of its company who gave it the longest service, who best understood its distinctive quality and lived its essence in a rare way, and who gave sure guidance to its affairs in a critical time. Many persons at Queen's and elsewhere have lost a close friend and a wise confidant.

Dr. John J. Deutsch prophesied that 'History is sure to include him among the few who will rank as the great builders of this University.'

Certainly his name and influence will carry on. The new Mackintosh-Corry Hall for social sciences carries his name and that of his successor. A new lecture series, the W. A. Mackintosh Lecture in Economics, has been established by members of his family. In these and in the traditions that he helped to foster, his name will be commemorated.

Other universities sought him as their head. He remained loyal to Queen's. He has left his mark indelibly on this campus.

James Alexander Corry

James Alexander Corry, C.C., LL.B., B.C.L., LL.M., LL.D., F.R.S.C., was installed as Principal of Queen's University on October 20, 1961.

Ernest C. Gill, Chairman of the Board of Trustees, in presenting Dr. Corry to Chancellor J. B. Stirling at the installation ceremony, said, 'Dr. Corry has a record of service that has already placed him among the great men of the University.'

He was indeed an obvious choice for the position. He had served for 25 years as Hardy Professor of Political Science, had been a leading figure in the establishment of Queen's Faculty of Law and acting Dean in its first year, and had served as Vice-Principal of the University for ten years. His services as principal or president of a Canadian university had been sought on more than one occasion. He was highly respected as a teacher and a scholar.

Dr. Corry was born and educated in Millbank, Perth County, Ont. He attended the University of Saskatchewan and graduated with a Bachelor of Law degree in 1923. The following year he was awarded a Rhodes Scholarship for Saskatchewan and attended Oxford University, graduating in 1927 with a Bachelor of Civil Law degree.

He joined the staff of the University of Saskatchewan in 1927 as a Professor of Law. In 1936 he came to Queen's as a Professor of Political Science. Subsequently he wrote a text on the political and governmental process, *Democratic Government and Politics,* which has had a profound influence on Canadian students of politics, and which has gone into four editions. An American edition, entitled *Elements of Democratic Government,* was also popularly received as a textbook. He was the author of *Soviet Russia and the Western Alliance* and numerous articles on legal, constitutional, and political subjects in various journals and periodicals.

He was a member and for two years chairman of the Canadian Social Science Research Council, a body devoted to stimulating and improving teaching and research in the social sciences. He was also a member of the Council for the Survey of the Legal Profession in Canada, formed to estimate the effects of recent social and economic change on the legal profession. For nine years he was a member of the Board of Governors of the Canadian Broadcasting Corporation. At the time of his appointment as Principal he was in Europe on a research fellowship awarded by the Canada Council, studying the effect of the welfare state on the individual.

Dr. Corry also took an active part in community affairs, serving as chairman of the Kingston Court of Revision and governor of Kingston General Hospital. He was active in the reorganization of the Kingston Children's Aid Society and had served as president.

So it was as a person thoroughly at home in Queen's and community and national affairs that he became the 13th Principal. It was a happy appointment in that he was fully conversant with the problems he was facing, had the unqualified approval of his colleagues, and knew what he wanted for Queen's.

In his installation address he outlined his assessment of the new responsibilities of universities in a rapidly changing society, a change from the conception of individual freedom to collective action through large-scale organization, both public and private.

He saw the new responsibilities as additions to, and not subtractions from, the older responsibilities.

These latter have included the education of men and women for the church, for teaching, for the older professions like law and medicine, and for entirely non-professional citizenship. The lives of many such persons across our country have been a prolonged instruction in civility, inducing reflection, restraint, second thoughts, personal responsibility, and community pride. From the wide scattering of such persons come many of the effective leaders of community opinion and public opinion, our defence in depth against the abuse of power, public or private.

So, if university education is to provide larger reservoirs of talent for public and private organizations, it must also feed in greater volume than before the scattered springs of thought and action in the wider community. If there are to be more controllers, there must be many more persons fitted to rally opinion for controlling the controllers. A community that is to remain free and become more civilized must always have the inner capacity to impose limits on the wielders of power. The newer responsibilities give more point than ever to the older responsibilities.

I know that becoming more civilized calls for more than I have asserted.

232

George O. Lilley photo

Without a vision beyond themselves, the people perish. It is widely held nowadays that we have become enslaved to the material and the immediate. The evidence for this point of view seems to me less than conclusive. I would rather say that our worst troubles come, not from the fading of vision but from an obscuring of the upward path in our immediate foreground. Nothing stays put around us any more; we lost our sense of direction in the fog of incessant change, and naturally we flounder. We can't relate what is happening all around us to the inherited values we still honour when we can see how to move. The first charge on the universities is to throw a steadier and longer beam from the lamps of reason.

These were the themes he outlined at the installation and these were the themes he was to develop and amplify during his seven years as one of Canada's leading educational figures, years that 'probably witnessed more challenge and change in higher education in Canada than the previous half-century had produced.' At the end of that period he had firmly established himself as a leading states-man and spokesman for higher education in Canada.

From the beginning Dr. Corry was faced with steadily increasing enrolments, which he regarded more as an aggravation than a problem. For years the administration had been talking about keeping the University small. During Dr. Mackintosh's ten years as Principal, registration had gone from 2,119 to 3,089. In his last *Principal's Report* he said that it was not to be expected that Queen's would increase its enrolment as much as some other universities, in view of the fact that 90 per cent of the students must live away from home. However, he said, 'it is evident that we have made provision up until now for our full share of the increase and have not left the responsibility to others.'

The enrolment during Dr. Corry's first year was 3,430, an increase of 9 per cent; the prediction had been for an increase of 6 per cent. Most of the growth was in the Faculty of Arts and Science and in graduate work. Dr. Corry took reassurance from the fact that Queen's was able to hold its place in quality, using the inter-university competition for scholarly awards as a criterion.

By his final year, 1967-68, registration had risen to 5,838. Queen's, which had an agreement with the Government of Ontario to have 5,000 undergraduates and 600 graduate students by 1970-71, had already overrun this target. With the growth in numbers came a changing and even turbulent climate. Dr. Corry needed all his considerable skills to cope with the situation.

234

There were many changes and additions to curriculum and buildings. A Department of Computing Science was set up to give instruction in both pure and applied aspects of computing. A School of Rehabilitation Therapy was started as a logical expansion of work in the health sciences and in response to the need for more practitioners with this training. The School of Nursing was reorganized. An Institute of Intergovernmental Relations was established to study systematically the relations of federal, provincial, and local governments. A full-fledged Faculty of Education was started under the title of McArthur College.

Physical facilities were expanded. When Dr. Corry assumed office, 437 women and 612 men were housed in university residences, a total of 1,049. By the time he retired, there were 1,853 single students in residence, and accommodation for a further 396 was under construction. Arrangements were started with the Ontario Student Housing Corporation to provide some much-needed housing for married students.

New buildings were provided for the Humanities and for the Departments of Chemical Engineering, Physics, and Biology. Construction was started on buildings for Mathematics and Psychology. Major additions were made to the Douglas Library, to Gordon Hall for Chemistry, Fleming Hall for Electrical Engineering, Macdonald Hall for the Law Faculty, and to the Students' Memorial Union and the Agnes Etherington Art Centre. Extensive renovations were also carried out in the old section of the Douglas Library, in Gordon Hall, the Old Arts Building, New Arts Building (Kingston Hall), New Medical Building, and the Craine Building.

Great care was taken to ensure that the physical expansion and increasing enrolment did not interfere with the quality of education. 'We have reason to think that we have improved in quality of education at the same time as we have been extending it to greatly increased numbers of students,' wrote Dr. Corry.

The cost of operating the University kept pace, from $5.7 million in 1961-62 to upwards of $17 million in 1967-68. Tuition fees did not increase on the same scale: for example, in the Faculty of Arts and Science they were $410 in 1961-62 and $500 in 1967-68. Governments, particularly the provincial government, became increasingly the main source of operating revenue.

It was apparent that new methods of fixing the amount of support would have to be worked out for the universities in Ontario, which

235

had increased from eight to 14. The system of each university presenting its own case to the Committee on University Affairs was no longer feasible, and new methods of determining support needed to be worked out. Dr. Corry, with Dr. Deutsch and Bernard Trotter, Director of Academic Planning, advocated a per-weighted-student formula for determining operating grants to universities on an equitable basis. Such a formula was adopted by the Government of Ontario and in use before Dr. Corry's term was up.

With growth and the increase in activity came the need for decentralization, and the Principal delegated decisions on many matters to others. The number of Vice-Principals was increased to four – Academic, Administration, Finance and Health Sciences. Deans were given supporting staff by means of associate and assistant deans and other officers, so that they could act more independently. Staffing at senior levels of such central academic services as the Douglas Library and the Registrar's Office were strengthened. The Principal himself appointed two executive assistants so that he could cope with the increasing demands on his time, not the least being an increasing involvement in the complex affairs of the Association of Universities and Colleges of Canada (AUCC) (over which he presided in 1964-65) and the Committee of Presidents of the Universities of Ontario (which he served as chairman from 1966 to 1968). In addition, he served for three successive years on the Council of the Association of Commonwealth Universities. How he managed to operate on so many fronts is a tribute to his administrative skill.

Out of decentralization and the problems inherent in expansion at Queen's and elsewhere emerged a persistent rising demand for reform in university government. The Duff-Berdahl Commission on University Government in Canada in 1966 recommended many changes. Although the report noted that Queen's had already embedded in its structures several of the desirable features proposed, Dr. Corry requested that the Alma Mater Society, the University Council, the Faculty Association, and the Faculty Boards prepare briefs summarizing their views on what changes were advisable at Queen's. Then the Senate appointed a committee under the chairmanship of Vice-Principal (Academic) F. W. Gibson to view the structures and procedures of the Senate. This provided the basis of a major reform of the Senate and the widening of its membership to include representatives of

236

the student body. Queen's University had moved with the times.

A lively sense of humour helped him to face with equanimity the spate of problems that threatened to engulf him. His capacity for enjoying a good joke was one of his most endearing qualities. When he was telling a story himself there would be a twinkle in his eye and a half-smile on his lips which grew into chuckles in anticipation and appreciation of the punch-line, and by the time that point was reached he would be shaking with merriment. His chuckle was infectious.

He used stories to illustrate or make a point, or just to enjoy the humour. At his installation dinner he referred to the unflustered way Dr. W. A. Mackintosh got to the root of a difficulty. 'An old Texan was watching an impatient fellow trying to unload a fractious packhorse on a steep mountain trail. After a while, he said: "Son, that horse has got you in a pretty fix. There's just two things to remember. T'ain't rainin' and nobody's shooting at you."'

Or he'd tell about the man, recently widowed, who took on another wife: 'For all they eat, I wouldn't be without one.'

Or Harry Truman's remark, 'If you can't stand the heat, stay the hell out of the kitchen.'

Or the catcher who went out to the mound to talk to Lefty Gomez, then in the twilight of his career, and said: 'You're not throwing the ball as hard as you used to.' Gomez denied the charge. 'I'm throwing as hard as I ever did. It just takes longer for the ball to get to the plate.'

Or the chap who was called upon to speak early in the program. 'I'm not used to coming on this early. I'm usually way down the line. By the time I stand up to talk I feel like Barbara Hutton's fifth husband – I know what I'm supposed to do; the problem is to make it interesting.'

Or the woman who asked a psychiatrist to examine her son. She said he sat in the back yard all day making mudpies and blowing bubble gum. 'What's wrong with that?' asked the doctor. 'Well,' the woman said, 'I just don't like it. And neither does his wife.'

He was once described as looking like a cross between Stephen Leacock and Carl Sandburg. He was not tall in stature, but he had a commanding presence. The humour was never far below the surface, but when he took a stand on an issue there was no ambiguity about his position. He had a quality he had often publicly admired in Dr. W. A. Mackintosh, 'the instinct for the jugular'. He had a special talent for cutting through the surface to the substance of a problem.

Dr. Claude Bissell, former president of the University of Toronto, wrote in his book *Halfway to Parnassus:* 'As so often in the history of higher education in Ontario, the Queen's point of view, idealistic but with a shrewd pragmatic hold on the actual, was influential, especially as it was expressed in Alec Corry, most humane of constitutional theorists.'

For exercise he liked mountain-climbing and walking. He was a familiar sight on the streets of Kingston at night, taking a walk. It was with shock and disbelief that it was learned that he had been attacked by hoodlums within a few feet of Summerhill while returning home one night. He was knocked to the ground, robbed, beaten. He required hospitalization for a few days, and it was a moment for rejoicing when he was able to return to his post, albeit bearing the scars of his ordeal. The Kingston Chief of Police, Bob Nesbitt, gave the affair his personal attention and the culprits were apprehended within 24 hours.

One of Dr. Corry's major undertakings was the preliminary planning for a multi-million-dollar medical sciences complex to be built by the University and the Kingston General Hospital, with the co-operation of other city hospitals. The complex, as visualized, would see the complete reconstruction of the hospital and the erection of a University health sciences building adjoining it. It meant a long-overdue updating of buildings and facilities to meet the needs of the University, the community, and Eastern Ontario.

Perhaps no single aspect of University development during Dr. Corry's tenure attracted more attention or required more discussion than that involving the Faculty of Medicine. Dr. E. H. Botterell was appointed Dean of the Faculty in 1962, and under his guidance a start was made to meet changing conditions. In 1968 Dr. Botterell was appointed Vice-Principal (Health Sciences), with overall responsibility for co-ordinating the Faculty of Medicine, the School of Nursing and the School of Rehabilitation Therapy, and representing the University in all joint projects involving the health sciences.

In 1968 Dr. Corry retired as Principal, in accordance with the deadline he had announced on his appointment to the post. He could step down with the satisfaction of a difficult job well done. He had guided the University through a trying period and left his successor with a solid foundation from which to carry on. Many honours came his way. He had been elected a Fellow of the

Royal Society of Canada. He had been appointed a member of the Canada Council and made a Companion of the Order of Canada. He had received the major alumni awards: the John Hammett Medal of the New York Society, the Montreal Medal, and the Toronto Branch's John Orr Award. And he received honorary degrees from 14 universities.

The Queen's citation read, in part: 'Here, over a generation, he enhanced by example and precept the repute of good teachers and scholars, preached the doctrine of excellence before it became a pedagogical cliché. ... With deep wisdom and sharp wit, he guided the expansion of this University on lines in keeping with its best traditions and its emerging needs.' At RMC he was cited as a good friend, a good neighbour, and a great Canadian. At Dalhousie: 'He is a scholar, an author, an administrator, but above all a teacher who already enjoys what Justice Holmes called "the subtle and post-poned power that comes only to the thinker and to the teacher, the assurance that even after he himself had passed from the scene, men and women will be moving to the measure of his thought and teaching." '

Although his retirement is extremely active, he does have more leisure to do the things he enjoys most, teaching and writing, and to spend more time with his charming wife, Alice. Two daughters, Madeleine, Arts '61, and Joan (Mrs. D. J. Crawford), Arts '65, are no longer at home.

In 1970, 13 of his addresses were bound together for publication as a book, *Farewell the Ivory Tower,* published by the McGill-Queen's University Press. In the foreword, Dr. J. E. Hodgetts, Principal of Victoria College, University of Toronto, wrote:

Two instructive messages emerge from a reading of these addresses. First, in determining the status and functions of the university, all participants must recognize the need for balance in seeking to reconcile such opposing but valid goals as autonomy and accountability, research and teaching, general and specialized instruction, and education as a private affair and as a public good. Finally, and most important, we must learn, in the phrase of E. M. Forster, 'to connect', to relate constantly the 'means for living' to a 'meaning for life'. If the university fails us here it will have abandoned its dreaming spires even as it has had to bid adieu to its ivory towers.

In 1971 he was the Massey Lecturer for CBC Radio's *Ideas* series, inaugurated ten years previously as a platform for original study or research by a noted scholar on a topic of contemporary interest. Titled *The Power of the Law,* Dr. Corry's six-part series was heralded as bringing 'a lifetime of active experience and quiet contemplation to bear on the crucial importance of law to life, politics, community and nationhood.' He brought wit, wisdom, and simplicity to a key problem of the Seventies – a growing disrespect for law in a revolutionary age.

From 1968 to 1970 he was consultant to the Department of Justice in an analysis of proposed changes in Canada's Constitution. Almost concurrently, 1969 to 1971, he was an adviser to the Secretary of State on the coming shape and structure of education.

In 1972 he produced a report entitled *Quest for the Optimum,* the result of a Commission to Study the Rationalization of University Research, undertaken jointly with Dr. Louis-Philippe Bonneau of the University of Montreal on behalf of the Association of Universities and Colleges of Canada.

This active retirement has also included terms as a visiting professor at Queen's, Carleton, McGill, and Duke. In 1973 he was made the recipient of the Royal Bank Award of $50,000 for his outstanding contribution to Canadian education. In announcing the award, the Royal Bank paid special tribute to Dr. Corry's 'leading role in encouraging and developing responsible student government at a time of continent-wide student unrest' and cited his vital advisory function in university-government relations during a period of unparalleled university expansion in Canada and increased government support.

With the $50,000 went a medal. The medal he kept. A large part of the $50,000 he gave to Queen's to found the Corry Lectureship.

In the same year he was called to the Bar of Ontario; the Law Society of Upper Canada conferred the Barrister-at-Law degree on him for his 'very great contribution to learning and to the law'.

At his installation it was said:

The eminence of his scholarship, the genuine warmth of his personality, and the wide acclaim that have greeted his appointment as Principal of Queen's provide the assurance of yet another era of notable progress during his term of office that will add new lustre to the history of Queen's.

The prophecy was amply fulfilled.

John James Deutsch

John James Deutsch, C.C., B.Com., LL.D., one of Canada's top economists and a 'roving royal commissioner', became the 14th Principal in 1968, in succession to Dr. Corry.

He came to the office as a person highly experienced in the ways of Queen's, in all that she had been, in all that she was, and in all that she aspired to be. Not only was he a graduate, but he had been a lecturer, Professor of Economics, Vice-Principal (Administration), and Vice-Principal 'without portfolio'. He had effectively reorganized and streamlined the University's structures and introduced modern business methods.

He had left Queen's in 1963 to accept appointment as the first chairman of the Economic Council of Canada, perhaps the most important in an impressively long list of assignments on behalf of governments, provincial and federal, Conservative and Liberal. When he came back as Principal-designate it was in effect a return to his spiritual home. The *Whig-Standard* said that 'one of Canada's great minds was coming back to his first love.'

He was raised on a Saskatchewan farm, the oldest of 17 children and the only one to obtain a formal education. His father, an immigrant from Bavaria, took up 160 acres 80 miles north of Regina in 1903, 50 miles from the railway and nearest town. With his wife, a young Hungarian immigrant, he drove to his homestead with a wagon pulled by a team of oxen. They built a sod hut and cleared land for planting. With a background like this, young John, if he had been born in the United States, would have been well qualified to become president of his country, in the tradition of Abraham Lincoln.

He went to Campion College in Regina for his high schooling, working at odd jobs to pay his way. Later he taught at Campion while taking extramural courses from the University of Saskatchewan and Queen's. When he had obtained all the academic credits he could in this manner, he secured a post teaching mathematics at

Wallace R. Berry photo

, Regiopolis College in Kingston, a job that paid $55 a month plus keep. He took eight o'clock lectures at the University, which was 18 blocks distant, and then hustled back to Regiopolis to teach. Needless to say, he did not have any time for student activities, politics, or nonsense. He specialized in Commerce and Economics and obtained a B.Com. degree in 1935. The next year was spent in postgraduate work and lecturing.

From 1936 to 1942 he was an economic research assistant with the Bank of Canada, and at one period he was on loan to the Rowell-Sirois Commission as director of research. He slipped back to Queen's in the winter of 1940 to teach economics.

The following year he was appointed secretary of the newly formed Joint Canada-United States Economic Council. In 1942 he became special wartime assistant to the Under-Secretary of State for External Affairs. Sandwiched in between was his participation in the establishment of the National Selective Service for Canada.

If there appears to be an overlapping of assignments in this and the following recital, it is because it is true. All his life, whether in university or government service, he showed all the ability of a juggler in being able to handle a variety of jobs with dexterity and skill. One of the secrets of his success was that he enlisted the assistance of the best talent available and then delegated full responsibility. He kept a careful eye on performance and progress.

After the war he went to Winnipeg as an editorial writer for the *Free Press,* on the invitation of the editor, Dr John W. Dafoe. He was a valued member of a team that included Victor Sifton, publisher, George Ferguson, executive editor, Grant Dexter and Bruce Hutchison. While there he served as a member of the Manitoba Commission on Adult Education. In 1946 he was back in the federal field as secretary to the Gordon Commission, classifying senior positions in the Civil Service. Later that year he joined the federal Department of Finance as director of its international economic relations division.

He travelled extensively, making two trips around the world, and attended many conferences, including the International Monetary Conference at Bretton Woods, the Conference on Trade and Employment at Geneva and at Havana, sessions of General Agreement on Tariffs and Trade at Geneva and Torquay, annual meetings of the International Monetary Fund and the International Bank for Reconstruction and Development at Washington and Mexico, and a meeting of the Consultative Committee, in connection with the Colombo Plan, at New Delhi, India. He was a member of the Canadian delegation to several NATO conferences and accompanied the Minister of Finance as an adviser on several occasions, including the Commonwealth Economic Conference in London and the Commonwealth Finance Ministers' Conferences in London and Sydney, Australia. He ranged far and wide, out of sight perhaps, but never out of mind; in 1953 he was appointed Assistant Deputy Minister of Finance, and the following year was named Secretary of the Treasury Board.

In 1956, as a change of pace, he assumed the position of Professor and Head of the Department of Economics and Political Science at the University of British Columbia. While there he served as a member of the Royal Commission on Newfoundland Finances, as chairman of the Natural Gas Distribution Enquiry Commission of Greater Winnipeg, and Industrial Inquiry Commissioner in the labour dispute in the forest industry of B.C.

In 1959 he returned to Queen's as Vice-Principal (Administration) and Professor of Economics. Three years later he was appointed general Vice-Principal. During this period he served on a committee which examined and suggested revisions to the Unemployment Insurance Act, was chairman of the Royal Commission on Higher Education in New Brunswick, and chairman of a committee to study the needs of higher education in Ontario.

In 1963 he answered a call from Prime Minister Lester B. Pearson to head up the Economic Council of Canada. He was given practically a free hand in setting up and running the organization, which ultimately consisted of a group of 25 businessmen and representatives of labour and agriculture, in search of a long-term economic policy for Canada.

Once the Council was firmly established, Dr. Deutsch was ready to move again. In 1967 he came back to Queen's as Principal-designate. When Dr. J. A. Corry had announced his wish to retire, there was much speculation as to his successor. Always the name of Dr. Deutsch was mentioned as a prime candidate. The scuttlebutt was right.

At the installation in Grant Hall on November 8, 1968, the academic procession was led by members of Queen's pipe band, while the brass band and cheerleaders performed outside. Upon the entrance of Dr. Deutsch, there was a flourish by a brass sextet from the Canadian Forces Band, Kingston, with music composed by Graham George, Queen's resident musician, based on the musical notes constituted by the letters D-E-U-T-S-C-H.

Official greetings were brought by the Hon. William G. Davis, Ontario Minister of University Affairs, and the Rev. Roger Guindon, representing the Association of Universities and Colleges of Canada. Honorary degrees were conferred: a D.D. for Louis Albert Vachon and LL.D.'s for William Grenville Davis, René Jules Dubos, Matthew Bullock Dymond, George Victor Ferguson, Arthur Koestler, Martin Meyerson, Jean Isobel Royce, and Pierre Elliott Trudeau.

In his address, Dr. Deutsch said that the university has become an immensely important institution in society, the great strategic resource, essential to the prosperity, health and the very survival of great nations. Knowledge, he said, not natural riches, not territory, is now the real basis of well-being and power in the world. As the conservers, transmitters and originators of knowledge, universities stand at the heart of this revolutionary phenomenon.

Dr. Deutsch pointed out that in the past seven or eight years Queen's had grown as much as during the previous 120. This sudden burst had brought its own special problems and new challenges. 'The chairman of the Board of Regents of the University of California remarked recently that "if a campus is completely unruffled in these tense times, you can be sure that it is sliding downhill." Mr. Chancellor, I can report that the Queen's campus is not completely unruffled.'

In connection with Dr. Deutsch's installation, the University, with considerable support from the Dunning Trust, arranged a symposium with the general title 'The University and the Ethics of Change'. The principal speakers were author Arthur Koestler, urban planner Martin Meyerson, geneticist René Dubos, and Prof. Northrop Frye. They dealt with ethical issues involved in influencing the mind, in influencing the physical environment, and in biological changes by way of defining the university's responsibility to deal with ethical issues.

Dr. Deutsch saw as one of his most urgent tasks the restoration and maintenance of a proper balance in the performance of the University's functions. Definition of this proper balance became the theme of his annual reports. 'We must define our overall size within which we seek to achieve a balanced development,' he wrote. 'We must recognize we cannot do everything well and be all things to all men. At the same time we must recognize a responsibility to respond to new needs where we have the strength and resources to meet them.

'We will choose to do those things which we can do well and will do as well as we can the things we have chosen.'

Major attention was directed toward the composition, functions and processes of the Senate, an implementation of the report on university government brought in by Dr. J. A. Corry's committee. The system was altered to give more adequate representation to the larger faculties, and there was an increase in the relative role of the teaching staff. Students were admitted to membership for the first time, and were also given representation on all Senate standing committees. Procedures for a certain amount of 'openness' were worked out.

Student participation in departmental committees was substantially extended. Students were given membership on the Faculty Boards. In fact, all overtures from the students for a greater share in the shaping of their destinies were given careful attention, with the result that in practically all instances a confrontation was avoided.

Dr. Deutsch's rapport with the students was impressive. He was always accessible for consultation and advice. He maintained an open mind in listening to suggestions. He adopted a liberal attitude of co-operation with the student leaders. As a result the students looked upon him as their friend. The story is told of a student in the School of Business who consulted him about a thesis he was writing on government financing. The Principal asked him to leave the matter with him for a few days. In the meantime he 'phoned the appropriate top level civil servant in Ottawa and enlisted his assistance. Then he gave the student the name of the man who was prepared to help him. Result: one happy customer, a young man who could scarcely believe that a Principal would take so much trouble for an undergraduate.

Dr. Deutsch looked on the alumni as an important constituency. As in the case of all Queen's Principals, he made a practice of visiting alumni branches and other gatherings whenever he could. He paid public tribute to alumni support, financial and otherwise, on all occasions, including Convocations.

Dr. Sidney E. Smith, former president of the University of Toronto, commented to Dr. Deutsch on the visits that a university head was expected to make to alumni branches.

'You're supposed to be a ball of fire by day and a bag of wind by night,' he said.

To which Dr. Deutsch wryly replied, 'And to have the stomach of a goat.'

Dr. Deutsch was sensitive to town-gown relations. One significant step was the appointment of a University Campus Planner to work in close co-operation with the City authorities and with the various university bodies concerned with the physical planning of the University. Major subjects of discussion were the problems of traffic circulation, parking, the new West Campus, land use, taxation, and housing.

The governance of those parts of the University engaged in education for the health science professions entered a new phase with the establishment of the Council for Queen's and Kingston Health Sciences Complex, QUAFHOP. Dr. Deutsch was chairman for the first two years. After many frustrations and delays, the essential new services were now about to be realized.

Other matters to which the Principal directed his administrative skills were in the area of Queen's relations with other universities, particularly with reference to federal support. Canadian studies, the nationalist debate, and faculty citizenship (at Queen's the percentages were found to be: Canadian 65, United States 10, United Kingdom 16, other 9), admission policies, high school

Kingston's Tercentenary, 1973: Principal Deutsch and Secretary of State Hugh Faulkner (centre figures) officially open the exhibition 'Heritage Kingston'.
Wallace R. Berry photo

247

liaison, post-secondary education, graduate studies, special admission (mature students, minority groups), curriculum overhaul, innovative approaches to teaching and learning, staffing policies (more flexibility, student-staff ratio, new sabbatical and negotiated leave), and the status of women.

And he had another star in his crown. Judge John Matheson, a member of the Board of Trustees, said he doubted there would still be a Queen's Theological College if 'it weren't that there was a valorous and devoted and very loving Roman Catholic Principal of Queen's University. He went to bat and he saved that institution.'

Building additions to the campus were of a spectacular nature. The Physical Education Complex, overwhelming a site previously occupied by the Gymnasium, the old School of Business building, the Faculty Women's Club and a rooming house, was a massive structure, shaped like a mediaeval fortress, which provided outstanding facilities for a wide range of sports activities as well as for teaching degree programs in Physical and Health Education. The new hockey arena perpetuated the name of Dr. John H. (Jock) Harty, and three large gymnasia were named for Prof. F. L. Bartlett, James G. Bews, and Prof. Marion Ross.

The George Richardson Stadium was moved in 1971 to the West Campus, where it was to have as neighbours McArthur Hall, home of the Faculty of Education, named in honour of Dr. Duncan McArthur, former head of the History Department at Queen's and one-time Minister of Education for Ontario, plus 12 residence 'houses' in two buildings, nestled around a social centre. This residence complex was named in honour of Dr. Jean Royce, and the names of 17 other Queen's folk were commemorated in the various houses. A 16-storey high-rise containing one-bedroom apartments became a prominent feature of the West Campus, and was given the name John Orr Tower, in memory of Dr. Orr's devotion of so much of his life to residence planning.

A new $2,000,000 Psychology building named in honour of Dr. George Humphrey, Charlton Professor of Philosophy 1924-47, was opened on Arch St., on the site of the old Jock Harty Arena. A new wing was added to Miller Hall, named in honour of Dr. E. L. Bruce, former head of the Department of Geology, and containing the Hawley Laboratories, with the name of another department head, Dr. J. E. Hawley. Goodwin Hall, a Mining Engineering building constructed entirely with private funds, was named in honour of Dr. W.

L. Goodwin, first Dean of the Faculty of Applied Science. The Arts-Social Sciences complex, named Mackintosh/Corry Hall in honour of two former Principals, was virtually completed. A start was made on the multi-million-dollar Health Sciences Complex. Jeffery Hall, for Mathematics, was opened, and plans were made to convert Ontario Hall for use by the Art Department.

In 1973 Dr. Deutsch advised the Board of Trustees of his desire to step down as Principal on October 1, 1974. It was his intention to remain at Queen's as Professor of Economics and to continue doing what he called 'odd jobs' for the federal government as they came up. With reluctance, the Board accepted Dr. Deutsch's decision.

Dr. Deutsch did indeed carry out odd jobs for the federal government and for others, as well. While still Principal, he served as a special adviser to a study on Maritime Union, and, as chairman of the committee, presented its recommendations late in 1970. He was appointed a member of the Commission on Post-Secondary Education in Ontario. He was an adviser to the Ford Foundation's Energy Policy Project, the only Canadian in the group. He was named by U.N. Secretary-General Kurt Waldheim to an 18-member international group to study the role of multinational corporations, again the only Canadian. The federal government named him to a 15-member committee studying the financial impact of pipeline development in the North. He chaired Ontario's Advisory Committee on Energy. He chaired the Board of the Centre for Resource Studies at Queen's.

The year he retired as Principal he was appointed a member of the Canada Council, chairman of the three-man committee of the Ontario Ministry of Health to examine the impact and implications of fiscal constraints on the operations of hospitals, chairman of the Tri-Level Task Force on Public Finance, and a member of the Ontario Council on University Affairs. He headed a committee to make recommendations on the future development of the Saint John campus of the University of New Brunswick. He was reappointed to the Advisory Group on Executive Compensation in the Public Service. He was made a director of the Private Planning Association of Canada. He was appointed by the federal Minister of Labour as a one-man Commission of Enquiry to look into the Canadian Railway Pension Plan.

With 12 other University heads, he participated in an official visit to the People's Republic of China, touring schools, hospitals, and factories in Canton, Shanghai and Peking, as well as six universities which formed the main object of the exercise.

He was a director of F. P. Publications Ltd., the Canadian Imperial Bank of Commerce, the International Nickel Co. of Canada Ltd., Alcan Aluminum Ltd., and Mutual Life Assurance. He was a member of the J. W. Dafoe Foundation; a trustee of the Canada Studies Foundation; and a director of the C. D. Howe Research Institute, the Institute for Research on Public Policy, the Bell Foundation set up by Maxwell Bell of Calgary, and the National Board of Directors of the Canadian Council of Christians and Jews. He was also a member of the Joint Bank-Fund Committee on Remuneration of Executive Directors, a part of the World Bank International Monetary Fund.

Dr. Deutsch received many honours and awards. He was given 17 honorary degrees, including one from Queen's in 1974 which cited him as 'a distinguished economist acutely sensitive to the political context of economic decisions and finely tuned to the common touch, himself a scarce resource in great demand by governments and their agencies. His quick and sure penetration to the heart of complex problems and his exceptional powers of judgment and vision have built over the past four decades an awesome record of public service.'

His awards included Companionship in the Order of Canada, Fellowship in the Royal Society of Canada, the Vanier Gold Medal of the Institute of Public Administration, and the Canada Council's Molson Prize of $15,000. Alumni gave him the John Orr Award (Toronto) and the Montreal Medal. He served as honorary president of the Alma Mater Society. Queen's new University Centre was named in his honour and so, at the request of the Faculty Association, was the drawing room at the Donald Gordon Centre for Continuing Education. The students presented him with an oil painting by André Bieler and a plaque recognizing his encouragement of athletics, the first to any Principal.

Dr. Deutsch had many articles and addresses published in scholarly and financial journals and was co-author of three books on Canadian economy. He had always been in great demand as a speaker, particularly on subjects of an economic or educational nature.

Once a cigarette smoker, three packs a day, he gave up tobacco in 1963. His hobby was work, to which he devoted most of his wak-

November 1974: John J. Deutsch addresses Convocation after receiving an LL.D. at the installation of his successor.   *Wallace R. Berry photo*

ing hours. He had no time for television except to catch the occasional newscast. While he was in Ottawa he became a member of the inner circle which belonged to the Five Lakes Fishing Club, up the Gatineau, where there wasn't much fishing, but lots of opportunity for dialogue with other mandarins. When he lived in Vancouver he bought a boat, and he and his wife and daughter enjoyed cruising among the islands. Back at Queen's, the family bought a cottage at Indian Lake, north of Kingston, where the Principal relaxed by working with his hands, clearing underbrush and doing odd outdoor jobs. He liked good music of all kinds and attended concerts whenever he got the chance.

He was of medium height, heavy set, solid, quiet spoken but direct, an intent listener, with a decisive and authoritative manner, modest but positive. He was described as a hard-nosed intellectual

251

and as 'an affable male Cassandra'. Peter C. Newman in *The Canadian Establishment* described him 'as probably the most remarkable and certainly the most practical of the great Ottawa mandarins.'

Dr. Deutsch died of cancer on March 18, 1976, at the age of 65. The news of his death came as a shock to his many friends and colleagues, most of whom had not known he was ill.

The funeral was held in St. Mary's Cathedral, which was filled to overflowing with many dignitaries from universities, government, and industry. Interment was made in the Queen's plot at Cataraqui Cemetery, where Principals Grant, Gordon, Wallace and Mackintosh are buried. After the ceremony there was a reception in Grant Hall, and friends signed a book of remembrance. A memorial service was held the following night in Grant Hall at which the Queen's Choral Ensemble sang Brahm's *Requiem,* and commemorative words were delivered by Dr. J. A. Corry, former Principal.

Tributes poured in from all over Canada. Many people – friends, colleagues, civil servants, politicians, editorial writers – said many laudatory things, and the phrase 'a great Canadian' was used over and over again.

To perpetuate his memory and his professional interests, a John Deutsch Memorial for the Study of Economic Policy was established. Originally conceived and discussed with him as a project to honour his retirement, the work will help promote the study and discussion of public policy in Canada.

A group of donors – Alcan, the Canadian Bank of Commerce, F.P. Publications, and International Nickel – commissioned a tapestry by Helen Frances Gregor to reflect the spirit and scope of Dr. Deutsch's important place in Canadian history. The tapestry will be hung in the John Deutsch University Centre.

Two honorary degrees were bestowed on Dr. Deutsch after his death, one by St. Lawrence University in Canton, N.Y., and the other by the University of Regina. His widow, Stephanie, received the degrees on his behalf.

Add to the list of 'Makers of Queen's' one more illustrious name, that of John J. Deutsch.

Ronald Lampman Watts

For Queen's 15th Principal, the search committee came up with a man who had served as a member of staff since 1955: Ronald Lampman Watts. He came to Queen's as a lecturer in the Department of Philosophy, held successive professorial ranks, switched disciplines from Philosophy to Political Studies along the way, and was Dean of the Faculty of Arts and Science when called to lead the University.

The new Principal was born in Japan to Canadian missionary parents (Anglican Church). His ancestry included pioneer shipbuilder John Counter and poet Archibald Lampman.

When he graduated from the University of Toronto (B.A. 1952), he was chosen a Rhodes Scholar for Ontario and proceeded to Oxford, where he obtained an Honours B.A. in 1954. It was from Oxford that he also received an M.A. in 1959, and a D.Phil. in 1962.

Described as a 'peripatetic political philosopher, who has crisscrossed the globe as freely as the campus', he has as the prime focus for this academic work the comparisons of federal systems around the world, and the lessons such comparisons offer for Canada. As lecturer, writer, analyst and consultant to evolving governments, he has been welcomed to Britain, the United States, Australia, New Zealand, Kenya, Nigeria, India and New Guinea. His experience abroad, encouraged largely by the Canada Council and the Ford Foundation, has been reflected in many publications – notably his books *New Federations: Experiments in the Commonwealth*, *Administration in Federal Systems* and *Multi-Cultural Societies and Federalism*, the last a study for Canada's Royal Commission on Bilingualism and Biculturalism.

His involvement with students, not only academically but administratively, was an important factor in his appointment as Principal. Early in his career at Queen's he served as don and then warden of

Three 'generations' of Principals at the installation of Ronald Lampman Watts, November 1974: left to right, Dr. Corry, Principal Watts and Dr. Deutsch
Wallace R. Berry photo

the first men's residence, McNeill House, and was closely associated with the planning of all subsequent student housing. He served as Dean of the largest Faculty, Arts and Science, from 1969 to 1974. Through his membership on provincial committees dealing with recruiting, applications, admissions and scholarships he had affected the lives of thousands of past, present and future students. 'He has not only been head of his fellow Deans in Ontario; on campus he has been the champion and spokesman of his academic colleagues and an active faculty representative on Senate and Council,' read his biography in the installation proceedings.

A former member of the executive of the Faculty Association, he chaired its Committee on University Government and also was a member of the Committee on Senate Structure and Procedures. He was chairman of the special and vitally important Senate Committee on Grievance, Discipline, and Related Matters, whose recommendations made a most significant contribution to the life of the University.

On November 8, 1974, in Grant Hall Dr. Watts was installed as Principal and Vice-Chancellor in what was described by the *Whig-Standard* as 'the kind of grand display of pomp and ceremony seen only on great occasions of church and state.' The academic procession was particularly colourful, with representatives from universities all across Canada. The arrival of the Chancellor's Party into the Hall was greeted with a flourish of trumpets.

J. D. Gibson, Chairman of the Board of Trustees, presented Dr. Watts to the Chancellor, the Rt. Hon. Roland Michener, who administered the pledge of office. He was invested with the robes of office by Dr. W. F. Connell, the senior member of faculty, and A. J. 'Tony' Wolman, President of the Alma Mater Society.

In his address, Dr. Watts spoke of the role of the university in modern society and about public disenchantment over the ability of education to solve all the world's problems, a belief that had gained popularity during the previous two decades. Too much was expected of education in general and of higher education in particular, with the result that 'at times the public seems to be on the verge of an unreasonable and irrational backlash against higher education itself.' The task of the university is 'not to train people for slots in today's society, but to educate today's minds that will shape the society of tomorrow, and to liberalize, civilize, and humanize people for the future.'

Honorary LL.D. degrees were conferred on the former Principal, Dr. John J. Deutsch, Dr. John R. Evans, President of the University of Toronto, Dr. Albert Birnie Hodgetts, teacher, writer and historian, and the Hon. Pauline McGibbon, Lieutenant-Governor of Ontario.

A keen and successful yachtsman, Dr. Watts is skipper of his own sailing craft 'Blue Peter', a C & C 27 cruising-racing sailboat. He has participated regularly in Lake Ontario Yacht Racing Association regattas, and won major trophies in 1973 and 1974. He was a member of the organizing committee for the world sailing Olympics in Kingston in 1976, serving as chief class officer, co-ordinating the competitors in the six Olympic sailing classes.

·He looks the part of a successful sailor, sturdily built, athletic, well co-ordinated, with quick reflexes. His most notable feature is a quiet smile, accompanied by a twinkle in his eye. He is reserved, but meets people easily and puts them at their ease. He is articulate and persuasive in argument, a careful and lucid speaker. His wife Donna has taught history in the Kingston Collegiate and Vocational Institute ever since coming to Kingston. A sister Margaret (Mrs. Peter Marsh), graduated from Queen's with a B.A. in 1959.

At 45, Dr. Watts was the youngest to assume the office of Principal since George Monro Grant, who came to Queen's at the age of 42. The records show that the Rev. William Snodgrass was the youngest of them all, at 37. The complete list of men who served as Principal and the age at which they came to office: Rev. Thomas Liddell, 41; Rev. John Machar, 50; Rev. John Cook, 52; Rev. William Leitch, 45; Rev. William Snodgrass, 37; Rev. G. M. Grant, 42; Rev. D. M. Gordon, 58; Rev. R. B. Taylor, 47; W. H. Fyfe, 51; R. C. Wallace, 55; W. A. Mackintosh, 56; J. A. Corry, 62; J. J. Deutsch, 57; R. L. Watts, 45.

There never has been a Principal at Queen's who has not had to cope with shortage of operating funds, and Dr. Watts is no exception. In fact, he came into office facing a record deficit and a deteriorating financial situation. However, as D. D. Calvin wrote in *Queen's University at Kingston 1841-1941,* 'Nothing in the history of Queen's is more astonishing than the way in which the founders and their successors were able to find answers to the money questions that beset them, to keep the College solvent, to do the seemingly impossible, to hold on grimly for the dawn of a better day.'

One of his first moves was the appointment of a Principal's Committee on Financial Restraint under the chairmanship of Prof.

The Principal setting a good pace in the students' United Way Bike-a-thon during half-time at the Reunion football game, 1974
H. Craig Campbell photo

L. G. Macpherson, formerly Vice-Principal (Finance). Out of the study made by this committee, plans effecting savings for the period 1976-1980 were produced, with measures built in to ensure that the quality of education would not suffer as a consequence. The report recommended a general belt-tightening, with the elimination of some positions, a reduction in budget for many departments and ancillary services, a campaign for alumni and public support, increased rentals, increased service fees, sale of excess University assets, the re-organization of central institutional support offices, and the like. Recommendations for reductions in academic staff ranged from the natural process of normal retirement 'to the painful and difficult problems of redundancy and economic necessity.'

There ensued a campus-wide campaign to save electricity and fuels in which the aid was enlisted of all members of staff to 'Turn Off for Queen's'; light levels were lowered, timers employed to shut off ventilating fans, temperatures lowered at night, showers limited to five minutes, running taps forbidden, use of office equipment restricted – everyone was asked to conserve and to submit ideas for conservation. Shades of Dr. McNeill! And the program worked. Dr. Watts was soon able to announce that substantial savings had been made in fuel and energy costs.

His appointment as Principal was for a five-year period. As this is written he has been in office less than two years. He has weathered such storms and disturbances as have arisen to date, and the future looks highly promising.

His vision of the Queen's of the future will strike a responsive chord. In an open letter to the alumni soon after taking office he wrote:

As we look ahead we must always keep in the forefront the University's primary function as a free community of individuals dedicated to the pursuit of truth and to the preservation and extension of human knowledge solely through reason. Our function is not merely further education, but higher education. It is the indispensable assumption of such a society that we are concerned with unique human beings not properly subject to standardized and standardizing processes. It follows that we should believe in persons, not methods or formulae. Furthermore, as a community whose processes are appropriately characterized by reason and civility, we must strive to continue the very special degree of co-operation, mutual support and rational accommodation which has existed among all the partners in the Queen's community – the students, faculty, staff, administrators, alumni, Trustees and benefactors.

In order to maintain a human scale of operation, Queen's University has recognized that we should not attempt to do everything and be all things to all men. We have realized that we must adopt a policy of selectivity. We must choose to do those things which we can do well and to excel in those things which we have chosen.

The choice of such priorities is almost always painful. Nevertheless, such choices are made all the more necessary by the increasingly stringent financial circumstances facing universities today. Queen's, however, has had a long tradition of finding the will to surmount periods of financial difficulty, and any anxieties I might have are lessened by the support and encouragement which have been offered to me by members of the Queen's community. I stand assured that we shall face the difficult times ahead together with confidence.

Well and truly said, Skipper. May you always have a fair breeze and a snug harbour!

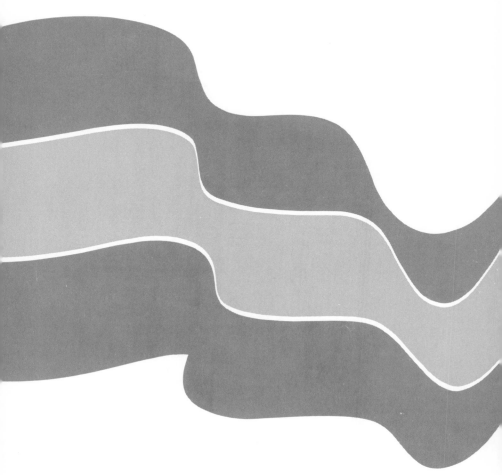

VIII
*The care
and feeding
of alumni*

Reunion 1972: Chancellor
Stirling welcomes H.A.
'Curly' Estabrook, Sc.'41,
and his wife Audrey
(Reece), Arts'41, to the Prin-
cipal's Reception in Grant
Hall.

Alumni as people

An alumni association in the western United States conducted a survey in the hope it would support an impression that the average age of alumni was getting younger and younger. They came up with a figure of 34 years. This fact was gleefully reported to the student leaders. One young lady shook her head mournfully: 'It's worse than I thought,' she said.

The History of Arts '34, as reported in the *Tricolor* for that year, included a reference:

The thought that in a few short weeks one will belong to that august body known as the Alumni is distinctly alarming. Somehow one always thinks of them as bewhiskered old gentlemen who spend their entire lives singing *Queen's College Colours*. It's all very depressing, but probably there is some fun in life yet – even for Alumni.

A few years ago, Bob Buller, Arts '71, conducted a survey designed to determine what the current crop of students thought of alumni. It turned out that the few who had ever given the matter any consideration at all thought of them as people at least the same age as their parents, which apparently removed them from the real world.

Now that the problem has been defined, considerable progress has been and is being made in improving the relationship between students and alumni.

Where are they now?

The heart and soul of the Alumni Office operations are the record files of the alumni, with their addresses, positions, and newspaper clippings recording their accomplishments. When the Alumni Association was organized in 1926, the University knew *who* her graduates were, but had only a sketchy idea of *where* they were. The addresses on file were badly out of date. At that time there were only 6,000 living graduates, but it was a monumental task for the newly appointed Alumni Secretary, Gordon J. Smith, and his staff of one, Anne Corrigan, to track down these people. It is to the credit of their tenacity that they succeeded to the extent they did. They did not complete the job, nor will it ever be completed, of course. There is a 30 per cent turnover in addresses in any one year, and no sooner are missing alumni located than others drift off into limbo. For most of these the loss is temporary, but there are some who become 'Lost Trails' for longer periods of time. A relatively small number are lost more or less permanently.

The tracking down of addresses is an art in itself. An approach is made to friends or relatives who might have news. There is a routine daily search through newspapers, telephone and city directories, trade magazines, house organs – any publication that might report the movements or appointments of professional people. There is much pleasure obtained from the successful conclusion to such a search.

At one time the Alumni Office used a form which was mailed periodically to all graduates and which asked for information of a biographical nature, useful for the graduate's permanent file. These were not always treated with the respect that might be desired. One caused a member of staff considerable bewilderment. She asked me if I had ever heard of a Luther Sharkfinger, whom she could not find in the records. Perhaps he was a former student? In any case, he was reported to have had a most interesting career. It seems he was currently employed in the numbers racket in St. Louis, Mo. Where we

262

Household effects: 16 out of 56 members in the graduating class of Medicine '59 were married and the fathers of children – 23 children, in fact, most of whom are shown above. Front row, left to right: Dr. and Mrs. Allen Ball with Lisa, Dr. and Mrs. Dick James with Nancy, Dr. and Mrs. J.D. Heslin with Jayme, and Dr. and Mrs. Wally Podeworny with Michael and Carol. Middle row: Dr. and Mrs. Jack Simpson with Shaun, Dr. and Mrs. R. Seymour with Karen, Dr. and Mrs. Floyd Bajjaly with Stephen and Michael, and Dr. and Mrs. S.V. Jarzylo with William. Back row: Dr. and Mrs. Bob Cranston with Donald, Dr. and Mrs. Hugh Friend with Linda, Peter and Susan, Dr. and Mrs. Gary Lewis with Christopher and Elizabeth, Dr. and Mrs. L.R. MacLean with Barry and Ian, and Mrs. Bob Smith with Bruce and Douglas   *D.G. Dewar photo*

263

had requested a short synopsis of career since leaving Queen's, there was the following:

1   ran guns for the loyalists in the Spanish War
2   climbed Mount Everest
3   won 30 games for the New York Yankees
4   was exhibit A in the Scopes monkey trial
5   won an Academy Award for performance in *Anne of Green Gables*
6   defeated Strangler Lewis two falls out of three
7   took a shot at an alumni secretary who asked too many questions.

A most interesting recital. Unfortunately, it didn't check out.

The Alumni Office has always been blessed with personnel who were willing to take great pains in tracking down missing alumni. Anne Corrigan, who served the Alumni Association so faithfully and well for 39 years, was a most effective sleuth and blazed a trail for others to follow. It was rare that she had to admit defeat of more than a temporary nature. One of her ploys was to publish in the *Review* from time to time a list of 'Lost Trails' in the hope that some of the readers could supply the necessary information. On one such occasion the *Review* had no sooner been delivered than her father reported that one person listed among the missing had appeared in the Corrigan backyard only a few days previously. This led to the adoption of the Standard Office Practice of taking one last look out the window before going to press.

When the new graduates were being added at the rate of 350 a year, the manual system of recording addresses and other vital information was practical, but when the output passed 2,000 annually, the systems became outmoded. When I joined the Alumni Office, the number of living graduates was 8,300. When I left, it was more than 37,000. The move to computerized records, begun in the spring of 1976, will provide a much more efficient operation. Computerization also poses a great challenge in that greater efforts will be called for to ensure that the all-important personal touch in alumni relationships is not lost.

Perhaps the most popular department of the *Review* is that devoted to vital statistics: births, marriages, deaths and news items about alumni, such as promotions, retirements, honours, distinctions, achievements. No muck-raking here; if a graduate runs afoul of the law, murders his wife, or is disbarred from his profession, you won't read about it in these columns. Information of this nature is just quietly filed away in a folder entitled *The Black Issue of the Review,* as a record of the human frailty that permeates us all, and as a warning to keep humble.

The popularity of the personal notes section was affirmed a few years ago when a survey was conducted to determine whether the magazine was doing the job for which it was intended. The bouquets and brickbats were about evenly divided. There were those who thought the magazine was a highly creditable publication, and there were those who called it a promotion of trivia and an embarrassment in times when the world was crying for leadership. The only common denominator was a general satisfaction with the personal notes section. This was an interesting appraisal, because many of the alumni magazines in the United States, which have become more and more sophisticated, have dropped personal notes.

At an American Alumni Council conference in Vancouver a few years ago, the *Review* was evaluated by a panel of senior editors. One of these commented: 'You seem to be labouring under the handicap that your editorial committee has not decided whether your publication is to be a magazine or a newspaper.' Probably true. On the other hand, perhaps this is not a defect, but a strength. Rationalization? Possibly. But the *Review* does have as its objective the purpose for which it was intended: informed good will.

But back to personal notes. There is no section in the magazine which requires more careful preparation. Some of the items are sent in. Many more are turned up in a search of daily newspapers, national magazines, professional publications, and other likely

266

sources. All require checking and rechecking. Once it has been determined that the person to whom reference is made is actually a graduate or former student, the spelling of the name and the class year must be authenticated, the facts must be verified. A simple note of five or six lines may require a score of checks. Even then a mistake may slip through, but the record of success is high. In only a few instances over the years has it been necessary to disinter a graduate reported deceased, unmarry a couple who had not been churched, or deny a birth that had not taken place. But the sword of Damocles is suspended by a slender thread, and the unwary editor is never free from fear of at least a verbal horsewhipping. One learns to live with the danger as an occupational hazard.

One mother was irate because her school-teacher daughter was reported married to a fellow member of staff. Not only was the report not true, the two were not particularly good friends. We never did track down to our satisfaction where this item originated or how it had managed to get into print.

One young lady was angry when her son's birth was announced, because we had reported her as married and as having taken her husband's name. She made it abundantly clear that while indeed she was married, ship-shape and Bristol fashion, she was retaining her own name, and she demanded that we move our editorial policies into the 20th century.

Some of the news items that come to hand are a sheer delight – such as the birth notice which appeared in the daily newspapers and was repeated in the *Review:*

> **Walker** – Douglas and Linda wish to advise Frank
> Tindall of a prospective Golden Gael, Jeff Douglas,
> born November 7, 1974, in Peterborough, slightly
> under 10 lbs.

Hank Wightman, Com. '47, when he was editor of the Napanee *Post-Express,* made up a special edition with a banner headline proclaiming to the world that he was the father of twins.

The *Review* has never run a Lonely Hearts Column, but on more than one occasion news of the death of a spouse has triggered an overture to the relict from a prospective suitor. Some highly successful marriages have resulted. Wrote one lady: 'You have no idea how it bolsters the ego to have college friends of so long ago remember you.'

268

The death announcements present problems of their own. Extra care must be taken in verifying the report of a death. One learned early on not to take as gospel truth mail returned with the notation 'Deceased'. The mail carrier may just have decided not to make a trip to the top of a hill for one measly letter.

One lady in Toronto, erroneously reported as having shuffled off this mortal coil, took it in good spirit after the initial shock had passed, and to this day, when our paths cross, waves her arms in menacing fashion and threatens, 'I'm coming back to haunt you.' One or two others in the same situation chose to take considerable and understandable umbrage.

At one time the *Review* reported deaths in considerable detail. In time this became impracticable, because of numbers, and it became the practice to publish little more than the name, class, degree or degrees, and position. This evoked a storm of protest – well, two or three comments – that such and such a distinguished personage deserved better treatment. So, longer obituaries were printed in special cases, a source of satisfaction to some and an irritation to others.

It is said that there is a book in the life of every man and woman. Certainly there is a wealth of material in the lives of most graduates of any university. Every issue of the *Review* highlights this point. Here are a few chosen at random: Karl S. Twitchell, a mining engineer of international renown; Mrs. T. J. S. Ferguson, 'year after year her choirs, groups and soloists have achieved outstanding results'; John Howard Sissons, 'who cast himself in the role of protector for Indians and Eskimos in the north and became a legend in his own time'; the Hon. Percy Page, coach of the world-famous Edmonton Grads and Lieutenant-Governor of the Province of Alberta; Helena Dickinson, 'author, philologist, and authority on liturgy and religious art'; Sir Aldington George Corphey, President of the Legislative Council of Jamaica; Dr. Edwin W. Bradwin, Principal of Frontier College, 'a muscular Christian'; Alice Chown, 'a pioneer in women's suffrage, women's trade unionism, and the international peace movement'. This is just a sampling of the fascinating life stories that surface in the course of preparing an issue for publication.

And consider these potential biographies: Dr. George E. Mac-Kinnon, 'a country doctor who never turned down a call'; Herbert F. Harris, one of that courageous band of fliers in World War One, 'shot down behind the German lines and for 19 months a prisoner of war'; Dr. Charles William Hedley Graham, a physician and inven-

269

tor of a railway crossing signal light safety device; W. A. Spence, 'the famous ace of Canada's Northland fliers'; Dr. W. G. Fralick, physician to many of the world's leading boxers, including Tunney, Dempsey and Firpo; Dr. John E. Hammett, distinguished surgeon, big game hunter, and doctor to the New York Yankees and such people as Joe Dimaggio and Marilyn Monroe; Col. C. F. Hamilton, liaison intelligence officer with the RCMP; Rev. Dr. John Pringle, 'Pringle of the Yukon'; or any one of that group of early women graduates in Medicine who went into missionary work in India and China; or any teacher, lawyer or doctor who pioneered in the West, or other frontiers; or those engineers who practised their skills in foreign lands or remote territories.

They are all part of the glory of Queen's University. May they rest in peace.

Dr. John E. Hammett and his wife Lyle with elephant they bagged on a safari in Africa

Association with the alumni records and the *Review* has a tendency to make one name conscious, even to have a mania about names. Early on I learned the correct spelling of George Monro Grant, Frank R. Leadlay, and William A. Mackintosh. There are several letters on file from irate alumni who had been incorrectly addressed on alumni mailings; you learn, in self defence.

I never met Rixton Rafter, to my regret, but his name long fascinated me. He graduated from Queen's in 1907, and was said to be the first blind person to obtain a degree from a North American university, and the first blind person to own and publish his own weekly newspaper, *The Enterprise News* in Arthur, Ont. In 1954 he was named 'Weekly Newspaperman of the Year' by the Ontario Weekly Newspapers Association. The citation read, in part: 'A touch typist, he produced all his own editorial and news copy. His phenomenal memory is common knowledge to his fellow-citizens. On many occasions he wrote a whole column of news with his mind as the only notebook. Never once did he miss an edition of this newspaper in his 45 years.'

A lusty character who surfaced during my time was Fleetwood Kingsley McKean, who was the ringleader of an unregenerate group which included Ding McGill, Don Brunton, Norm Alcock, Cooch McMaster, I. D. McKenzie, Doug Annan, Dave Rigsby, Jack (Rubber Legs) Mitchell, Harvey Marshall, Ken Clarke and Nick Paithouski. It took a good man to stand out in this motley crew, but McKean was a Viking at heart – he could have posed for the central character in the comic strip 'Hagar the Horrible' – and wherever devilment was taking place he was there front and centre, just the sort of company mothers warn their offspring against. At the same time he was manager of the football team and President of the Engineering Society and held a host of other positions. Fortunately he was never saved, and remains a colourful personality to this day.

En route to retirement, he discovered a mine, invented a new process for cleaning molybdenite, and spent almost 30 years complicating life for the Ministry of Transport. In case the name doesn't ring a bell, I'll confess that he was never known as Fleetwood or Kingsley, but rather as 'Pappy' or 'Dick' McKean.

And then there was Ruben Frederick Wethenbach Nelson; I don't know what his mother called him, but around Queen's he answered to 'Butch'. A one-time Theological student, Butch was in the forefront of a myriad of student activities and was a popular campus crusader. He graduated with an honours degree in Philosophy, and has been involved in social service, federally and privately, in the Ottawa area. Perhaps it is just as well. The name 'Rev. Butch Nelson' on a church signboard might have raised a few eyebrows.

The name of Kees Wouter Kort always gave the proofreaders trouble. Was it Kees Kort or vice versa? Of the fact that Kort was a good football player there was no doubt whatsoever.

*

A 1933 Journal *reported that two Varsity students had taken advantage of a football weekend to make a tour of the new Gymnasium. Their guide was a janitor who took great pride in pointing out the features, and his sales pitch was a paean of praise for Queen's. The visitors absorbed the remarks without comment, but as they departed one was heard to say: 'Can you beat that! Even the janitors have it!'*

Hark! The herald angels thundered!
Arts! Arts! 1900!

Wallace Hall resounded with this yell when William J. Russell turned up for his class reunion a few years ago. He was the only member on hand, but that didn't prevent him from having a wonderful time, and he regaled all who came within range of his voice with tales of Queen's at the turn of the century. He had played football with the legendary Guy Curtis and at the age of 80 he suggested in all seriousness that he might suit up and join the Gaels for a play or two. He was disappointed when Coach Frank Tindall was not receptive.

Another team-mate of Guy Curtis, the jaunty James Falkner, Class of Arts '03, was one of those who attended the reunion in 1954. He was better known to the students of his day as 'Jofakis'. There was a ditty that went:

Queen's football team has two good men
And these two men are brothers
Dunc Falkner is the name of one
Jofakis is the other.

The story behind the nickname is that when Jim Falkner's studies began to suffer because of his involvement in athletics, his father wanted him to stop playing. But Jim's team-mates persuaded him to stay with the team, and his name was concealed in the lineup by an illegible scrawl which the sportswriters interpreted as 'Jofakis'. And it was as Jofakis that he was known to the end of his days.

I well remember one reunion when the registration headquarters had been set up in the common room on the second floor of the Students' Union. An elderly gentleman made his way slowly up the stairs, and, short of breath, paused at the door. He peered into the room, looking, searching for a familiar face. When one of the staff approached him, he asked in a quavering voice, 'Where's all the old gang?' No one had the heart to tell him that he was probably the sole survivor.

Many classes make gifts to the University to mark their graduation or a memorable reunion. Scholarships have been set up, books have been donated to the library, trees have been planted, rooms have been furnished in the residences. The Class of 1910 gave the University the iron gates which stood for more than 50 years beside Grant Hall. For all those years the Convocation processions passed through the gates en route from Kingston Hall to Grant Hall. When campus planning dictated their removal, the gates were transferred to the Arch St. entrance to Summerhill, the Principal's residence. Nine members of the Class, back for their 60th anniversary reunion in 1970, happily took part in a re-dedication ceremony.

Alex Edmison, Permanent President of the Class of Arts '26, was not able to attend his class reunion in 1941 because he was overseas with the Canadian Army, but his thoughts were with those who were at Queen's for the occasion. He wrote to say that Bud Thomas and Hugo Ewart were prevented from attending for the same reason, and he commented: 'What an uncertain thing Life is – three more unlikely soldiers never lifted a 1926 Red Room tea-cup, or 'phoned for a 25-cent Kingston taxi, or took an ice cream soda at the Superior, or tried to get a ticket for the Plumbers' Ball. ...Hope to see you all five years hence.' And he did, and for many a successful reunion thereafter, including the 50th in 1976.

Reunions are happy occasions, and many of those who come back to the campus take the trouble to say so afterwards. Austin Cross, Arts '23, wrote in his column in the Ottawa *Citizen:*

To those who go back after some years, and whose visits are all too rare, the change that will most impress you will be the emancipation of women. Notably the emancipation of women's legs. If you wanted to see that much of a lady when I was at Queen's, you had to marry her. But the cheerleading girls wear the briefest of plaid skirts, and then during cheerleading stunts, they turn cartwheels. Appropriately enough, the girls wear panties of yellow, blue and red, the Queen's colours. One girl in yellow unmentionables was the athletic type, and she stood on her head as much as half a minute, while gentlemen cheerleaders jumped through her legs. Truly, education has advanced since my day.

J.E. MacKay had a comment in similar vein after he came back for his 60th reunion in 1974. He wrote: 'My wife and I thoroughly enjoyed the Reunion, perhaps as much in our impression of the

Reunion 1963: Members of Arts '49 regroup around the tree they planted at the Students' Union when they graduated.   *D.G. Dewar photo*

spirit of the students as in meeting former classmates. We got a special kick out of the performance of the band and the cheerleaders at the Saturday box luncheon. No girls in our time stood bare-legged on the shoulders of young men!'

Thomas Carlos Lennox, Class of Science '11, was so inspired at the prospect of seeing old friends at his 50th reunion in 1961 that he wrote a song to the tune of *Home on the Range,* which he entitled *Daisies of Queen's* and dedicated to all the college sweethearts. He arranged for Fred Love, a Theological student, to sing the song. One of the verses:

> *O take me once more, to Ontario's shore*
> *Where many a harbour light gleams*
> *Where the flowers are fair, yet none can compare*
> *With the beautiful daisies of Queen's.*

275

All joined in enthusiastically on the refrain:

Queen's, Daisies of Queen's
Their beauty adorns all our dreams
For many are fair, yet none can compare
With the beautiful Daisies of Queen's.

The spirit of John Wilkes, perhaps the most colourful rake of the 18th century, was invoked by members of Arts '24 and '25 when they held a reunion in 1938. Wilkes was one of the leaders in the infamous Hell Fire Club, and he was adopted by the Artsmen as their patron saint. A notice was prepared:

There will be a meeting of the Hell Fire Club in Kingston on Saturday, October 29. The club was founded in London, England, in 1703, and has had a long and distinguished career. An opportunity to extend and enforce this record will be provided this Reunion Weekend, the occasion of the McGill game. Only persons of unimpeachable bad character are being invited – for the society prides itself above all else on being select.

The latter-day John Wilkes was none other than than eminent historian Gerry Graham, a hardened sinner, and his fellow conspirators were George Carson, Dave Rankin, Ross Winter, Eric Cross, Norman McLeod, Mace Mair, Mac Haig, Gordon Sinclair and Harold Cave.

Wilf Eggleston, Arts '26, long-time newspaperman, author and freelance writer, summed up neatly the reactions of many when he wrote in the Ottawa *Journal* after attending his 45th reunion:

The years bring hardening of the arteries to some and softening of the brains to others. I admit to bias. I came away with two deep convictions. The respect and affection we felt nearly half a century ago was well founded on realities. The subsequent generations have more than lived up to the early dreams. Queen's will be a mighty force in the Canada of tomorrow.

The mail must go through
(but please don't go to any trouble on my account)

A perceptive toiler in the alumni vineyard, Robert F. Goheen, once remarked: 'If anyone harbors the notion that the alumni of any university form a solid, homogenized phalanx of nostalgic, reactionary "old grads", let him read my mail for a week.'

Bang on, Brother Goheen, bang on!

Complaints provide an opportunity, of course, to explain, to palliate, to assuage, to smooth ruffled feathers, not always successfully, but at least enough to show understanding and sympathy. Where complaints do not surface, the damage may be irreparable.

Not all complaints are legitimate. Investigation sometimes reveals that the charges are unreasonable, or without basis in fact. No matter.

Many of the excerpts from letters which follow are in response to appeals for money. In some cases there have been threats to cut Queen's out of wills, or at least out of annual support. Some of the most sweeping statements have come from persons who had never gotten around to making a contribution, ever. Some go so far as to demand that their names be taken off the mailing list. These instructions are carried out, but not until after there has been a letter from the Alumni Office expressing regret. At the same time permission is asked to continue sending the *Review,* to which all graduates are entitled as a constitutional right. This is invariably granted, at least by default – no instructions to the contrary. It is illuminating to check up on disgruntled correspondents years later and find out that in many cases all has been forgiven and forgotten, judging from contributions received in the interim.

Probably the most concerted protest from the alumni body came over the Board of Trustees' proposal to erect a building on the Lower Campus. From far and wide the protests came in by mail, by telephone, in person, through University representatives. They decried the threatened violation and desecration of one of the last major green areas of the campus. People who apparently had never

277

thought of the University for years now were united in demanding that not one single blade of grass be disturbed. The protests prevailed. The building was erected elsewhere, and a very fine building it is – Stirling Hall on Queen's Crescent. The Lower Campus now covers a huge underground parking area, but it is still verdant, still a playing space, still a green oasis among limestone buildings.

Another storm of protest arose over the demolition of the Jock Harty Arena on Arch Street, which left Queen's temporarily without hockey facilities. This situation was rectified soon afterward with the inclusion of a new and improved Jock Harty within the physical education complex.

Here is a sampler of other letters from over the years.
I feel that I am living on the edge of a precipice, and I am in mortal fear of being pushed over the edge by the skullduggeries of Messrs. Trudeau, Benson and Co., who are insulated against the pains and anxieties of their own extortions and to whom it never seems to occur that thievery is no less thievery because the thieves pass laws that confer legality upon their thievery. ... May the new year see our deliverance from the pestilence of predatory, Pecksniffian politicians and their janizaries.

*

I have precious little left over to contribute to the Alumni Association's various funds. Even if I did, I am afraid that I would feel obliged to send it in aid of the starving millions in the Sahel region of Africa. ... Besides, I am beginning to lose whatever faith I had in the universities of this country. Perhaps somewhat naively, I expected that they would educate young men and women towards a more profound understanding of the demands of justice – and of common humanity both in this country and especially in the underdeveloped nations of the world. ... I was wrong. I have discovered that our university graduates come out, not changed, but merely confirmed in the selfish middle class values that they had received from the cradle.

*

Please remove my name from your mailing list. I do not make enough money to contribute to such funds, and if I did I would contribute to more useful ones, such as political refugees, etc. As things stand, and bearing in mind the world's resource crisis, you are wast-

278

ing time, money and Canada's paper with these valiant pleas to an impoverished Queen's graduate.

*

Friends in Canada have written to tell me that when you inserted the birth announcement I sent you, you changed my format and as a result have seriously embarrassed and compromised me. WE ARE NOT MARRIED, and I feel it was wrong, unimaginative and libellous of you to assume that we are.

*

Please remove my name from your mailing list. For 43 years I have looked forward to having my son enroll at Queen's. To date, all he has received has been an invitation from Coach Trimble [sic] to attend pre-school football training camp! ! ! P.S.: He was accepted at Western!

*

It has always been my belief that educational expenses should be met by a combination of student fees and government grants, and not be dependent on grants or endowments from alumni. For this reason I have little or no intention of ever making any such donations to either the University or the Alumni Association.

*

I would be very happy to contribute to the Alumni Fund as soon as I receive confirmation of the fact that the space left by the moving of Richardson Stadium will be kept as a 'green area' for use by interfaculty teams, general recreation of Queen's students, a teaching area for outdoor activities in the physical education faculty.

*

Is it in harmony with the traditions and principles of Queen's University to hold alumni gatherings, dinners, etc. in breweries, distilleries, etc.?

*

I do not like the public relations officers you send out. I like neither their quality, nor what they say. If I am to believe they truly represent the universities, down with the universities!

279

Please do not send any more 'begging letters' to me when you cannot find a place at Queen's for our daughter who has graduated with 60 per cent from Grade 13.

*

I do not intend to make any more contributions until Canada stops co-operating with the Communistic enemies of the U.S.

*

I got a little close to the Queen's students celebrating this fall in Toronto. I doubt if I want any part of my money going to educate these 'boys will be boys'. However, I really reserve my largest objection to the fact that neither the university or the Alma Mater Society takes any responsibility.

*

It has long been my conviction that several members of the faculty have been retained beyond their period of usefulness to Queen's. When I can be satisfied of a wise administration I shall be more than happy to contribute.

*

After five years in the RCAF, I obtained a first-class honours degree from Queen's, and learned to despise it in the process.

*

I have been advised that my obituary appeared prematurely in the current issue of the *Review*. Naturally I expect to be resurrected and would appreciate receiving an explanation as to the origin of the rumour.

*

In three years at Queen's I never received any financial help from Queen's bursary program, although I asked for it. The worm has turned!

*

It has come to my attention recently that the University Building Committee is not making the best use of funds presently at their disposal. For the time being, the same amount of money will be pledged to other universities with which I have been associated.

I am appalled to think that someone has succeeded in renaming our time-honoured alumni reunion weekend with the slushy, sentimental Americanism that is the 'Homecoming' of every second-rate college below the line. The name is embarrassing, the sentiment revolting.

*

This is not intended to be smart Alex. Just a simple expression of opinion. ... Money should come from government. Government control is less to be feared than Big Business, e.g., General Motors. University graduates by Gallup poll are very reactionary (where is the cultural heritage? Christ, Socrates, etc.).

*

For a number of years my wife and I have been glad to contribute to the Alumni Fund, but have changed our minds since the Kingston meeting of Mr. Diefenbaker. I understand that a goodly number of the hoodlums at that meeting were first-year students and as such would be staying in residence. My wife and I are not particularly interested in helping to provide a roof for the shelter of such hoodlums.

*

Many thanks for your May-June issue with its excellent coverage of the spring graduations, including the distinguished recipients of honorary degrees. One wonders if the array of 12 good knights would not have been enhanced by the appearance of even one distinguished woman graduate.

*

No further donations unless Master of Education degree used after my name.

*

You can write me off as a dead loss because when the epidemic of 1918 struck. ... [this letter was received in 1964].

*

Although my name is difficult to spell, people at Queen's have managed to do it correctly for four years. Why don't you of the Alumni Association do the same?

281

I will be happy to vote when I see two candidates of the 1950-plus vintage. This is a boat-race, not an election.

*

The picture of the Class of Medicine '41 on the back cover of the last issue is out of place. It belongs in *Mad Magazine,* where its sick vulgarity would be appreciated.

*

Thanks for nothing! A couple of years ago you refused to accept our son after Dr.—— had made very liberal donations to Queen's for the past 20 years.

*

It is bad enough to be married, separated from my husband, and trying to bring up my daughter all alone, but then to have mail addressed to my maiden name reaching my home for the cleaning women to see!

*

I wish to register my protest over beer and games of chance being offered as inducements presumably to encourage Queen's men to turn out to an annual election.

*

The proudest name Queen's has had was 'The poor man's university'. Principal Grant established the fair treatment of all, including women, and his professors established sound teaching. And the poor men established democratic principles of equal rights for all, a square deal for everybody. Let's keep it the Poor Man's University!

*

I dislike carrying a dead man's middle initial. Perhaps you can get my name straight so that I can send you another cheque and receive all communications from Queen's with the proper name on the label.

*

Since all publishing companies and even the Royal Bank in sending out its newsletter, take pains to get correct degrees for their addresses, it should not be too much trouble to do so.

282

It has been drawn to my attention that the crop of dandelions on the campus is scarcely in keeping with the general appearance of the university grounds. Would it be impertinent to suggest that the application of the chemical weed killer 2-4-D would not only remove the weeds, but also have public relations value. Although I have allocated my contribution to the Alumni Fund for general expenses I would be quite happy if it were 'dedicated to the dandelions'.

*

I will be sending you $5 each year provided that you maintain prompt, efficient delivery of the *Queen's Review* and any other pertinent publications to the address shown above. Also, I expect a reasonable amount of co-operation on your part should I wish to secure tickets to home football games for relatives and/or friends as well as for myself.

*

I feel like Sinclair Lewis when his Alma Mater tried to acclaim him. At the banquet when he was called on he rose and said 'When I was a student here none of you would give me a pleasant look, but now when my name is a public word you gather to acclaim me. Now, you can all go to hell!' That exactly expresses my sentiments, so I'd say you can take my name off your list as far as this fund is concerned.

*

My address is still the same as it has been for five years. I just realized I haven't received a *Review* since last Fall. I don't really think I'M lost – but somebody is!

*

I understood that I should be regarded as a permanent contributor and would not be asked for anything more during my lifetime. Since then I have had many appeals from your office. How do you account for this? I will be very pleased to leave my estate to someone else if you don't want it.

It might be gathered from the foregoing excerpts that the Alumni Association and the University receive nothing but complaints. The opposite is closer to the truth; there is a preponderance of bouquets. Queen's graduates like their University and don't hesitate to say so or to indicate their approval by contributions.

One of the most heart-warming letters in recent years was this one, sent to the Principal's Office:

Dear Mr. Principal,

My husband and I would like to tell you how favourably impressed we are with Queen's University. ... Our first impression came when our son received a refusal from the Faculty of Medicine. Someone had taken time to explain the huge number of applications received and the large number of qualified people who had to be refused acceptance. It was not one of those 'We regret to inform you...' notes (which sound like a death announcement in wartime) that he received from other universities. When he was accepted this year at McMaster, Queen's alone wrote to congratulate him. This letter took time and effort and was greatly appreciated for its humanity.

This fall one of our twin daughters went to Queen's. When we took her to Adelaide Hall, we were greeted by students who took all her bags. A large paper daisy was on her residence door, with 'Welcome Nancy' on it. A girl immediately greeted her and introduced her to her neighbours. We parents were greeted and given coffee and cookies.

I was so moved and grateful for this greeting to Nancy that tears came to my eyes. I was also feeling sorry for her sister, who was with us. We had earlier installed her at another university after spending a great deal of time finding her room, carrying her bags and settling her in, alone. Not one person greeted her.

The pre-registration information that Nancy received was written with care and thoughtfulness for the individual. Yes, they were form letters, but someone had made an effort to make the student feel like a human being and not a number.

The prefect on Nancy's floor at Adelaide wrote her a personal letter in advance, telling her when to come, what extras to bring to make her room more personal, etc. Her Orientation was well planned. She had fun and made friends.

Having come from a small town with small schools where everyone called me by name, I have felt sorry for my children and others in their bouts with computers. The efforts of Queen's to keep its 'humanity' are especially appreciated.

And this one was written to the Parents Association:

...We have felt very fortunate in having a closeness to Queen's and having our youngest of five children graduate from such a fine university. ... I especially like the size of the student body and the concern between teacher and student. I know this (smaller size) means disappointment for many, but a greater advantage for those who are accepted. ... Our best wishes for future success.

The case for the Defence rests.

*

Do the students of today feel the same way about Queen's as they did in days of yore? Very much so.

A few years ago when radicals on many campuses were making life interesting for those in authority, a group of 30 students, at their own expense, erected a billboard in downtown St. Catharines, that proclaimed to the world that 'Queen's is the ONLY University.'

Photo by Denis Cahill, St. Catharines Standard

285

Memorabilia

A delightful by-product of alumni work has been the acquisition over the years of all sorts of memorabilia, notably pictures of student and staff executives and activities, but also a wide variety of mementoes of life at Queen's. Some records are irretrievably lost, but an amazing amount of material still comes to hand as graduates clean out their attics or as descendants look for a repository for personal treasures belonging to members of their family.

The collection now includes upwards of 1,500 pictures. The oldest now goes back to the Class of Medicine 1865 – though the record belonged for many years to the Class of Arts 1876. There is a good representation of old *Journals, Golden Words,* yearbooks, directories, handbooks, football programs, reunion souvenirs, pennants, paperweights, medical instruments, minute books, buttons, badges, academic and athletic medals – anything with a Queen's crest or the Queen's colours on it, or any connection with the University at any period.

All these items are useful to an organization dedicated to the promotion of nostalgia as a stock in trade, to the preservation of heritage, to the nourishment of the Queen's spirit. They are displayed at times of Reunion. They are a valuable resource for the *Review.* They are a tangible link with the past.

There is a wealth of material available for display purposes. The Alumni Office has long been promised museum space, and when that day materializes some very interesting displays can be arranged: World War One, World War Two, sports, student activities in all their manifestations, reunions – there are literally scores of possibilities. Think of what a display could be made, for example, under the title *A Canadian To Remember,* showing the honorary degrees, medals, and distinctions collected by Dr. B. G. Ballard in the course of a lifetime as an outstanding research scientist, or the collection of athletic trophies, awards, and pictures accumulated by Frank R.

"Pep" Leadlay, one of the greatest athletes ever to wear the Tricolour uniform.

The University has a rich heritage. May alumni always help to preserve it.

The author with some treasured sports memorabilia, including the 1893 cap of the legendary Guy Curtis

Index

Alumnae 60th, 90
Drama Guild, 50th, 47, 75th, 91
Newman Club, 73
Queen's Journal 100th, 91
Queen's Quarterly 60th, 58
Radio Station CFRC 50th, 90
School of Business, 87
University's 100th, 37, 39, 40, 117, 121
University's 125th, 72

Applied Science, Faculty of, 39, 53, 58, 70, 72, 89, 104, 173
April Fool, 91, 94
Arkley, L.M., 50
Armstrong, Alvin, 134
Arnup, J.D., 73
Aroutunian, Dr. Amasasp, 61
Art Centre, Agnes Etherington, 66, 99, 143, 225, 235
Arts, Faculty of, 46, 173, 202, 208, 216, 221
Arts and Science, Faculty of, 70, 72, 80, 86, 94, 173, 253, 255
Arts 1876, 285
Arts 1900, 273
Arts '26, 274
Arts '54, 58
Arts Festival, 100
Arts Journal, 58
Arts Society, 6, 48, 100
Arts and Science Undergraduate Society, 70
Associated Medical Services Inc., 93
Association of Universities and Colleges of Canada (AUCC), 236, 240, 245
Atherton, W.H., 187
Athletic Board of Control, 44, 124, 127, 154, 162, 172, 181
Athlone, Earl of, 40, 194

Austin, L.J. 'Blimey', 29, 50, 63
Austin, Margaret, 63

B

Bajally, Floyd, 150
Baker, Grant, 166
Baker, Manley B., 50, 119
Baker, Tim, 78
Baker, W.C., 36
Balfour, R.O., 100
Ballard, B.G., 286
Ban Righ Fireside Program, 98
Ban Righ Foundation for Continuing University Education, 94, 101, 143
Ban Righ Hall, 24, 49, 51, 54, 124, 201, 202, 215, 226
Ban Righ House Council, 24
Bands, Brass & Pipe, 31, 33, 44, 153, 187
Bank of Canada, 229, 243
Bannister, J.W., 49
Barker, Reg, 158
Barnabe, Ed, 148, 152, 159
Barriefield, 53, 131, 133
Bartlett, F.L., 49, 80, 156, 248
Baseball, 124
Bater, Robert B., 93
Bates College, 110, 120
Batstone, H.L. 'Harry' (Red), 28, 125, 149, 152, 157, 158
Bayne, Arthur S., 180
Bayne, D.B. 'Don', 151, 159
Beals, C.S., 64
Beck, Paul, 150
Becker, Henry, 81, 82
Beer Brewing Contest, 101
Beggs, Joyce, 61
Bell Telephone Co., 25
Bellringer, Frank, 28

Benidickson, Agnes (Richardson), 96
Bennett, The Rt. Hon. R.B., 188, 194
Berry House, 41, 65
Berry, N.E., 41, 62
Berry, W.R., 49
Bertram, Alice, 43
Beta Sigma Chapter, Nu Sigma Nu, 180
Bevan, Bob, 150
Beveridge, J.M.R., 70
Bews, James G., 248
Bews, Mal, 148
Beynon, Tom, 152
Bieler, André, 80, 120
Biochemistry, 33
Biological Station, Lake Opinicon, 49, 215
Biology, Department of, 70, 235
Birchall, Air Cmdr. L.J., 70
Bissell, Claude, 238
Bissonette, N.L., 187
Bitter Grounds, 75, 100
Black, Mathew, 72
Blake, Diana, 105
Blazer, Queen's official, 17, 18, 58
Boag, T.J., 96
Board of Trustees (see Trustees)
Boarding houses, 40, 60, 172, 184
Bogstad, Finn O., 94
Bolton, Eleanor T.R., 80
Bond, Jack, 149
Boo-Hoo, 122, 130, 147, 153, 170
Booth, C. Jackson, 160
Border Cities Star, 175
Boston Marathon, 93
Botterell, E. Harry, 87, 238
Boucher, D.W., 41, 80
Boucher, Mrs. D.W., 41, 43

Boucher House, 41, 183
Bowell, G.S., 48
Boyd, Eldon M., 106
Boxing, 156, 166-168
Braccia, Gus, 150, 151
Bradburn, A.M. 'Brad', 93, 106
Bradfield, R.D., 106
Bradwin, Edwin W., 269
Branigan, Dinny, 29
Brennan, Chris, 151
British Weekly, 117
Britton, J.C. 'Bubs', 28, 152, 159
Broadbent, Alan, 198
Broadbent, J.A., 198
Brockington, Leonard W., 5, 12, 48, 57, 62, 75, 80, 135-140, 185, 197, 220
Brooks, Ron, 151
Brovedani, J.M., 50
Brown, H.A. 'Hank', 130, 150, 159
Brown, James H., 70, 106
Brown University, 229
Browne, Roland, 29
Bruce, E.L., 50, 248
Bruce, Lou, 150, 158, 161
Brunton, Donald C., 271
Bryce, Beatrice, 89, 106
Buchan, John, 57, 136
Buller, R.F. 'Bob', 261
Burley, Norm, 149
Burns, R.M., 78
Burns, Robert, 136
Burr, R.C., 106
Business, School of, 72, 87, 225
Bus-It, 91
Buttars, John, 76

C

CFRC, 14, 49, 50, 82, 90

CKWS, 134
CNRM, 186
COTC, 33, 36, 37, 73, 75
Cadavers, 54
Caldwell, George, 159
Calgary, 217
Callander, T., 36
Calvin, D.D., 40, 201, 256
Cameron, Donald, 3, 7
Cameron, J.C., 80
Cameron, M.C., 6
Camp Outlook, 90
Campbell, Dave, 153
Campbell, P.C., 211
Campbell, P.G.C., 50, 119, 183
Campbell, W.A. 'Bill', 80, 125, 130, 149, 157, 158
Campling, C.H.R. 'Chuck', 93
Campus Bookstore, 93
Canada Council, 239, 249, 253
Canadian Broadcasting Corp., 232
Canadian Establishment, The, 224, 252
Canadian Imperial Bank of Commerce, 70, 87
Canadian Institute of Guided Ground Transport, 87
Canadian National Railway, 68, 87
Canadian Officers Training Corps, (see COTC)
Canadian Pacific Railway, 58, 87
Canadian Press, 181, 189
Canadian Union of Students, 69, 76, 84
Canvin, David, 81
Cape Vincent, N.Y., 25
Capitol Theatre, 29
Cappon, James, 36, 110, 111, 116, 121, 143, 193, 203, 216

Carmichael, Norman, 12
Carnegie Corporation, 201, 218
Carruthers Hall, 226
Carson, George, 276
Carson, Dr. George, 159
Carson, Orrin A., 80, 149, 151, 158
Carter, J.H. 'Howie', 158
Casgrain, Senator Pierre, 187
Cataraqui Cemetery, 121, 127
Cataraqui River, 131, 132
Cave, H.M., 80, 276
Cays, F.A., 62
Centennial celebration (see Anniversaries)
Centre for Resource Studies, 87
Chair of Social Science, 186-190
Chalmers Church, 218
Chamber Singers, 98
Chantler, P.D. 'Pee Wee', 150
Chaplains, 42, 43, 44, 53, 106, 140, 220
Charters, J.W. 'Jim', 127, 150, 158
Chartier, M. Louis, 189
Chemical Engineering, 81, 215, 235
Chernoff, Gerry, 29
Chesterfield, Lord Bowden of, 100
China, 249, 270
Chochla, M.A. 'Mo', 198
Choral Ensemble, 98, 252
Chown, Alice, 269
Chown, G.Y., 111, 203
Chown Hall, 54, 225
Chown, Tom, 151, 152
Christ's Hospital, 206
Churchill, E.C. 'Ed', 66, 68
Churchill, Rt. Hon. Winston, 118
City Hall, 172
Civil Engineering, 225

Dalhousie University, 48, 59

Dances, 31, 44, 98, 99, 101, 104, 172, 173, 177, 209

Dancing, 29, 31

Davies, Robertson, 29, 61, 133

Davies, Rupert, 189

Davis, Steve, 151

Davis, Hon.William G., 100, 245

Day, Jack, 167

Day, R.C. 'Weenie', 28

Day Care Centre, 89

Dean of Women, 24, 43, 89, 120

Debating, 29

Deguire,E., 187

Delahaye, J.L. 'Jack', 149

Delahaye, J.S., 50

Delta Omega Kappa, 178, 180

Democratic Government and Politics, 231

Denison Mines, 161

Depression Years, 23, 24, 25, 109, 113, 208, 215

de St. Remy, Elizabeth H.D., 198

de St. Remy, Mac, 198

Desjardins, Dorothy, 62

Deutsch, John James, 68, 70, 79, 85, 91, 121, 230, 236, 241-252, 256

Dewar, D.G., 68

Dexter, Grant, 243

Dickey, Herb, 28

Dickinson, Helena, 269

Diefenbaker, Rt. Hon. John G., 64, 280

Dobson, W.A. 'Bill', 159

D.O.K. Club, 180, 183

Dolan, Eddie, 149

Dollar Bill, 128-134

Domesday Book, 141

Donald Gordon Centre for Continuing Education, 94, 105, 250

Donnelly, Brian, 78, 151

Dorn, Peter, 87

Dorrance, R.L.

Dots, The Two, 62

Douglas, A. Vibert, 54, 62, 121

Douglas, James, 201

Douglas Library, 46, 49, 58, 89, 93, 115, 136, 143, 202, 226, 235, 236

Douglas, Maj.-Gen. H.E.M., 39

Drama Guild, 29, 47, 61, 75, 89, 99, 204

Drinking, 53, 100, 101, 131-133

Drum Majorettes, 153

Duff-Berdahl Commission, 236

Dubos, Réné, 245

Duncan, A.R.C., 70

Dunlop, H.W. 'Hal', 157

Dunning, Chancellor Charles Avery, 47, 60, 135, 215

Dunning Hall, 98, 225

Dunning Trust, 47, 245

Dupuis, Nathan, 193, 216

Dyde, S.W., 193

Dyer, Peggy, 153

Dyer, Sandy, 153

Dymond, M.B., 245

E

Eagleson, Melva, 80, 106

Eaman, Keith 'Skip', 151, 152, 159

Earl, R.O., 62, 119

Earl Hall (Biology), 70, 235

Earle, F.E. 'Frank', 159

Economic Council of Canada, 241, 244

Edgett, G.L., 80

Laverty, A.M. (Padre), 42, 43, 106, 140, 220
Law, Faculty of, 59, 64, 72, 104, 225
Law, Mike, 152
Law Society of Upper Canada, 59, 240
Lawler, 'Chummy', 28
Lazier, S.S., 105
Leacock, Stephen, 237
Leadlay, Frank R. 'Pep', 125, 127, 130, 149, 157, 158, 271, 286
Leander McCormick Observatory, 6
LeCaine, Hugh, 94
Leckie, N.M. 'Tout', 158
Lederman, W.R., 59
Legal Aid Office, 91
Leishman, Morris A., 180, 181
Leitch, Rev. William, 256
Lenard, Al, 127, 150, 152, 158
Leng, John S., 42
Lennox, T.C., 275
Leonard Hall, 91
LeRoy, Barry, 76
Letondal, M. Henri, 189
Levana Society, 49, 71, 78, 173
  Candlelighting ceremony, 60, 78
Lewis, Arthur E. 'Curly', 149, 158, 160, 161, 162
Lewis, Gary, 150, 158, 160, 161
Lewis, Jack, 148
Lichty, George, 8, 9
Lichty, Jan, 76, 82
Lilles, Heino, 151, 152, 157, 159
Logan, J.R. 'Tip', 127, 150, 152, 159
London Times, 140
Long, Marion, 46
Lord Simcoe Hotel, 72, 76

Lord, T.V., 62
Love, Fred, 275
Love, H. Morris, 96
Lovell, Sir Bernard, 100
Lower, A.R.M., 62, 66
Lower Campus, 71, 277, 278
Lundy, C.S. 'Sam', 148
Lyons, Bishop, 187

M

MacCallum, Elizabeth, 51
MacClement, W.T., 36
MacCormick, Rector, 194
Macdonald, Sir John A., 68, 185
Macdonald Hall, Sir John A., 59, 64, 81, 225, 235
MacDonell, Glenn, 82
Macdonnell, Anne, 29
Macdonnell, Hugh, 158
Macdonnell, Hon. J.M., 60, 117, 182, 212
Macdonnell, Mary L., 62
Macdonnell, P.M., 50, 120
MacDougall, J. Lorne, 179
Macgillivray, John, 36, 179
MacGregor, J. Arnot, 184
MacGregor, Marge, 44, 153
MacGregor, Rob Roy, 29, 62
Machar, John, 256
Mackay, G.J., 36
MacKay, J.E., 274
Mackinnon, G.E., 269
Mackintosh, Agnes, 230
Mackintosh, Helen, 230
Mackintosh, W.A., 19, 61, 73, 119, 121, 136, 143, 211, 212, 221-230, 234, 237, 256, 271
Mackintosh, Mrs. W.A., 230
Mackintosh-Corry Hall, 94, 230, 249

Mackintosh (W.A.) Lecture in
Economics, 230
MacLaren, J.F., 64
MacLaren, Walter, 29
Macklem, Peter, 61
MacMillan, H.R., 73
MacNeill, R.D., 176
Macphail, Alexander, 26, 36
Macphail, Peter, 152
Macpherson, Bud, 28
Macpherson, Lawrence G., 70,
106, 221, 257
Mair, Mace, 276
Manitoba, 213
Maracle, Muriel, 188
Marat, Jean, 171
Marquis, T.G., 160
Marshall, Harvey I., 68, 271
Mascots, 122, 130, 147, 153,
160, 170 (see also Pierce, Alfie)
Masefield, John, 136
Massey Lectures, 239
Massey, Raymond, 47
Massey, Rt. Hon. Vincent, 118
Masterton, Bob, 161.
Mathematics, Department of, 235
Mathers, Donald M., 94, 105
Mathers, Helen, 94
Matheson, D.C., 62
Matheson, John, 50, 117, 203
Matheson, John Ross, 248
Maubourg, Jeanne, 189
Maughan, George B., 166-168
McArthur College (see Also
Faculty of Education), 70, 72,
248
McArthur, Duncan 36, 188, 248
McArthur, Helen, 188
McCalla, Doug, 68
McCallum, Mary, 51
McCarney, Hal 'Moose', 159, 165

McCarthy, Dan, 152
McCarthy J.R., 73
McConnery, Lorne, 152
McCuaig, C.H., 62, 127
McDonald, Leo, 28
McDonald, Tupper, 159
McDougall, J. Lorne, 80, 106
McDonell, J.S., 124, 160
McGibbon, Hon. Pauline, 256
McGill Daily, 76
McGill, H.F. 'Ding', 271
McGill-Queen's University Press,
78
McGill University, 8, 26, 53, 61,
64, 78, 118, 147, 153, 166-
168, 171, 178, 202, 218
McGinnis, Norah (Glen), 180
McGinnis, T.A., 33
McGregor, D.A., 217, 219
McIntyre, Don, 152
McKean, F.K. 'Pappy', 271
McKean, Jim, 152
McKee, Bill, 28
McKelvey, G.J. 'Gib', 28, 150,
206,
McKelvey, J.L. 'Red', 126, 149,
158
McKelvey, Ross, 127, 150, 158
McKenzie, George, 152
McKenzie, I.D., 271
McLaughlin Hall, 44, 215
McLaughlin, Col. R.S., 51, 57,
215, 216
McLaughlin, Mrs. R.S. 'Adelaide',
51, 57, 215, 216
McLaughlin, R.T. 'Ron', 13, 57
McLaughlin, W. Earle, 68
McLeish, Archibald, 118
McLellan, Gord, 153
McLeod, Norman, 276
McLeod, P.A.'Pres', 80, 149

Richardson Memorial Stadium 3, 26, 29, 33, 44, 53, 61, 89, 91, 124, 147, 149, 153, 156, 202, 248, 279

Ridout, Godfrey, 73

Rigsby, D.L. 'Dave', 87, 271

Ritchie, Robin, 152, 159

Riviera, 31

Robb, D.A. 'Don', 159

Robb, Wallace Havelock, 133

Roberts, Goodridge, 208

Roberts, J.A.G. 'Jack', 150, 159

Roberts, Leslie, 227

Robertson, E.M., 80

Robertson, J.K., 62

Robertson, J.L., 193

Robertson Theological College, 193

Robinson, Ken, 28

Rodden, M.J. 'Mike', 157, 158

Rogers, Norman McL., 96, 194, 195

Roosevelt, Eleanor, 50

Roosevelt, President Franklin D., 33, 49, 118

Root, Claude, 150

Roscoe, Muriel, 51

Rose, Bruce, 62

Ross, Arthur E., 124, 159, 160, 194

Ross, Marion, 106, 248

Rotary Club, 68, 94

Roundheads, 57

Roy, Don, 150

Roy, James A., 62, 128, 134

Roy York Cafe, 31

Royal Bank, 68

Royal Bank Award, 240

Royal Canadian Air Force, 37

Royal Economic Society, 229

Royal Exhibition of 1851 Scholarship, 213

Royal Military College, 42, 70, 94, 227

Royal Society of Canada, 120, 218, 229, 238, 250

Royal Visits, 61, 69, 91, 92

Royal York Hotel, 25

Royce Hall, Jean, 94, 101, 248

Royce, Jean I., 80, 245

Rubin, Jerry, 78

Rugby, 15, 17, 209

Russell, William J., 273

Rutledge, L.T., 50

Ryan, H.R.S., 104

Ryerson Polytechnical Instit., 114

S

Sadie Hawkins Week, 31, 44

Safrance, Chuck, 150

St. Andrew's University, 213

St. Catharines, 285

St. James Church, 127

St. Lawrence River, 25

St. Lawrence College, 84

St. Lawrence University, 252

St. Mary's-on-the-Lake Hospital, 42

St. Thomas *Times Journal,* 175

Salari, Pete, 150, 159

Salaries, staff, 60, 202, 203, 216

Sandwell, B.K., 4, 194, 195

Sapientia et Doctrina Stabilitas, 19

Sargent, B.W., 106

Saskatchewan, 6, 223

Saunders, Lois, 116

Saylor, Jim, 149

Scarecrow, 99

University of Saskatchewan, 241
University of Syracuse, 162
University of Toronto, 8, 28, 50,
  60, 93, 101, 118, 153, 171,
  202 (see also Varsity)
University of Virginia, 6
University of Western Ontario, 6,
  8, 93, 120, 147, 148, 153, 154
University, Victoria, 78, 118
Urban and Regional Planning,
  School of, 87
Uzbalis, Vic, 150
United States, 33, 49, 69, 75, 142

V

Vachon, Dr. L.A., 245
Vaghy Quartet, 98
Van Buskirk, Rick, 151
Vancouver, 217
Vancouver Daily Province, 217
Vandalism, 26, 76, 52-53
Vanier Cup, 147, 151
Vanier Gold Medal, 250
Vanier, Jean, 100
Vanier, Pauline, 73
Van Koughnett, Kevin, 91
Varsity/Varsity Blues, 10, 28, 76,
  148, 149, 151, 161, 162, 166,
  272
Veale, Fred, 149
Veterans, 42, 43
Victoria College, 6, 118
Victoria Cross, 39
Victoria Hall, 94
Victoria School, 187
Victoria University, 78, 118
Vietnam, 69, 75
Vincent, C.J., 80
Viscount Alexander of Tunis, 44
Voss, Carl, 28, 150

W

Wade, George, 152
Walker, E.A., 106
Walker, C.E., 50
Walker, D.F. 'Doug', 151, 152,
  267
Walker, N.L. 'Liz', 126, 149, 159
Wallace, Elspeth (Mrs. C. Baught),
  220
Wallace Hall, 100, 126, 273
Wallace R.C., 5, 13, 36, 39, 41,
  42, 47, 51, 117, 119, 121, 126,
  135, 165, 213-220, 226, 256
Wallace, Mrs. R.C., 213, 215,
  218, 220
Wardle, Dorothy, 43
Ware, Lebo, 29
Warren, Fred, 152
Warrender, A. Brian, 153, 160
Wartime Prices and Trade Board,
  224
Waterloo-Lutheran University,
  151
Watertown, N.Y., 55
Watertown Times, 55
Watson, E.E., 106
Watson Hall, 235
Watson, John, 36, 113, 117, 193,
  203, 216
Watson, Ted, 46
Wattsford, George, 105
Watts, Ronald Lampman, 70, 86,
  94, 105, 253-258
Waugh, Doug, 148
Waugh, Douglas O., 87, 91, 96
Waugh, Freeman 'Casey', 166-
  168
Webb, Jack, 105
Webster, A.'Sandy', 47, 91
Webster, Charles, 160